P9-DNR-570

EVALUATION IN TEACHER
EDUCATION

COMMISSION ON TEACHER EDUCATION

Appointed by the American Council on Education

E. S. EVENDEN, Teachers College, Columbia University, *Chairman*

RALPH W. TYLER, University of Chicago, *Vice Chairman*

HAROLD BENJAMIN, University of Maryland

MILDRED ENGLISH, Georgia State College for Women

HARRY M. GAGE, Lindenwood College

HELEN HAY HEYL, New York State Education Department

CHARLES W. HUNT, Oneonta State Teachers College (New York)

HAROLD E. JONES, University of California

FRED J. KELLY, United States Office of Education

LEWIS MUMFORD, Stanford University

SHELTON PHELPS, Winthrop College*

W. CARSON RYAN, University of North Carolina

PAYSON SMITH, University of Maine†

ALEXANDER J. STODDARD, Philadelphia Public Schools

FRANK W. THOMAS, Fresno State College (California)

GEORGE F. ZOOK, American Council on Education, *ex officio*

KARL W. BIGELOW, *Director*

* Retired in 1943.
† Chairman from 1938 to 1942

EVALUATION IN
TEACHER EDUCATION

By

Maurice E. Troyer and C. Robert Pace

LB1731
.T86   71159

Prepared for the
Commission on Teacher Education

LB1731.T86   ST. JOSEPH'S UNIVERSITY   STX
Evaluation in teacher education.

3 9353 00037 5970

AMERICAN COUNCIL ON EDUCATION

Washington, D.C.

1944

COPYRIGHT 1944 BY THE AMERICAN COUNCIL ON EDUCA-
TION. PUBLISHED MAY, 1944. SECOND PRINTING APRIL,
1945. THIRD PRINTING DECEMBER, 1946. FOURTH
PRINTING SEPTEMBER, 1950

Brief parts of this report may be quoted without special permission
provided credit is given. Permission to quote extended passages may
be secured through the Commission on Teacher Education, 744
Jackson Place, Washington 6, D.C.

Foreword

IN RECENT YEARS the term "evaluation" has been increasingly employed in educational circles. It has suggested the importance of systematic and continuous judgment not merely of the accomplishments of persons and the outcomes of processes but also of the values in terms of which accomplishments and outcomes must be estimated. In other words it has implied a critical analysis of educational purposes as well as of possibilities and attainments in relation to such purposes.

The various programs for which the Commission on Teacher Education has been responsible and with which it has been associated have paid a great deal of attention to evaluation. This book is a report growing out of that particular aspect of the Commission's experience. Like other reports in the same series it sketches the Commission's work, describes and analyzes specific practices employed in certain colleges, universities, and school systems, and sets forth the authors' own interpretations and conclusions.

The book has been prepared by Maurice E. Troyer, who was associate in evaluation on the staff of the Commission, and by C. Robert Pace, his assistant. Dr. Troyer came to the Commission staff from the faculty of the School of Education at Syracuse University in February 1940, and returned to that institution in July 1943 as professor of education and director of the bureau of field services. Dr. Pace left the research staff of the General College at the University of Minnesota in September 1940 to accept a Commission fellowship in evaluation, being assigned to Teachers College, Columbia University. From September 1941 to September 1943 he was attached to the Commission's central staff. He is now in the training division of the Bureau of Naval Personnel.

The Commission wishes to express its appreciation to Dr. Troyer and Dr. Pace, as well as to the many others whose participation in evaluation activities in connection with the cooperative study of teacher education has helped to make this valuable report possible. The manuscript was reviewed for accuracy by the institutions whose programs are reported. The authors have, of course, been free to express their own views and they assume joint responsibility for all statements made. The action of the director in recommending, and of the Commission in authorizing, publication of the report does not necessarily imply endorsement of all that is contained therein.

KARL W. BIGELOW
Director

Acknowledgments

BECAUSE THIS volume is in such large measure a report of what other people have done, the task of acknowledging everyone's contribution to it cannot be met completely in any brief space. It goes without saying that our major debt is to the many teachers, supervisors, and administrators in the colleges and school systems with which the Commission has been privileged to work. Their attempts to evaluate a great many aspects of teacher education, and their reports to the Commission have provided the basic material for our descriptions and analyses. Furthermore, these individuals generously furnished us with data regardless of when the particular program was initiated or the part played by the Commission in its development. The final revision of the manuscript was prepared with the help of critical comments supplied by the institutions and school systems in question. Our experience in working with these people in a great variety of circumstances has been invaluable.

Special contributions to our work as the staff in evaluation, and to the progress of enterprises in the field, were made by persons who, for varying lengths of time, were financed by the Commission or on that body's recommendation were granted fellowships by the General Education Board. This group comprised the following: Warren R. Baller, Robert N. Bush, George P. Deyoe, Vivian V. Edmiston, John Chester Junek, Lee H. Mathews, Donald J. McNassor, Daniel C. McNaughton, Earl E. Mosier, Ida E. Scheib, and Laban C. Smith.

We are also indebted to Ruth E. Eckert, Alvin C. Eurich, Irving D. Lorge, Louis E. Raths, and Ralph W. Tyler, who served on more than one occasion as consultants in the field or at evaluation conferences.

Three members of the Commission on Teacher Education— Mildred English, W. Carson Ryan, and Ralph W. Tyler—constituted an advisory committee to review the manuscript at various stages of its development. We wish to acknowledge their helpful service in this connection. We are under similar obligation to the director and other members of the Commission staff who have given us freely the benefit of their judgment and experience.

M.E.T.

C.R.P.

Contents

ix

I

Background for Evaluation in the Cooperative Study

WHAT IS EVALUATION in education? It is the process of judging the effectiveness of educational experience. It includes gathering and summarizing evidence on the extent to which educational values are being attained. It seeks to answer the questions: "What progress am I making?" and "What success is our educational program having?" Teachers, administrators, and students are daily making value judgments about the effectiveness of their procedures in the attainment of their goals. Thus evaluation, whether recognized as such or not, goes on continuously in all education.

CHARACTERISTICS OF EVALUATION

Evaluation makes use of measurement but is not synonymous with it. How do the two differ? Measurement refers only to observations that can be expressed quantitatively. It is concerned with the question of "how much." Evaluation recognizes the need to know how much but it is especially concerned with the question of "what value." This emphasis upon *values* distinguishes evaluation from measurement most clearly. Evaluation presupposes a definition of goals to be attained; the evaluator draws upon any source of evidence, quantitative or qualitative or descriptive, that may be useful in judging the degree to which those objectives are attained.

What are the tasks involved in the process of evaluation? Obviously, one is the formulation of objectives. What goals am I trying to reach? What are the purposes of this course? What aim are we seeking to realize in our educational program? Usually a statement of objectives is somewhat abstract. We say we

1

want students or teachers to think critically, to develop whole-some personalities, to become responsible citizens. But precisely what do we mean by responsible citizenship, wholesome personality, or critical thinking? What does a person do who is a responsible citizen? What behavior do we look for in deciding whether one possesses a wholesome personality? General objectives, therefore, must be defined more sharply in terms of the specific behavior implied by them. This is a second main task in evaluation. A third task is to identify the sources of evidence we can use in observing such behavior. Where shall we look to find evidence of responsible citizenship? What are some of the opportunities students have to display responsible citizenship? A fourth task is to develop methods for getting the evidence we want. We may discover tests, rating scales, questionnaires, and other instruments that will serve our purpose. We may need to construct new forms. Or we may need to work out some scheme of firsthand observation, some method of collecting anecdotes, some way of pooling judgments. Finally, we must interpret the results we gather in the light of our goals or objectives. This fifth task requires summarizing and integrating a variety of evidence. It requires considering the degree of confidence we can place in that evidence. It is, in short, the task of making the best possible judgment concerning the meaning and importance of our data. These, then, are five major tasks in the process of evaluation. This is not to say that everyone who evaluates engages in these five tasks consciously and deliberately, nor that the process of evaluation is a fixed sequence of steps. It is to say, however, that what people do when they evaluate can be classified and analyzed in some such manner as we have suggested.

What are some of the purposes and values of evaluation? Why do we evaluate? One very clear reason is in order to judge the effectiveness of an educational program. The unit for evaluation may encompass the total offerings of a college, it may be a single course, or it may be a fairly coherent aspect of a total program—such as general education, student teaching, or orientation and guidance. We undertake to evaluate the program because we hope thereby to improve it. By knowing its strengths and weaknesses we are enabled to plan more intelligently for its improvement. Similarly, we may evaluate the progress of an individual—ourself or someone else. And again, we do it because we hope thereby to advance progress, to attain greater success because we have found out what was holding us back. We know that knowledge of results aids us in learning new skills. So likewise, an evaluation of our status and progress helps us to improve that status and to make further progress. By analyzing our experience, resources, and programs we help to clarify them and to bring our efforts more directly in line with our purposes. Thus evaluation is a technique that can and should lead to the continuous improvement of education.

What sorts of evaluation do we find in schools? And under what conditions do we find them? Probably the commonest sort is that which a teacher makes of the students in his class. The college teacher, for example, gives an examination at midterm and at the end of his course. Perhaps he also assigns a term paper or some other report to be prepared outside of class. Perhaps, further, he has gained during the course some general and some specific impressions regarding contributions that individual students have made in class discussions, in private conferences, or in formal oral reports. On the basis of a student's performance in all these areas he makes a judgment, an evaluation, which is transmitted to the student in the form of a letter grade. What the instructor looks for when he reads the student's examination papers, and considers other evidence he has accumulated during the year, constitutes his objectives. In common practice the objectives in this sort of evaluation are concerned with informational and intellectual outcomes. Does the student know the basic facts and concepts in the subject matter he has been studying? Less frequently in actual practice, the objectives include ability to organize, apply, and interpret these facts intelligently.

The evaluation which a teacher in a nursery school makes of her pupils is not essentially different, so far as the process is concerned, from the evaluation which a college teacher makes. The process is the same, but the objectives, the sources of evidence, and the form of the final appraisal are different. Instead of knowledge and understanding of economic principles, the nursery school teacher is concerned with the development of physical coordination and skills, better eating habits, ability to work and play happily with other children. Instead of looking at examinations and reports, the nursery school teacher observes how the children behave at the lunch table, in the sand pile, at games, and elsewhere. Perhaps she keeps a chart showing what the children eat at lunch. Perhaps she jots down brief anecdotes in a notebook to remind her of how Billy or Mary acted in a certain situation. Instead of summarizing her evaluations in a letter grade, the nursery school teacher writes a report to parents. She says that Billy has been doing better at lunch; he eats more than he did last month and has developed a liking for string beans. He is a little small for his age and does not show quite as much initiative as the other boys in situations requiring physical coordination. But he is very polite, seldom cries, and almost always participates actively in discussions following the story hours. To be sure, the evaluations of the college professor and the nursery school teacher differ in almost all details. But in both evaluations there are objectives, either explicit or implied. In both there is a more or less systematic collection of evidence of students' progress toward the objectives. In both there is a final synthesis and interpretation of this evidence. And both are evaluations made by the teacher of the students.

Another very common sort of evaluation is that which individuals make of their own courses. A teacher finds that the number of student failures in his course at midterm is larger than usual. He may decide that this is entirely the students' fault, or he may try some special means to help those whose achievement has been disappointing to him. He notices that student participation in class discussions is sluggish. He sees that some students fall asleep during his lectures. Or again, he may note with satisfaction that students' term papers are especially well done and reveal a genuine grasp of the materials in the course. He observes in class discussions and private conferences that many students are questioning their previous beliefs, are developing new attitudes which he believes to be sounder and more appropriate than their old ones. He is sensitive to all these things, and many others, because he is a good teacher, because he genuinely wants to make his course better. He may observe and gather his evidence informally, or he may use more systematic means. He may, for example, ask students to write anonymously their criticisms of the course and their suggestions for its improvement. He may even have students fill out a questionnaire in which they rate various aspects of the course—the lectures, the required readings, the term papers, and so forth. In doing all these things he is evaluating his own course and himself.

Student self-appraisal is a variety of evaluation that is also practically universal in all education. Students are concerned about their grades. They judge their own progress informally, and if the grade they get from the teacher is lower than the one they think they deserve, they are likely to say so to the teacher. They are almost certain to say so to their associates and they usually cite evidence to justify their belief. Of course, many of these self-appraisals may be in error, may even be deceptive rationalizations. The quality of self-appraisal usually depends a great deal upon how important the outcome is to the student. If it concerns the choice of an occupation the student may talk at length with friends, interview men in that occupation, read books about it, call on a vocational counselor, take aptitude and interest tests before coming to his decision. By and large, teachers and evaluation specialists have devoted much more time to evaluating students and courses than they have to developing competence in students to evaluate their own progress. But a recognition of the prevalence of informal self-appraisal, plus an increasing conviction that the development of ability in students to make wise decisions for themselves is a major goal of education, should lead teachers and evaluators to develop the techniques of self-evaluation more systematically and thoroughly in the future.

Evaluation of the total program of an institution, or even a major aspect of the total program, is found much less frequently than the kinds of evaluation which have been described above. Relatively few institutions have, in fact, undertaken thorough-going self-appraisal. Schools and colleges are periodically surveyed by regional accrediting agencies, but these surveys have been in the past concerned primarily with the possessions of the school—its library, the quality of its staff, physical plant, its endowment—rather than with the products of the school, or progress toward the attainment of its educational objectives. In recent years some accrediting agencies, notably the North Central Association of Colleges and Secondary Schools, have modified their policies radically in recognition of the importance of local purposes, thus giving impetus to institutional self-evaluation. Some colleges which have experimented boldly with new methods and materials of education have also made intensive evaluations of their programs. The General College at the University of Minnesota and Bennington College are outstanding examples. Public and private schools associated with the eight-year study of the Progressive Education Association, colleges associated with the Cooperative Study in General Education of the American Council on Education, and school systems and colleges associated with the cooperative study of teacher education of the Commission on Teacher Education have, in varying degrees, attempted appraisals of major parts or of all of their programs. And their number is increasing. Worthwhile evaluations, institutional in scope, are not beyond the financial resources of any school or college. Techniques developed at research centers can be adopted or modified in the light of local purposes. Evaluation can be made an integral and ongoing part of the instructional program.

The varieties of evaluation can be summarized briefly. There is evaluation of individual progress, of single courses, of total programs or major parts thereof. There is evaluation in regular or normal settings and in experimental settings. There is evaluation as an ongoing, continuous activity and evaluation that is periodic. And there is self-evaluation and evaluation by others. It may be helpful to keep these varieties and conditions in mind as specific activities in different schools and colleges are examined.

Perhaps a word should be added about evaluation as research. Much appraisal is not research but a program of evaluation may include research in it. The research may take the form of developing precise techniques of measurement for relatively complex objectives, or it may take the form of systematically assembling and analyzing data in relation to a clearly stated hypothesis. It is, in fact, difficult to judge whether an evaluation is or is not research. Scientific research may be defined as the testing of hypotheses in a carefully described or controlled setting. When evaluation consists of studying an educational program, the goals of which are stated and the curricular materials described, when students' behavior is observed and analyzed in relation to those goals, and when these things are done carefully with appropriate techniques and reasonable methods for checking conclusions, evaluation is research. This kind of evaluation is by no means limited to university research centers, for more and more schools are undertaking broad appraisals as an integral part of their educational program. Local and cooperative evaluations can be strengthened by drawing upon the resources of research specialists; and graduate schools and research specialists can improve the significance of their studies by working in evaluation programs in the field.

What sorts of evaluation do we find in teacher education? All the types we have just described are found in teacher education. There is evaluation of students by teachers in single courses, evaluation of teachers by supervisors and administrators, evaluation by teachers of their own courses, evaluation by students or teachers of their own progress, evaluation of major aspects of programs of teacher education. Some evaluations are ongoing and continuous, others are periodic. Some are in experimental settings, and others are not.

Within the total program of teacher education certain major aspects have been, more commonly than others, the subject for evaluation, the center of evaluative effort. For example, as a student progresses through the sequence of experience that constitutes a program of teacher education, he finds his attention directed quite naturally at several points to evaluative activity. The institution likewise finds its attention drawn to evaluation at certain points in the same program. One of these is the point of initial selection. The student must decide whether or not he wants to be a teacher, and in doing this he must consider what teaching as an occupation means and judge his own liking and fitness for it. The institution must decide whom to admit, and on what bases. And it will want to know if its selection program is providing better prospective teachers. Perhaps the college also has a program of orientation and guidance designed chiefly to help students choose their occupation in full recognition of its demands and of their fitness to meet those demands. General education and the sequence of professional courses tend to become further units for evaluation, both for the student and the college. As the student engages in practice teaching, he again finds himself in a situation that impels self-appraisal; and the college finds a focus for judging the level of competence attained by the student and produced by its program. Upon graduation the student must get a job. And the college must draw together evidence of the student's competence in order to make its recommendation. Once on the job the individual wants to prove and improve his competence; the school system will make available to him programs for continued study such as study groups, workshops, field trips, and so forth. The progress of the individual and the values of these programs become focal points for evaluation at the in-service level. Thus, in teacher education, a series of major aspects of the total program is found to offer frequent opportunities for evaluative activity.

ORGANIZATION AND PURPOSES OF THE BOOK

What is the plan and organization of the present book? Because, in teacher education, evaluation has tended to center around the sequence of areas or topics we have just described, we have taken this sequence as the framework for our report. Each chapter of the book is devoted to a description and analysis of evaluative efforts in one of these major areas: selection, orientation and guidance, general education, professional education, student teaching, follow-up, growth of individual teachers in service, evaluation of in-service programs. In each of these areas we have generally considered evaluation not only from the standpoint of the institution but also from the standpoint of the individual, both student and teacher. And we have generally concerned ourselves with the interrelationships of these areas as well as with the appraisals of specific courses, programs, or procedures within the areas. Another reason for this chapter organization derives from the different functions and special interests of faculty members. Different educators, by virtue of their specific jobs, have a major interest in different aspects of professional education. Some have major responsibility for the selection of students or for their orientation and guidance. Some have major responsibility in the area of general education. Some are primarily interested in the program of student teaching. Some are especially concerned with the growth of teachers in service. These major functions and interests may overlap in intricate ways; nevertheless, evaluation problems in the different areas have their peculiar nature and setting. Although it may be desirable to have a total staff participate in a broad program of evaluation, few colleges or school systems have, as yet, undertaken such comprehensive appraisals. We have, therefore, chosen to organize our discussions in the light of conditions that are approximately representative of teachers' interests and activities in evaluation at the present time. We hope that, in this way, each reader will find a discussion fairly closely related to his own special interests.

It is true, of course, that there are general procedures in evaluation, and tasks which will be encountered, regardless of the particular subject or area being evaluated. Not all of these common procedures and tasks are described in equal detail in each chapter. The task of formulating objectives, for example, is discussed at length in the chapters on evaluation in general education and professional education, but mentioned only in passing in the other chapters. In the final chapter, however, some of these common tasks are summarized and analyzed, and the critical discussions of them in previous chapters are referred to.

What are the major purposes of the book? We have said that evaluation is an activity found, in various stages of development, in all schools and colleges. Recognition of the prevalence of evaluation, and of its importance, was clearly manifested at the Bennington planning conference of the Commission on Teacher Education.[1] At that conference, representatives from the schools and colleges that were selected for participation in the cooperative study of teacher education included evaluation among the major problems with which they and the Commission should be concerned. Moreover, they recommended the establishment of a service division in evaluation and this recommendation was carried out. The major purpose of the division was to provide assistance to men and women in the cooperating schools and colleges who were working on problems of evaluation. And this is the major purpose of the present book. By discussing some of the problems of evaluation, and by describing what has been done in some of the schools and colleges associated in the cooperative study, we hope that others in teacher education will find useful suggestions and insights for their own evaluation programs. We hope they will find ways of extending their evaluative activities, will get a better understanding of both the hazards and the possibilities of different techniques and procedures, and above all will gain a clearer concept of the potential role of evaluation in any educational program. How can we get started on a program of evaluation? What are some of the problems we are likely to face? What are some of the difficulties we might avoid? What have other people done? How can we improve the bases of our evaluation? All these questions are the concern of this book.

SOURCES OF MATERIAL

What is the background and what are the experiences and data from which the book is written? Because the experience of the Commission's total program provides the setting for the

[1] *Bennington Planning Conference for the Cooperative Study of Teacher Education: Reports and Addresses, August 21 to September 1, 1939* (Washington: American Council on Education, 1939).

activities of the evaluation division, we need to describe briefly this framework. The cooperative study of teacher education emphasized implementation rather than research and survey. Its purpose was to work with groups on their problems rather than to organize a program or to present formal recommendations. It was to work through and to develop local leadership, and to stimulate thinking and experimentation on basic problems in teacher education. Because there were obstacles to the free play of local initiative, the staff of the cooperative study became increasingly interested in how changes were brought about—in the strategy of effective planning. They and the Commission believe that, in the long run, greater progress in teacher education would be made by each institution striving to improve its own program than by any national organization trying to lay down standard recommendations. Thus, in the cooperative study, responsibility for the development of programs and procedures remained within each institution.

All this had a direct bearing on the philosophy and services of the evaluation division. It meant that there were no comparative studies, no tests centrally developed for use by all the cooperating centers, no prescribed sequence of steps for each to follow in evaluating itself. There was, in other words, no evaluation of schools and colleges by an external agency; rather, there was a working with schools on evaluative tasks chosen by them.

In carrying out its policy of working with schools and colleges the division on evaluation provided a variety of services. It sought to develop local leadership by sending people to workshops, to visit other schools, to study at research centers, and to conferences on evaluation. It assembled files of tests, rating scales, questionnaires, forms for recording anecdotes, and other evaluative techniques; and it circulated these, together with suggestions for their use, among the cooperating schools where evaluations were being undertaken. It sent consultants to help local groups plan next steps in the evaluation programs they were starting or carrying on.

The most extensive of the services of the evaluation division comes under the heading of consultant services. The two staff members of the division, for example, made a total of sixty-nine visits to twenty-nine different institutions. Eight of these institutions were visited once; six were visited twice; and fifteen were visited either three or four times. In addition to its own central staff the evaluation division provided the services of other consultants to many institutions in the study: specifically, to nine institutions concerned with evaluative problems in general education, and to sixteen institutions concerned with evaluative problems in professional education. Likewise, either one or two full-time consultants in evaluation were provided by the division for thirteen different summer workshops carried on within the cooperative study. Fifteen brief local or regional conferences, organized for the study of numerous problems, were similarly served by consultants in evaluation.

Two important conferences on evaluative problems were conducted by the divison. The first, held at the University of Chicago, February 14-19, 1941, was attended by thirty-eight participants from twenty-nine centers in the cooperative study. Its purpose was to discuss problems of procedure and techniques in evaluation being faced in the several participating units. Group meetings were organized in three areas—general education, pre-service professional education, and in-service education—but a major part of the time was devoted to individual conferences between participants and consultants. The second conference, held at Ohio State University, March 23-26, 1942, was attended by thirty-seven participants from twenty-seven centers in the cooperative study. Its purpose was to hear, discuss, and analyze reports on evaluative activities from the several centers. Nineteen such reports were given, and some major issues in evaluation were explored and summarized. Five consultants were available for individual conferences and special discussion groups.

On all of these activities—conferences, workshops, consultant services—written accounts have been accumulated. Consultants have sent in reports of their work to the evaluation division. Reports of workshops and conferences have been made. Moreover, each institution in the cooperative study has made an annual progress report to the staff of the Commission and has prepared a final written report summarizing its work during the three years of the cooperative study. Many of these reports from institutions contain special sections describing evaluative activities, and many have been supplemented by special detailed reports to the evaluation division. All of these reports, therefore—from the staff, from consultants, from special enterprises, from institutions—comprise the basic data for the present book. And to these must be added experiences, impressions, ideas of the evaluation staff retained in memory but not set down in the written records.

SOME SPECIAL EMPHASES

The variety of projects in the schools, the relationship of projects labeled evaluation to other problems in teacher education, and differences in attitude toward evaluation are quite naturally reflected in the reports accumulated in the Commission's offices. Moreover, the evaluative problems in teacher education and the manner of working on them have been conditioned by the philosophy and operating procedures that resulted from cooperative planning among participating institutions, the Commission, and its staff. These two factors—local autonomy and a philosophy of cooperative action—lead to several special emphases in this book. We have a special concern with the contributions which evaluative activities can make to the total program of teacher education and with ways in which evaluative activities can be carried out consonant with democratic philosophy and conducive to change.

The relationship between evaluation and instruction was a problem frequently encountered in the cooperative study. Many writers have pointed out that the bases for evaluation should be as broad as the objectives of the instructional program. Students and faculty alike tend to focus their learning and teaching efforts on the outcomes for which they will be held accountable in the final appraisal of their work. The appraisal, therefore, must not be limited to the qualities most readily measured, but must attempt to collect evidence with respect to all the goals that are professed. This relationship between instruction and evaluation is generally recognized and accepted. But there is another type of relationship with which we have been concerned. To what extent can the process of evaluation itself be educative or instructive? And to what extent can instruction and learning themselves be evaluative? If evaluation is to be a learning experience for the people evaluated, then the conditions under which evaluation takes place should be similar to the conditions under which effective learning occurs. The student must be motivated—that is, he must see in the evaluative device an opportunity to find out something he genuinely wants to know about himself; he must know the results; he must participate in the activity. Granted this, what modifications in the procedures for giving tests, rating scales, and so on, are called for? And what implications follow for the development and use of evaluative techniques and results?

Another problem is the relationship between evaluation and guidance or, more broadly, personnel work. If the function of the counselor is to help pupils make better decisions for themselves, how can tests, questionnaires, and other tools common to personnel and evaluation work contribute to this objective? How may participation in evaluative processes lead the student or teacher to a better understanding of himself, of his strengths and his weaknesses? How may competence in self-evaluation be developed?

Changes recommended as a result of some appraisals are never made. Action is blocked or resisted. Some colleges or school systems, surveyed, judged, and admonished by a group of experts, continue to operate in the same way they did before the survey. Some teachers, rated by their supervisors or principals, complain that the ratings are unfair. Some students, examined by their teachers at the close of a term or instructional unit, complain that the examinations are unfair. Some committees on evaluation find that their proposals are shelved. The procedures of evaluation are, in short, clearly related to administrative problems. How may a program of evaluation operate so that the people who are affected by the outcomes do not fear or reject those outcomes? If an evaluation should not only measure status and change but should produce change, what implications follow for the way in which the evaluation should proceed?

Back of all these problems and relationships—with instruction, personnel, and administration—lies the problem of relating evaluative procedures to democratic philosophy. If such a philosophy means belief in the uniqueness and worth of every human individual and in the equality and brotherhood of all individuals, then what we do in education—the way we teach, guide, administer, and evaluate—should foster and strengthen those beliefs. Do we, as supervisors or principals, help teachers feel their own worth and integrity when we determine their security and advancement by ratings which we seldom discuss with them or whose value they doubt? Do we, as teachers, promote students' belief in the importance of group welfare and common purposes when nearly all our classroom procedures are competitive? Do we, as evaluators, exemplify democracy in action when we give batteries of tests to students out of relation to purposes real to them, and pass out the results without regard to their effect on the attitude, security, and motivation of the students? Perhaps we do, but we need to consider many of our practices repeatedly and very consciously for their consonance with our democratic faith.

Throughout the book, reflecting our experience in the cooperative study, we shall be concerned with the procedures and the purposes of evaluation: with procedures that are in harmony with democratic and cooperative concepts and with purposes besides the common one of measuring status or change.

II

Initial Student Selection

W HO WILL BE good teachers? How can we identify the potentialities and the levels of skill and competence that should be expected of those who seek to prepare for teaching? In short, how shall we decide whom to admit to our professional education program? These questions define the problem of student selection. The problem of evaluation of student selection is to discover how well the questions have been answered in actual practice. But also, the process of selecting students for professional preparation is itself essentially evaluative in character. We have said that evaluation includes several tasks—formulating general objectives, defining them specifically, identifying appropriate sources of evidence, developing and using appropriate means to get that evidence, and finally interpreting it in the light of our objectives. Selection also involves these same tasks. We must decide what kinds of people we want and do so with some degree of definiteness. We must decide how and by what means we can identify these people. And we must interpret the results. Thus selection and evaluation are closely related.

Just as evaluation implies objectives so a program of selection implies some concept of who will be good teachers. The development of such a concept, however, is a task of the entire educational profession and not solely of those who operate the selection program. Recognizing the hazards in trying to characterize the good teacher, the members of the Commission on Teacher Education attempted in a recent publication to sketch at least the broad outlines of such a concept.[1] They said that the good teacher should possess intelligence, breadth of knowledge plus special insights in some areas, emotional soundness, integrity,

[1] *Teachers for Our Times, a Statement of Purposes by the Commission on Teacher Education* (Washington: American Council on Education, 1944).

respect for personality, understanding of the community, and good citizenship. They said further that the good teacher would be fond of children and youth; have an understanding of human growth and development, of the learning process, and of the techniques of evaluation; would have a sound social philosophy supported by conviction and knowledge; would be a good citizen of the school; would possess scholarship; and would believe in the worth of his work. Few will quarrel with the broad outlines of this conception. Yet one cannot help being aware of how few of these qualities we deliberately and systematically appraise in the selection, preparation, and certification of teachers.

To select or reject students on the basis of some of these qualities of the good teacher might not be appropriate at the freshman level, because of the lack of sufficient or convincing data on certain traits at that time. Moreover, it is the function of the professional program to develop some of these qualities. Selection is a continuing process. Some selecting can be done at the time of entrance. Some will result from personal counseling and professional orientation courses. Some will occur by the very nature of the tasks students encounter in the total professional program. The value of a well defined concept of the good teacher lies in its use as a framework through which to view all professional teacher education. Selection practices can then be complementary whenever they occur, rather than contradictory at different points in the professional program. In the present chapter, however, we shall be concerned primarily with initial selection.

SOME CONDITIONS INFLUENCING SELECTION PRACTICE

No single formula or program for the initial selection of students can serve all institutions equally well. Circumstances tending to hinder or expedite the development of selection programs vary from college to college. For example, selection practices may be influenced by state legislation. In some regions the conditions of supply and demand, and of teachers' salaries, may be a decisive factor. In some colleges the major task of selection occurs at the freshman level; in others it does not occur until the junior year. There are, likewise, variations among colleges in the provision of remedial instruction, in the interest in research studies of selection practices, and in the inclinations of local leaders.

Laws make the selective admission of students difficult in some states, while in other states selective admission is mandatory. The state universities in Ohio and Nebraska, for example, must accept nearly all applicants who are graduates of accredited high schools. If a student's high school scholarship has been poor and if he has made a low score on the college aptitude test, he can be dissuaded from entering the school of education or admitted on probation, but he cannot be refused entrance to the university. At both Ohio State and Nebraska Universities relatively unselected students enter the professional School of Education as freshmen. Many of them do not have a very clear notion of their chances of success in college or, indeed, any very strong conviction that they wish to become teachers. Under these circumstances it is not surprising that orientation courses have developed, and that these courses have served a selective function. Properly used, such orientation courses, together with facilities for personal counseling, enable the college to *guide* out rather than kick out those students whose potentialities lie in directions other than teaching.

In contrast, the enrollment of students in the state teachers colleges of New York and New Jersey is regulated by the state department of education in accordance with the size of the schools and the qualification of the students for entrance into teacher training. In New York during the last ten years, a program of selective admission based on tests of students' knowledge, academic skill, health, and personality has evolved. A similar program has developed in New Jersey where, in addition, emphasis is placed on sending counselors into high schools to recruit eligible students. Both programs illustrate some of the possibilities of selection at the freshman level and both are described in greater detail later in the chapter.

Local conditions of supply and demand, salaries, and prestige sometimes combine in ways that limit the development of selection programs. For example, in some regions where teachers' salaries are low, there are not enough applicants for admission to colleges of education to meet the demand in the field. Under such conditions, the impetus to develop selective programs has made little headway. There are some colleges in which the students and staff in the department of education are looked down upon by the influential members of other departments with the result that fewer students prepare to teach than are needed. It is possible, however, to develop more favorable attitudes toward teaching by administering a selection program which noticeably improves the quality of students. For instance, the quality of students in home economics education, physical education, and public school art at Syracuse University has been markedly improved in the last five years by strict adherence to selective criteria even though such adherence gave the institution, temporarily, fewer students than it could have placed. While such a solution is difficult, and may be still more difficult if low salary rather than low prestige is the obstacle to be overcome, it does indicate that having fewer students than can be placed is not always a good excuse for delaying the development of a selection program.

In many colleges, students do not enter professional education programs until some time after their initial enrollment as freshmen. Students at Wayne University, Stanford University, and the College of William and Mary, for example, do not begin their professional study until the junior year. The lower-division work in such institutions is devoted largely to general education. During this time however, if the student is in the immediate environment of the professional school, there is opportunity to gather detailed information concerning his qualifications for professional preparation. Many institutions have not taken advantage of this opportunity. They have continued to admit to the professional school anyone who has made a satisfactory academic record during the first two years. Other institutions have developed selective admission programs based on much more than academic records. Wayne University is one of these; its program of selection is described later in the chapter. ·

The specific factors considered in a selection program—at the freshman or the junior level—will be affected in part by the extent to which the institution assumes responsibility for remedial instruction. Some colleges do not offer any courses except those they believe to be of college quality. They do not, in other words, provide specific opportunity in their programs for helping students overcome deficiencies which, in their opinion, should have been overcome in high school. These institutions should feel an obligation to reject deficient students. Other colleges, believing that they have a responsibility to provide appropriate educational opportunity for all who wish to enter, do not limit their offerings in this way. Educability rather than past achievement thus becomes the major basis for selection. Remedial instruction can be willingly offered.

Research likewise has given some impetus, during the past decade, to the development of selective admission programs. Many studies have revealed that teachers colleges have not attracted as able students, judged by tests of academic aptitude and knowledge of school subjects, as have universities and colleges of liberal arts. The publication of such data has stimulated leaders in teacher education to take stock of their student personnel, and to explore ways in which the quality of students could be improved.

There is yet another factor that determines, to a large extent, the presence or absence of a selection program. The faculty must believe that it is important to get students of the highest quality to prepare for teaching. Unless there are men and women on the staff of an institution who believe that few jobs are as profound, exacting, or important as the job of giving direction to the mental, social, emotional, cultural, and physical development of children and youth, the need for initial and continuous selection of high-caliber personnel for the teaching profession may not be apparent or seem urgent. In short, there must be sensitivity to the need for improving the quality of individuals who go into teaching, and the vision and ingenuity to do something about it, if an effective program for the initial selection of students is to be developed.

Because we are interested primarily in evaluation we will not consider further some of the factors influencing selection programs that we have mentioned above—factors such as laws, teacher supply and demand, salaries. But we shall discuss further such factors as the time at which initial selection occurs, the characteristics of the college's education program, and the framework within which the selection program operates; for these factors have rather direct implications for the techniques and procedures of student selection and appraisal.

SELECTION AT THE FRESHMAN LEVEL

As already noted, procedures for selecting freshmen are in existence at the state-supported institutions for the preparation of teachers in New York and New Jersey. Information is available on how these programs have been working. We shall present the relevant facts in some detail.

THE PROGRAM IN NEW YORK

Selective admission to teacher education has been in operation in New York since the spring of 1932. We shall describe briefly how the program developed, how it now functions, and what attempts have been and might be made to judge its effectiveness. In July 1932 the board of regents of the University of the State of New York authorized the commissioner of education to establish a regulation limiting the registration of students in state normal schools and teachers colleges, in accord with the capacity of each school and the qualifications of students for teacher training. A committee, consisting of two representatives of the state department of education and one from each of the ten (now eleven) state teachers colleges, has had responsibility for planning and implementing selective admission, subject to the approval of the commissioner.

Expansion and operation

Prior to 1932 some of the institutions had been using high school scholarship, as revealed by an average of the regents' examinations, as a criterion for admission. It was thus only natural that, in the first year of the statewide program, the average of regents' scores was still used as a main basis for admission. But the committee was convinced that factors other than academic competence contributed to success in the professional education of a teacher. Consequently they administered to applicants in 1932 psychological, English, diagnostic, physical, and teacher-prognosis examinations, and they also asked high school principals to rate applicants from their schools on character and personality. Data from the tests and ratings were not used this first year in deciding who should be admitted, but they were studied in each institution in relation to the success of those who were admitted. Each institution summarized the data relative to its own students, and the state committee summarized for all institutions. Subsequently the diagnostic and prognosis tests were dropped; the psychological and English tests and a reading test were added to the regents' examinations as sources of data to be used regularly in the selection program. The committee also recommended the continued use of principals' ratings and physical examinations. In 1934 and 1935 the institutions were encouraged to use the personal interview experimentally as a means of gathering data about applicants; from 1936 to the present time such interviews have been consistently used by all of the institutions. A personal-inventory blank came into use in 1935. Since 1938 a voice-and-diction examination administered by a speech specialist in each institution has been a regular part of the admission procedure.

The most recent expansion of the selective admission program has been the development of a personality-and-speech rating scale. The scale was developed by a subcommittee of the state committee on selective admission. After some preliminary study, the committee selected eight major headings for the scale as follows: personal appearance, social adaptability, enthusiasm, emotional qualities, breadth of experience, use of English, voice and diction, and speech defects. The meaning of these major headings was defined by substatements under each, and there was a total of thirty-four items in the scale on which each applicant was to be rated. The rating is made by a member of the college staff following a fifteen- or twenty-minute interview with the applicant.

Currently, the selective admission program operates as follows: during April the psychological, reading, and English examinations are administered in each of thirty centers throughout the state. Responsibility for their administration is divided among the institutions; the time and place of the examinations are widely publicized among the high schools of the state. When the student takes the examinations, he also fills out an application and personal-inventory blank, and designates the institution he hopes to enter the following September.

All the information gathered at the examination centers is distributed to the several colleges according to the choices indicated by the applicants. Each college then obtains ratings on the student's character and personality from the high school principal on a form supplied by the state department of education. In due course, the applicants are invited to appear at the institution of their choice for health and speech examinations, and for personal interviews. The physical examination is given by a physician employed by the college—usually the director of the health service. Speech tests are given by staff members of the speech department. Personal interviews are held between the applicant and each of two to four staff members. At one institution, for instance, each applicant interviews three staff members; at the close of the day the interviewers, together with the speech examiner and the college nurse or doctor, meet to review what they have done and to discuss doubtful cases.

The problem of how one can summarize the data in order to reach a decision on the acceptability of individual applicants is always perplexing. In New York much of the information obtained is in the form of test scores and numerical ratings—scores on regents', psychological, English, and reading examinations, and ratings on speech and personality. These numerical data are weighted and combined into a single numerical index. In the current scheme of weighting, the factor of high school scholarship (regents' examinations) counts for four-tenths; intellectual ability and skill in English and reading, three-tenths; personality and speech, three-tenths. Data from the principal's rating, the physical examination, and the personal-inventory blank are not included in the combined index. These are supplementary factors to be used in whatever ways seem wisest in the local colleges. Health factors, for instance, have not been included in the state formula for weighting because they sometimes must be considered on an all-or-none basis: it would be difficult to develop a formula that would weight the presence or absence of active tuberculosis so as to eliminate an otherwise highly desirable candidate. One might question, of course, whether some of the items in the personality-and-speech rating scale, now included in the combined index, do not also operate in a similar all-or-none way. As a matter of fact, the items concerned with speech defects have recently been eliminated from the combined index. We shall return to this problem of weighting later in the chapter.

Evidence of success

In 1940 the state committee assembled data to show the extent to which various factors operate or are held important in the selection of students by different institutions in the state. Each institution was asked to classify, according to the major contributing factor, each applicant who had been refused admission. These data are shown in Table I. The 812 students classified in the table comprise approximately 30 percent of the total number of applicants. About 55 percent of all applicants were accepted. The remainder withdrew before committee decision. From the table it is evident that two-thirds of the total rejections were said to have been made for academic reasons. But differences in emphasis among the colleges are also apparent. It is interesting to note that the academic factor was considered the major reason for rejection in only 32 percent of the cases at institution E, whereas it was the controlling factor in all of the rejections at institution G. Institution E is the only place where a majority of the rejections was based on personal qualities. No explanation of these differences is forthcoming from the table. It would doubtless be helpful for all the colleges to discuss together the different methods they use in considering evidence relative to the personal qualifications of applicants.

The state committee issues an annual report summarizing the results of selective admission. From the reports each institution

TABLE I

REASONS FOR THE REJECTION OF 812 FRESHMAN APPLICANTS IN 1940
BY TEN NEW YORK STATE TEACHERS COLLEGES[a]

Institution	Number Rejected	Percentage of Applicants Rejected for			
		Academic deficiencies	Personal qualities	Physical disabilities	Miscellaneous
A	112	67	21	12	—
B	34	91	6	3	—
C	122	82	4	2	12
D	4	75	25	—	—
E	166	32	51	17	—
F	262	75	8	4	13
G	26	100	—	—	—
H	23	70	26	—	4
I	59	66	—	7	27
J	4	50	50	—	—
Percentage of total		67	18	7	8

[a] Data from *An Analysis of the Results of the Selective Admissions Program of the New York State Teacher Education Institutions Preparing Elementary School Teachers, 1940–41,* compiled by Herman D. Behrens (Albany: University of the State of New York, State Education Department, 1941, mimeographed), p. 13.

can compare the outcome of its own practices with that of the other institutions (not individually identified) and can make local modifications in certain standards and procedures. For quantity and quality of scholarship, however, standards are fixed by the state committee. Data in the annual reports are not recorded in such a way as to permit year-to-year comparisons on all of the factors now included in the admission program. One can, however, show the average scores of applicants over an eight-year period on the regents' examinations. These scores are comparable from year to year; since the beginning of the selection program, high school scholarship has been the most influential factor in determining the admission of candidates to the teachers colleges.

Table II shows the median scholarship ranking on the com-

TABLE II

COMPARISON OF THE STANDINGS ON HIGH SCHOOL SCHOLARSHIP OF ALL FRESHMAN CANDIDATES WHO APPLIED FOR ADMISSION, WERE ADMITTED, OR REJECTED AT TEN NEW YORK STATE TEACHERS COLLEGES, 1934 to 1940[a]

Year	Group	Number	Regents' Examination Percentiles		
			Q_1	Median	Q_3
1934	Applied	2,390	75.9	79.1	83.0
	Admitted	1,672	76.8	79.8	83.6
	Rejected[b]	718	73.1	75.9	80.4
1935	Applied	2,668	75.9	79.3	83.3
	Admitted	1,696	76.6	80.0	84.0
	Rejected	547	73.1	75.8	79.6
1936	Applied	2,953	76.4	79.7	83.7
	Admitted	1,893	76.9	80.3	84.3
	Rejected	568	74.6	77.6	80.6
1937[c]	Applied	2,773	76.5	79.7	84.0
	Admitted	1,901	76.9	80.1	84.2
	Rejected	410	73.3	75.7	78.4
1938	Applied	3,079	77.4	80.9	85.2
	Admitted	1,626	79.3	82.9	86.7
	Rejected	1,091	75.3	77.8	80.9
1939	Applied	3,265	78.1	81.7	86.1
	Admitted	1,518	79.7	83.1	87.3
	Rejected	1,305	76.4	79.4	83.2
1940	Applied	2,763	78.1	82.1	86.4
	Admitted	1,509	79.5	83.2	87.3
	Rejected	812	76.4	79.5	83.7

[a] Data from *An Analysis of the Results of the Selective Admissions Program of the New York State Teacher Education Institutions Preparing Elementary School Teachers:* 1938–39, p. 44; 1939–40, p. 24; and 1940–41, p. 23.

[b] Withdrawals were tabulated with rejections in 1934 only.

[c] Includes data from only nine of the ten colleges.

bined regents' examinations for every other year, 1934-40. The picture is one of consistent improvement, not only on the part of those who were admitted but also of those who applied. At first glance it may appear that an increase in median percentile from 79.8, for those admitted in 1934, to 83.2 in 1940 is, after all, only 3.4 points and relatively unimportant. Note, however, that the median percentile of those accepted in 1940 is only 0.4 of a point less than the 75th percentile of those admitted in 1934. This marked improvement in scholarship over the eight-year period is evident throughout the whole range of scores, for the 25th percentile (79.5) of those admitted in 1940 is only 0.3 of a point less than the median for 1934. Moreover, each year the median of those rejected is approximately the same as the 25th percentile of those accepted. In short, the selective admission program in New York has been effective in improving the scholastic level of students who are college entrants. This has, indeed, been the major emphasis of the New York program. Yet it must be clear that many factors besides high school scholarship are playing a significant role in the selection program. For example, about one-fourth of the applicants who are rejected have better scholarship records than the typical student who is accepted. One must assume that these superior students are rejected on the basis of factors other than scholarship, yet these factors are but vaguely defined and their relation to scholarship largely unexplored.

Need for more evidence

Beyond the simple comparison of accepted and rejected applicants in scholarship, there are many other ways of judging the effectiveness and the validity of a selection program. Some of these have already been attemped on a small scale; others will perhaps be carried out at some future date. For example, one small-scale study showed a correlation of 0.55 between high school scholarship (regents' examinations) and scholarship (grades) during the first year of college. Studies are in progress at four of the state teachers colleges of the reliability and validity of the data obtained from the speech and personality ratings. Other studies have been recommended to the colleges by the state committee on admissions. Among these are the following: a follow-up study of the relationship between admissions factors and student success in different specialized fields; a follow-up study of applicants who were refused admission; and a follow-up study of applicants who completed all requirements for admission but who did not enroll.

The emphasis given to follow-up studies is an important one. Moreover, one should not be content with follow-up studies of academic success, for, broadly conceived, the purpose of a selective admission program is to select students who will succeed not only in college but also as teachers in service. Improvement in the quality of applicants on the factors measured by regents', psychological, English, and reading examinations may be at the expense of important personality traits.[2] The development of the rating scale for personality and speech and its incorporation in the combined index has increased automatically the recognition given to personal factors; therefore, any comprehensive study should pay special attention to the validity and significance of these factors for ultimate success. Finally, out of a comprehensive follow-up study may come a clearer statement of the purposes of the New York selective admission program. To some extent purposes can be inferred from the techniques and procedures used in the selection program; but they should be made explicit.

DATA FROM NEW JERSEY

New Jersey is another state where the teachers colleges have cooperated in an effort to improve the quality of their students. They now recruit applicants who rank in scholarship almost without exception above the 50th percentile of their respective high school classes. This has been accomplished partly through an organized program of conferences with high school principals, superintendents, deans, directors of personnel, and meetings with groups of prospective candidates, to clarify the basic philosophy of careful selection and to gain a common understanding of the benefits resulting from it. The program of selection is similar to that in New York state. High school records,

[2] A study of pupil-teacher relationships, reported in Chapter VIII, reveals this possibility

interviews, speech tests, entrance examinations, and medical reports, provide the basic data on which the applicants are accepted or refused. As in New York, there are extensive data showing that the scholastic level of freshmen accepted in the colleges has risen from year to year. While the two programs differ in details they are enough alike to make it unnecessary to present statistics on the success of the New Jersey program.

One study in New Jersey[3] is reported here because it suggests an important area for further investigation. Applicants for admission to the state teachers colleges were compared with students in sixteen high schools who anticipated going to colleges of liberal arts and universities to pursue curricula other than teacher education. All students took the regular entrance examinations for New Jersey teachers colleges, including subject-matter tests in mathematics, English, history, biology, and general science. In about half the schools those seeking admission to the teachers colleges made higher scores on a majority of the subject-matter tests than those intending to go to liberal arts colleges or universities. In the other schools, the reverse was true. Few of the differences were statistically significant. But, in one school all test results favored the students interested in teaching, while in a second school the significant differences were all in favor of the other group. Furthermore, variations between the two categories of students were almost as great among different subject-matter areas within schools as among schools. The study itself throws no light on the causes of this variability. It seems likely, however, that interviews with high school teachers and principals in schools where the divergences are greatest would uncover at least some of the influences at work. Emphasis in the New Jersey program upon conferences with principals and upon personal recruiting could lead quite naturally to such an interview study.

Both the New York and New Jersey programs would profit from careful follow-up studies of the college success and the success after graduation of the students who are selected. Mean-

[3] Martha Downs, *A Comparative Study in Student Abilities*, Faculty Bulletin, Supplement No. 2 (Newark: New Jersey State Teachers College).

while, other institutions concerned about the quality of their students may find encouragement in knowing that relatively extensive selection programs can be carried out on a statewide basis. The experience in New York and New Jersey may likewise be useful to those who are concerned with the development of an admission program within a single institution.

A SELECTION PROGRAM AT THE JUNIOR LEVEL

When students do not have to be selected for professional training until the junior year, or later, the college has an opportunity to find out more about them than it can when selection must be made directly from high school. There is more time to collect helpful data. Students are older, and readier for vocational preparation. More of them have had experience that appears to be predictive of success in teaching. And in the majority of institutions most of them will have spent their first two college years on the same campus. There is, in short, opportunity to observe, interview, test, and study cumulative records for evidence of students' potentiality for teaching.

The College of Education at Wayne University is in a position very favorable to the development of a comprehensive program of admission. The university is part of the Detroit public school system, and the schools look to Wayne as the chief source of new teachers. Members of the College of Education staff who advise students in their major areas are also supervisors in the Detroit schools in special subject-matter areas. Under these conditions, the staff could escape neither concern nor responsibility for the quality of students preparing to teach.

Wayne University has taken advantage of this unique opportunity to develop a selection program that is quite extensive. From each applicant the college obtains data relative to academic aptitude and achievement, physical and mental health, personality and professional promise. The American Council on Education Psychological Examination is used as the index of academic aptitude. Academic accomplishment is judged by performance on the Cooperative tests in English, General Culture, and Contemporary Affairs, the Detroit Handwriting Scale, the Stanford Achievement and Dictation Test in Spelling, and by records of previous scholarship at the university. A general physical examination, special tests of hearing and speech, an interview with a psychiatrist, and performance on the Bernreuter Personality Inventory provide data relative to physical and mental health. Ratings on personality and probable fitness for teaching are obtained from six instructors, four public school principals, the curriculum adviser in the student's major field, an officer of a social agency where the student has given service, and, if possible, from a former employer. The responsibility for taking all these tests, interviewing the proper people, and doing whatever else may be required to complete the admission procedure rests upon the student. The college issues directions for the student's use, sets aside definite periods when various tests will be administered, and then leaves to the students the job of carrying out the directions and taking the tests.

SAMPLE TECHNIQUES AND PROCEDURES

Some of the techniques Wayne uses are commonly employed elsewhere—the psychological examination, a record of previous scholarship, and a physical examination. Some techniques are similar to, but perhaps more detailed than, techniques used elsewhere—for instance, the use of three of the Cooperative tests, tests of spelling and handwriting, and special examinations in hearing and speech. Other techniques are rarely found elsewhere, yet they play a very important part in the Wayne program. We have selected three of these for illustration.

Principals' rating

Each applicant must interview four school principals in Detroit. If the student attended the local schools he can select one of the principals. The others are assigned by the college. The interviews are brief—usually about fifteen minutes—and all that is asked for is a general rating on the student's probable success as a teacher. A copy of the form which the principals fill out is reproduced on page 32.[4] On the five-point scale, with 5

[4] *Admission Status of 2,188 Applicants for Teacher Education: Research Studies in Selective Admission and Placement, No. 2* (Detroit: Published by Authority of the Board of Education of Detroit, Nov. 1, 1940, mimeographed), p. 111.

PRINCIPAL'S REPORT OF INTERVIEW WITH APPLICANT

Name of Applicant _____ Date _____

To School Official:

The College of Education believes that these reports turned in by school officials after applicants for admission to teacher education work have interviewed them are important aids in its selection procedure. Valued estimates are thus secured from those under whom these future teachers may later work. Other data, such as intelligence test scores and college marks, are relatively easy to get but they are not the only important factors that should be considered in attempting to predict future teaching success.

It will be greatly appreciated if you will give this applicant an interview and return this report blank to the College of Education as soon as possible. Please check (√) on the scale below approximately where you think this applicant would stand. It is of course understood that your rating is given usually after only a short interview. No applicant will be accepted or rejected solely on one individual's rating or on any one of the several other criteria used in the selection program. However, the combined ratings of the principals or their assistants are given much weight in the consideration of the personal fitness of candidates for teaching.

Estimate of Probable Success as a Teacher

Superior prospect	Good prospect	Average but below desired standard	Very doubtful prospect	Definitely undesirable prospect

Please add additional significant comments.

_____   ___ _____

To the Applicant: The first responsibility of school principals and their assistants is the efficient direction of their schools. You should therefore arrange for the interview in advance.

To the Principal: Please return to College of Education. This report will be kept absolutely confidential. Lower part will be cut off at dotted line as soon as blank is received.

_____   _____
Signature of School Official   Title and School

indicating "superior prospect," the average of the four principals' ratings on the typical candidate is 3.82 with a standard deviation of 0.50.

Psychiatrist's rating

Another important feature of the Wayne program is an interview with a psychiatrist or psychiatric social worker. Prior to the interview the student writes a brief description of himself in relation to the following instructions:[5]

1. Please tell us how environmental influences have contributed to your personality. These usually include:
   a. Home, family, and parental
   b. School and outside work
   c. Social and friend relations
2. Please try to analyze your personality strengths and weaknesses.
3. What are the features and opportunities of teaching that attract you to it?

This statement provides the starting point of the interview. Brief notes are recorded by the psychiatrist under five topical headings as follows: health and vitality, school and community adjustment, childhood and youth history, personality and emotional factors, and physical characteristics.[6]

The psychiatrist's observations and judgments are then written on the rating blank reproduced on page 34. The notes on this particular blank describe a boy of average intelligence but with serious emotional conflicts that might not be discovered by an untrained interviewer.

Social agency's rating

Applicants to the College of Education at Wayne must have had 100 hours of work experience—in the evenings, on holidays and weekends, or during the summer—with boys and girls in one or more of Detroit's social agencies, such as Boy Scouts, YMCA clubs, and so forth. The social agencies cooperate with

[5] *Ibid.*, p. 122
[6] *Ibid.*, p. 123.

PSYCHIATRIC SOCIAL WORKER'S OR PSYCHIATRIST'S RATING BLANK

NAME John Jones   BY Mary Smith, Psychiatric Social Worker

DATE 1-3-41   AT My office

I. Success in Social Relationships: Evidence of emotional immaturity as shown in narcissism, egocentricity, neurotic symptoms, poise or lack of poise, alertness, directness, school and community adjustment, lack of opportunity for normal emotional development.

This young man of [foreign] parentage gives the impression of being an inhibited, elusive, unstable person. He is definitely in a confused state over his recent dismissal from a seminary where he had been preparing for the priesthood for 8 years. He was very cagey at first but when he does try to explain or justify this dismissal his efforts at expressing himself are stilted and unconvincing because of his ambivalence of feeling. His rationalizations . . . seem weak and indicate a lack of integrity or instability which might interfere with his dependability under all circumstances. . . . [Once] he expressed great humiliation and said his whole purpose in life was to be reinstated at the seminary after a 2-year period. Again, later he said he thought he would eventually marry.

The effect of his foreign background on his speech has not been successfully overcome in spite of 8 years' training in the classics. This was shown in his pronouncing "dey" for they; "true" for through; "wid" for with.

He admits lack of experience in leadership, saying that he had "never had anything to do with anything with youth." His lack of insight into the need to understand the particular types of children with whom he deals in order to adjust his methods and information to them is seen in his complete lack of knowledge of the mental status of children at Wayne County Training School where he had had some religious training while at the Seminary. He lacks . . . insight into the differences between mentally retarded and delinquent children.

II. Significant Experiences (experiences which have contributed to the student's own personality development and which should aid in teaching):

8 years' training—seminary preparing for priesthood.

III. Physical Characteristics and Appearance (significant attitudes relating to possible relationship to personality factor):

Short, stocky build. Dark complexion. Sharp, piercing brown eyes. Mature appearance.

Speech affected by foreign accent on some words.

Wears glasses.

				X[a]		X
IV.	Superior prospect	Good prospect	Average but below desired standard	Very doubtful prospect		Definitely undesirable prospect

[a] This supplementary rating was given by John Smith, Psychiatrist.

34

REPORT BLANK FROM SOCIAL GROUP WORK AGENCIES

Name of student _____   Address _____   Telephone number _____

Name of agency _____   Address _____   Type of student leadership _____

Student's schedule of group leadership _____   Total clock hours completed in your agency and inclusive dates _____

Directions: Please fill in report blank on each of our students helping you in your program at this time. Rate the student by checking one of the five classifications which in your judgment would most closely identify the student's work and ability with respect to the items listed below. If you have been satisfied with the student on an item you should rate him "good average" or "superior," of course taking into consideration that he will usually be a freshman or sophomore preteaching student who has had no professional training either for group work or regular teaching.

	4. Superior	3. Good average	2. Low average	1. Poor	No evidence on which to base judgment
1. Worker secures good rapport with group; gets on well with members; secures confidence and is "at home" with them; is pleasant and patient					
2. Willingness to learn; open-minded and adaptable; has good attitude in using suggestions of supervisor...................................					
3. Studies and respects personalities of all members of his group; aids them in adjusting even outside the specific group situation.........					
4. Uses cooperative and democratic rather than dictatorial methods in group leadership..					
5. Conscientious and responsible in matters of record-keeping and other necessary administrative or routine matters......................					
6. Seems to have proper balance in his own emotional life as it relates to group or supervision......................................					
7. Stimulates individual or small group to creative work; resourceful in aiding them to plan, execute, and evaluate their projects..........					
8. Has a desirable combination of interest in the children and in the program of the group...					
9. Consistent in policies in administering necessary disciplinary control within the group..					
10. Appearance and appropriate grooming..........................					
11. Vital and energetic; uses own personality to the best advantage of the program...					
12. Analyzes job and considers implications of his work................					

Your estimate of this student's probable chances of success in teaching are:

_____

Please add additional remarks if you think they would be helpful. All reports and remarks will be confidential.

Space for remarks

Signature of Supervisor _____   Position _____   Date _____

Address of Supervisor _____   Telephone number _____

NAME_____ SEX____ AGE____ STANDING_____ CURRICULUM_____

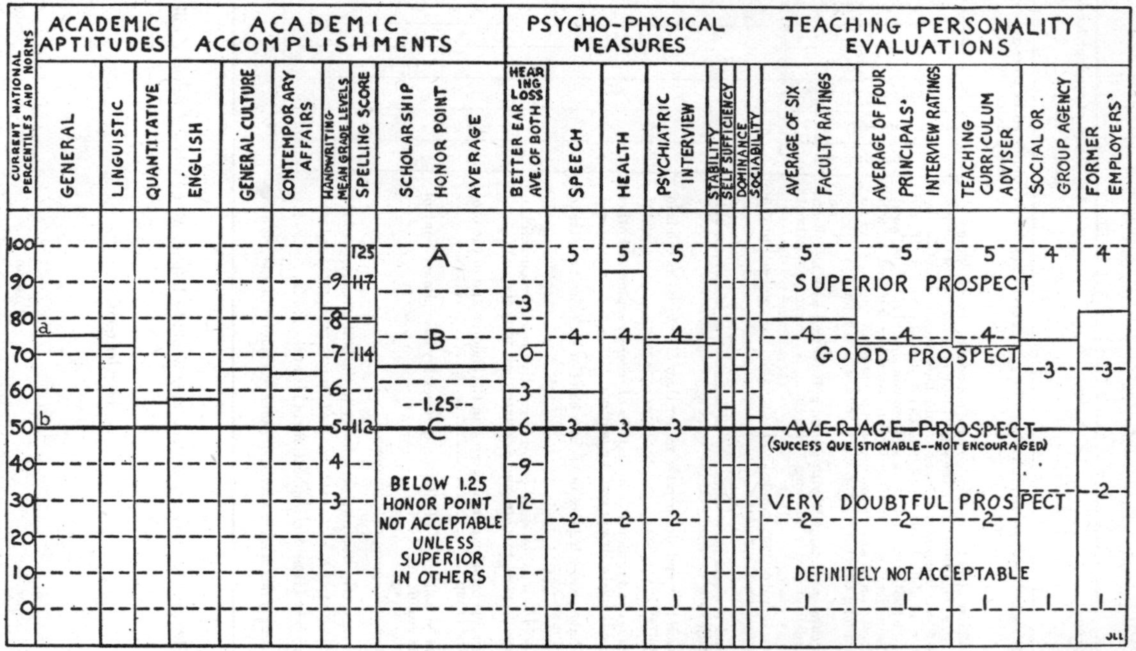

CURRENT NATIONAL PERCENTILES AND NORMS	ACADEMIC APTITUDES				ACADEMIC ACCOMPLISHMENTS					PSYCHO-PHYSICAL MEASURES					TEACHING PERSONALITY EVALUATIONS				
	GENERAL	LINGUISTIC	QUANTITATIVE	ENGLISH	GENERAL CULTURE	CONTEMPORARY AFFAIRS	HANDWRITING MEAN GRADE LEVELS	SPELLING SCORE	SCHOLARSHIP HONOR POINT AVERAGE	BETTER EAR HEARING LOSS AVE. OF BOTH	SPEECH	HEALTH	PSYCHIATRIC INTERVIEW	STABILITY / SELF SUFFICIENCY / DOMINANCE / SOCIABILITY	AVERAGE OF SIX FACULTY RATINGS	AVERAGE OF FOUR PRINCIPALS' INTERVIEW RATINGS	TEACHING CURRICULUM ADVISER	SOCIAL OR GROUP AGENCY	FORMER EMPLOYERS'
100								125	A		5	5	5		5	5	5	4	4
90							9	117		-3-									
80							8		B		4	4	4		4	4	4	3	3
70							7	114		-0-									
60							6		-1.25-	-3-	3	3	3						
50							5	112	C	-6-									
40							4			-9-									
30							3		BELOW 1.25 HONOR POINT NOT ACCEPTABLE UNLESS SUPERIOR IN OTHERS	-12-	2	2	2		2	2	2	2	2
20																			
10											1	1	1		1	1	1	1	1
0																			

Rating bands (right side):
SUPERIOR PROSPECT
GOOD PROSPECT
AVERAGE PROSPECT (SUCCESS QUESTIONABLE—NOT ENCOURAGED)
VERY DOUBTFUL PROSPECT
DEFINITELY NOT ACCEPTABLE

REMARKS:

PREPARED BY:

a Solid lines within individual columns indicate local medians.
b Heavy long line indicates "theoretical average student"—American Council Psychological and Academic norms. (Red lines should be drawn in by hand by the staff to indicate standing of a particular applicant.)

the university in making these experiences available to students and the students work under the supervision of regular leaders in the agencies. The leader then reports, on the blank reproduced on page 35, on the effectiveness of the student's relationship with boys and girls and with the agency.

THE PROFILE CHART

All the rating scales, report forms, and test papers are turned in to the examiner's office. There all the results are transcribed to percentile scores, and these scores for each student are entered on an individual profile chart. A folder is then prepared for each student which includes the profile and copies of the ratings and reports. The actual ratings, with the comments on them, can be referred to conveniently in order to clarify the numerical ratings when necessary. The profile chart is Wayne's solution to the problem of summarizing the mass of data gathered on each applicant for admission. New York, it will be recalled, summarized a large part of its data in a single numerical index. At Wayne the information on each of the factors considered in the selection program is recorded separately; then the over-all pattern of data is examined. An applicant low in certain qualities may be admitted if he has compensating strengths; or one who ranks consistently high in most qualities may be refused because of a serious deficiency in a single quality. Within the over-all pattern, however, some factors are generally considered more important than others. The width of each column in the profile chart, reproduced on page 36, is a rough approximation of the significance attached to the factor it describes.

Over a period of years, it has been possible to develop local norms for all factors covered in the applicant's profile. They are represented by the solid lines within each column on the chart. The heavy line across the chart at the 50th percentile represents national norms for those tests on which these are available.

Out of experience in using these tests has also come the setting of critical points below which an applicant's admission is withheld or granted only on condition. The critical points vary with the field in which the applicant proposes to do his major work. For example, a score on the Cooperative Contemporary Affairs Test below the national 20th percentile will admit the student only on condition, and implies a need for remedial work, but for social studies applicants a score below the 50th percentile carries a condition. These critical points, together with other information about the factors included in the admission battery, are described fully in a manual of interpretation prepared for the Wayne staff by the college examiner.

With all this information available, the dean of the School of Education then inspects the profiles and folders and decides on the applications. In this process he classifies the applicants as unconditionally acceptable, conditionally acceptable, or unacceptable. Doubtful cases are referred to a committee on student recommendations for review and group judgment. The applicant may be recalled for further interviews and tests.

EVALUATION RESULTS AND QUESTIONS

In attempting to evaluate the selective admission program, an impressive array of data has been analyzed by the Wayne staff, and only a small part of it can be reported here. Table III,

TABLE III

SUBSEQUENT STATUS OF APPLICANTS TO THE COLLEGE OF EDUCATION, WAYNE UNIVERSITY[a]

Item	June 1939		September 1939		February 1940		Total	
	Number	Percent	Number	Percent	Number	Percent	Number	Percent
Applicants for admittance........	80	100	540	100	247	100	867	100
Applicants who completed entrance procedure....................	55	68	348	64	205	83	608	70
Applicants admitted.............	51	64	324	60	143	58	518	60
Applicants who enrolled..........	47	58	312	57	141	56	500	58
Students likely to graduate.......	41	50	259	48	116	47	416	48

[a] From an unpublished manuscript in the files of Wayne University.

to begin with, reveals that many students who apply for admission are not accepted. Specifically, during a twelve-month period, 4 out of 10 applicants fail to be admitted (60 percent are admitted). Most of those who fail, however, do so not because their performance on the admission battery has been judged inadequate but because they do not complete the tests and interviews that are required. According to the table, there were 608 applicants who completed the tests and interviews and 518 of these people were accepted. Thus 90 were rejected on the basis of test and interview results. This number may be contrasted with the 259 students who did not complete the admission procedure. No reason is given for so many incompleted applications. It would be worth knowing, however, how many of these students withdrew because they felt the procedures were too complex or because they felt they were not doing well in the tests and interviews. This large number of incompleted applications is, of course, not undesirable if the factors that account for it are known to be predictive of failure in the professional program.

In 1940, 54 percent of the students who were admitted were accepted conditionally—that is, they were judged to have deficiencies which must be removed before eventual certification. Three-fourths of this group accepted conditionally were judged as having some serious defect. Remedial work is provided for these students and further tests are given from time to time to measure their progress.

Laboratories have been set up for those deficient in speech, writing, reading, and spelling. Personality problems are worked on through the counseling services. Orientation courses are, at present, also giving attention to these factors. The difference between the number who drop out after having been admitted and the number admitted with basic deficiencies would seem to indicate that students are quite successful in removing their deficiencies, or that regulations regarding the removal of basic conditions by the time of graduation are not carefully enforced, or that the description of a deficiency as "basic" is not so serious as it would appear. In any case, a study of the resources which prove most useful to students in the removal of basic conditions would be helpful locally as well as to other teacher-educating institutions.

Exhaustive statistical analyses have been made, not only of all of the factors included on the profile chart but also of the single items on the application blank on which the student records personal data relative to his educational experience, home and family background, socio-economic status, and recreational activity. Intercorrelations, factor analyses, and studies of the reliability of differences have been made using *admissions status* as the criterion—that is, students not admitted have been compared with those admitted. Some of the results of these studies have been summarized by Reitz as follows:

There is no single and outstanding predictive measure of admission status among the seventy-two variables studied, although various statistical procedures yield a number of statistically significant differences between means or proportions of such groups as "admitted" vs. "not admitted," and "admitted" vs. "total applicants." This finds its explanation in several facts. Most variables yielding significant differences do so only because of the relatively large number of cases involved in the calculations. Practically all of the differences in themselves are not large enough in terms of the respective scales to become noticeable and critical in the case of an individual to be selected. For instance, the average percentile difference on the linguistic part of the Psychological Examination for the nonadmitted and admitted groups is about 10 percentiles only. In the case of honor-point average the difference is less than 0.2 of a point. Most of the distributions of measures for any groups studied, such as "admitted" and "nonadmitted" are highly overlapping. Other variables yield large differences because they are merely anticipations of the final admission or nonadmission judgment on account of their function and place in the admission procedure, such as the ratings of the Committee on Students. [This rating is not part of the profile.] But most important is the reason that the array of variables composing the admission process functions as a whole in the arrival at the final judgment of admission status. . . .

Combining the discriminatory prediction powers yielded by . . . statistical procedures . . . , the following grouping by significant levels of the variables and attributes studied is seen to result. . . . [The only factors listed below are ones included in the profile.]

High Statistical Discrimination
    Curriculum Adviser's Recommendation
    Psychiatric Social Worker's Summary Rating
Substantial Statistical Discrimination
    Psychological Examination Linguistic Score Percentile

Honor-Point Average
Psychological Examination Gross Score Percentile
Former Employer's Report
Speech Test Rating
Average of Principal's Rating
Handwriting Quality
Fair Statistical Discrimination
Average of Faculty Ratings
Health Report Rating
Bernreuter Dominance-Submission Percentile
Contemporary Affairs Test Score Percentile
Low or Chance Statistical Discrimination
Psychological Examination Arithmetic Score Percentile
Spelling Score
Bernreuter Self-Sufficiency Percentile
Bernreuter Sociability Percentile
Hearing Loss
Bernreuter Neurotic Tendency Percentile (under 30)

One of the most gratifying findings with reference to the evaluation of the admission process is the actual operation of a relatively great emphasis upon personality factors. Of the identified variance [between admitted and not admitted], only 29 percent is due to an academic factor, whereas 71 percent is due to such personality factors as "Interview Personality," "Dominance-Self-Sufficiency" or "Autonomy," "Youthfulness" or "Plasticity," "Personal Professional Fitness for the Respective Field of Specialization," and "Socio-Emotional Adjustment and Stability." This emphasis is in significant contrast to the emphasis upon academic and scholastic factors of some years ago. However, these personality factors are far from being adequately identified and reliably measured. Their validity is only tentatively established. Whether or not the factors found to actually underly the program are the factors for which a conscious effort is exerted, and whether or not they have desirable relationship to success and growth in teaching, await further determination.

It is felt important to repeat that the findings and implications listed above present only a bare minimum of those which the data permit, nor are the implications necessarily identical with those which cooperative thinking of the faculty might arrive at. In view of this fact, it is recommended that efforts be made to bring about a greater familiarity with the data on the part of all those concerned with the selection process, in order that the maximum benefit to college policies and procedures be obtained.[7]

[7] *Ibid.*, pp. lviii ff.

Ultimately, the improvement of selection practices depends on the extent to which relationships can be established between factors identifiable at the time of entrance and success in teaching. Wayne is now engaged in establishing some of these more significant relationships by means of follow-up studies. But what is meant by "success in teaching" is extremely difficult to define precisely; the use of a vague criterion of teaching success necessarily means that only vague and unstable relationships can be established between it and factors that might be used to predict it. Improving the bases of prediction will be a long-time, difficult, and complex job and one can perhaps afford to be patient.

An important recent development in the program at Wayne University is a trend toward the administration of admission procedures in orientation courses during the freshman year rather than during the semester immediately preceding enrollment in the College of Education. Early knowledge of strengths and weaknesses affords the student and counselor an opportunity to plan and carry out a remedial program. If an intelligent choice of vocation can be reached during the freshman and sophomore years, the number of students whom the institution must exclude arbitrarily from further training can be reduced. Even though institutions may not technically be allowed to admit students to their professional schools until the beginning of the junior year, there seems to be little reason why the selective process cannot be made to serve a guidance function during the first two college years. The selection data can, of course, also serve a guidance function during the last two years of college if they are readily available to and used by both students and advisers.

The extensive analyses of the admission program that have been initiated at Wayne should, when carried through to include follow-up studies of graduates, be extremely helpful to other institutions with similar programs. Equally helpful to Wayne and other colleges would be a more specific statement of the purposes of the selection program and a more critical review of the tests and other devices used in relation to those purposes. Such a statement might well result from a follow-up study.

BASIC CONSIDERATIONS AND PROCEDURES

As one looks back over the factors that are included in these various selection programs, the need for some classification and analysis of them is apparent. The several factors vary in their importance and in the manner in which they are handled among the different colleges. Two guiding questions, however, can be set forth. The first question is this: What degree of importance does the institution attach to this factor? Stated another way, how important is this factor or characteristic for the good teacher? The second question is: To what extent does the institution assume responsibility for effecting improvements in students' status with respect to this factor? The first question refers broadly to a concept of the good teacher; the second refers specifically to the goals of the instructional program of the college. We can raise these two questions with respect to specific factors.

There are, for example, many factors that are important for the good teacher that also represent specific objectives of their professional education. Knowledge of a given subject matter, interest in current affairs, competence in working and planning with boys and girls would be examples. It may be appropriate to consider some of these factors in selection at the junior level or higher, but for the most part they are rightly regarded as capacities the college is seeking to develop. Then, there are factors that are important for the good teacher that are also objectives of education but not necessarily of professional college education. For instance, to develop students' skills in reading, spelling, and speaking are definitely basic objectives of education, and of special importance for prospective teachers, but few colleges consider it their responsibility to teach skills which students should have acquired in elementary school. Therefore, the college should select students who already possess these skills to a degree sufficient for college and professional success. If the college offers remedial instruction the requisite degree of skill needed for entrance may be less than otherwise. Also relevant to the way in which such skills will be valued by different colleges will be the time at which selection occurs and the importance of the skill for the particular teaching field the student plans to enter.

Then, finally, there are factors that are generally recognized as fundamental to teaching success but that are not primary goals of education. Intelligence, health and vitality, and emotional stability would be examples. No one would deny that educators are concerned with the intellect, or with health, or personality. But, by and large, colleges do not at the present time assume responsibility for increasing the intellectual ability of students, or for developing emotional stability in those who are disorganized, or for raising students' energy output to anywhere near the same extent as they assume responsibility for increasing students' knowledge, skills, and understanding. Since the former are not, in fact, main objectives of teacher education, and since at the same time they are almost universally considered as essential characteristics of the good teacher, it follows that colleges should select students who already possess them to a satisfactory degree.

We do not, of course, know what the requisite amount should be but we can act on best guesses. We know something about the relation between students' scores on tests of academic aptitude and subsequent grades in college. We know that the task of spending six to nine hours a day with growing, active boys and girls demands energy and vitality. Physical examinations can yield important data relative to students' fitness for meeting this demand. Supporting evidence can be gained from questionnaires and ratings relative to past and present successful accomplishments and to participation in sports and games and other nonsedentary activities. We know that much of the teacher's work is personalized, is conducted in face-to-face human relationships; and we believe that in teaching intelligence and vitality must find their expression within the bounds of normal emotional stability. The judgments of psychiatrists and clinical psychologists along with records of students' past behavior can be used to eliminate clear cases of emotional imbalance. Personality tests can be useful in locating cases that should come to the attention of specialists. In dealing with factors of this kind —intelligence, health and vitality, emotional stability—we have the kind of data that can, and should, be used for initial selection at the freshman as well as the junior level.

In classifying all three types of factor discussed above we referred to a concept of the good teacher and to the objectives of the particular college. The close relationship between a selection program and the objectives of the educational program was thereby emphasized. Student selection is conceived as the beginning of the teacher-educating program. It is the beginning of evaluation in the institution, the beginning of the students' college career, the beginning of guidance, and in some schools of remedial work. Subsequent phases of the program can build on these beginnings with continuity if the functions of the selection program are clearly seen in relation to the over-all program.

The problems of selection are identical in no two institutions, for they do not begin at the same points, have the same resources, or the same kinds of student. Nevertheless, any school attempting to improve its selection practices will be faced with the problem of where to begin and how to proceed. There are five tasks that will be faced. Working agreements will need to be reached with respect to (1) the competencies or characteristics a teacher should possess, (2) the levels of competence to be required for admission, (3) the evidence that can be used to identify competence, (4) the means to be used for gathering the evidence, and (5) the interpretation that can be justified from the data gathered. We can illustrate how a group might approach these tasks with particular application to some of the factors that are commonly deemed important in the good teacher. Health, intelligence, and certain basic skills and knowledge might be considered as among such generally accepted qualities.

Most teacher-educating institutions would say without hesitation that their graduates should be healthy. In saying this they are not only recognizing a professional responsibility but are also defining an area which might be one concern of their selection program. As a particular concern of this program, however, the quality "health" must be defined more specifically. One approach to such a definition might be to call in a group of parents, principals, teachers, and doctors to discuss the characteristics of a desirable teacher from the health standpoint. A committee so constituted would provide a balance of the theoretical and the practical. The doctor is a source to whom to look for expert technical knowledge; members of the college staff must understand and accept any program that develops if it is to be a functional part of the larger program of the college; principals have practical experience with public school teachers to contribute; and parents often have definite ideas about teachers who pass on any illness or maladjustment to children. Such a group might begin by asking itself, "What kinds of health deficiency would you not want a teacher of your children to have?" Some colleges have found that this negative approach to the development of criteria leads to a consensus more rapidly than a direct positive approach. It will be easy for the group to say that active tuberculosis should be sufficient cause for rejection. In considering less obvious health deficiencies conflicting ideas will arise. For example, what attitude will they take toward an applicant who has a deformed hand, or who wears a hearing aid, or who is crosseyed? In debating the policy of accepting such students they might decide that the degree to which the student has adjusted to his condition should be given serious consideration. If there is evidence that he does not respond emotionally to his deficiency or make others feel uncomfortable in his presence, he may be acceptable and in fact desirable. Decisions will seldom be clearcut; debate should be profitable.

There will be difficulty, too, in deciding on the emphasis which verbal aptitude or so-called "general intelligence" should receive in the selection program. The group could easily agree that no one who is mentally deficient should be admitted. They might even agree that they would not want anyone admitted whose IQ fell below the average of the boys and girls with whom he will eventually work. They might set the standard still higher. But the higher they go the more dependent they should be on the researches of psychologists and educators regarding the significance of intelligence in college success and in teaching, for at these higher levels the total pattern of one's abilities and traits may be more significant than any single item.

In considering a skill such as English usage, the committee will face many of the same problems. A college applicant whose ability to recognize incorrect grammar, punctuation, and sentence structure is equivalent to that of a high school junior may with some help and encouragement improve markedly in college; but an entering student who performs at the eighth-grade level may have a deficiency for which the college or university desires to assume no responsibility. In such a case the college staff is faced with two alternatives. Either they exclude him from the group preparing to teach, or they admit him *and* assume responsibility for helping him to improve. The decision may rest partly, too, on the teaching field the student is seeking to enter. For instance, it is quite possible that a teacher in the creative arts need not be so proficient in the fine points of English usage as a teacher in language arts. In the absence of experimental data one will need to make decisions arbitrarily, drawing upon his common sense; but eventually these decisions can be improved by statistical studies of students' subsequent performance.

For information about students' health the sources of data will be the student himself, his parents, and the doctor. Health questionnaires may be useful, especially if they serve a guidance function. The means of collecting most of the data will be technical and can appropriately be left in the doctor's hands. A special problem may arise in reporting and interpreting health data. The ethics of the medical profession rightly hold health information confidential. This need not be a handicap to a selection committee. If the doctor is willing to pass on the fitness of the candidate, the candidate can be referred to him for explanation of an adverse decision by the selection committee. If the doctor has information about an accepted student that may

be useful to the personnel division he can inform the division of
that fact if, through staff meetings and other devices, he has developed a sensitivity to some of the ramifications and problems
of student selection and guidance. The student can become the
carrier of information between doctor and counselor, or can
give permission to the doctor to transmit such information.

With other factors of admission the sources of evidence are
more varied. Helpful information can be gained from the student himself, his parents, former teachers, guidance or administrative officers, community agencies he may have served, former
employers, and so on. Questionnaires or checklists, rating scales,
anecdotal records, recommendation blanks, interview reports,
high school grades, aptitude and achievement tests, or a combination of these in a cumulative record are suggestive means
for collecting needed information.

The final task involves interpreting the evidence. Data can
be plotted on a profile—as at Wayne University—and the significance of the profile can be clarified by reference to descriptive notes from interview blanks, ratings, and questionnaires.
The final decision to accept or reject an applicant can seldom
be made with a satisfying degree of confidence except in the
case of students whose qualifications are uniformly high or
markedly deficient. Usually the total pattern of the student's
abilities, skills, and attainments will need to be studied. A student may rank among the best in all qualifications save one, and
that one be so serious that it should be the controlling factor in
acting on his application. A student may present a generally
mediocre record yet give evidence of such seriousness of purpose, conscientiousness, and persistence that his acceptance
would be justified. This self-propelling quality may compensate
for numerous small deficiencies and even some large ones. Between the extremes of outstanding qualification and outstanding
deficiency there is a middle range of applicants about whom
much argument and difference of opinion can be reasonably
expressed. Only by building up as rapidly as possible a file of
data on the subsequent success of admitted candidates can one
eventually make decisions in this middle range with a minimum

of unfairness to the institution and the students. For initial selection, decisions will for some time be based on group probabilities rather than individual diagnoses. When the college is in a position to develop an efficient program of orientation and guidance large numbers of students in this middle range can be admitted and subsequently helped to reach appropriate decisions. Under these conditions decisions can be more personalized.

When the program of initial selection has been developed cooperatively, drawing upon the ideas of people who have a stake in the outcome, the basis for continuity in the larger program has been laid. The close similarity between the problems of initial selection and the problems of orientation and guidance described in the next chapter lends special importance to the need for laying such a groundwork of understanding and effective working relationship.

III

Orientation and Guidance

A<small>M</small> I sure that I should prepare to teach? How can I make good plans for becoming a teacher? The quality of a student's answer to these questions will depend on comprehensive and valid knowledge of himself, of the competence required of teachers, and of the resources that might be useful to him in developing such competence. That students should be able to answer these questions with increasing insight is a growing concern in teacher education.

Selection programs, as indicated in the preceding chapter, can give some help to the student in determining his potentialities for teaching. But the decisions are usually made for him. Selective admission for entering freshmen can do little more because personal contacts prior to enrollment are generally too meager to permit effective individual guidance. Selection of students for the professional school some time after initial enrollment in the institution of which it is a part provides opportunity for effective guidance. The trend in professional schools that admit students at the beginning of the junior year is toward less emphasis on selection as an institutional prerogative and more on helping the student find his own way, less tendency merely to tell the student, "You can or cannot prepare to teach here," and more effort to help him see desirable directions for his educational effort.

Professional schools without extensive selective admission policies have relied on the standards of their education program to assure that only graduates of high quality find their way into the profession. But unless there is a personnel and guidance program to bring all of the data together about individual students, and to provide counseling service, this rather nebulous thing we call the educational program of an institution is not

50

likely to fulfill a continuing selective function with rhyme or reason to the students.

As colleges and universities expanded in size, students tended to lose their identity. Students had four or more instructors. Instructors had one-fourth or less of a student. Deans and counselors had time for only those who were in serious difficulty. Most students could not identify staff members to whom they could look for help in the intelligent planning of educational programs to meet their individual needs. Most staff members lacked the time and ability to counsel with students on other than the meeting of routine requirements. Partly to overcome these difficulties, orientation courses have been developed in some institutions to enable students, under guidance, to study themselves and plan for the future.

How can we help students size themselves up in relation to the requirements for success and satisfaction in the teaching profession? How can we help them plan for the future? How can we help them appraise their progress? The emphasis placed on evaluation by these questions is clear. In the orientation programs we describe in this chapter, evaluative activity is, in fact, a basic feature of the instruction. Within the courses evaluative activity is focused on individuals as well as on the effectiveness of the program as a whole.

EMPHASIS ON STUDENT PLANNING

The basic goal of the educational orientation course for freshmen in the College of Education at Ohio State University[1] is *intelligent life planning.* Then, more specifically related to teacher education and to the college are the following major goals: (1) to aid the student to make the everyday adjustment in personal living necessitated when one is transplanted from an environment in which he grew up to one which is, for the most part, strange, void of many of the opportunities and restrictions

[1] For a more detailed statement of purposes and description of procedures, see L. L. Love *et al., Student Planning in College* (Columbus: Ohio State University Press, 1941); and A. J. Klein, ed., *Adventures in the Reconstruction of Education* (Columbus: College of Education, Ohio State University, 1941), Chapter II, pp. 33-62.

that existed in the old environment, and filled with many opportunities and restrictions that are new; (2) to bring about in
the student an interest in and understanding of the competencies that are demanded of teachers; and (3) to help the student
plan intelligently for growth toward such competencies, and to
open up opportunities whereby the student may put his plans
into action.

These needed traits which the student learns to understand
and plan toward have been described by the faculty as "Major
Factors of Competency for Teaching." An outline of these factors follows:[2]

1. Expressing in action a clearly formulated social and educational
   philosophy
   a. Possession of an educational philosophy which functions in
      teaching
   b. Contributing to school and community life
   c. Helping students to clarify their values
   d. Accepting responsibilities to the school as a whole
   e. Representing the ideals of the profession
2. Expressing in action and developing in pupils effective personal
   and community relationships
   a. Applying the principles of healthy social adjustment in
      personal living and in dealing with others
   b. Applying the principles of healthful living, mental and
      physical, to personal living and to teaching
   c. Interrelating school and community in teaching
   d. Using the various media of communication: oral and writ-
      ten expression, the fine arts, crafts, and music in teaching
3. Effectively promoting the growth and development of boys and
   girls
   a. Consciously applying the principles of child development
   b. Dealing effectively with individual differences among stu-
      dents
   c. Consciously applying the principles of functional guidance
      procedures in teaching
   d. Participating constructively in the extracurricular program
      of the school
4. Utilizing all available resources—in men, materials, and techniques—in the learning process

[2] A more complete statement of the "factors," in which each point is amplified
by a paragraph, is found in L. L. Love et al., op. cit., pp. 22-29.

a. Utilizing the process of planning in daily living and in teaching

b. Utilizing proficiently a wide range of materials and methods of instruction

c. Continuously evaluating educational aims, processes, and results

d. Knowing the subject matter in one's teaching fields and using this knowledge to increase the students' intelligence about the world in which they live

e. Carrying out appropriate and effective methods in the management of pupils both in and out of the classroom, and in other relationships

f. Applying critical reflective thinking (scientific method) to the solution of problems and teaching for it in school situations

These factors, together with the purposes of the orientation course stated above, form the framework within which the course is organized, the evaluation of individual progress is judged, and the program as a whole is appraised.

PURPOSES AND OPERATION OF THE PROGRAM

The emphasis upon gaining familiarity with the college, with the profession of teaching, and with oneself—all basic to intelligent life planning—is appropriate, for freshmen at Ohio State University are a relatively unselected group. Their presence in the College of Education suggests that they have tentatively chosen teaching as a career. But actually few of them have made carefully reasoned choices. Some have made good choices without knowing why they are good. Some have made poor choices without knowing why they are poor. The orientation course, therefore, is required of all freshmen in the College of Education.

The students spend six hours each week in more or less formal class activity. Out of this six hours, a two-hour period is set aside each week for group meetings of about fifteen students with their faculty adviser and his assistant. These are known as conference sections. There is another two-hour period of laboratory activity while the remaining two hours are for lectures, panel discussions, movie demonstrations, and similar large group activities. The course carries five regular quarter-hour credits.

The students for whom a faculty member is adviser for the first two years make up a conference section. The adviser has available to him personnel information about his students from all the university sources. These arrangements help to promote the integration of personnel and instructional responsibility. Each conference section chooses a committee that works with the adviser in planning the program for that group. Planning takes in such considerations as the discovery of university resources, the arrangement of opportunity to discuss ways of using these resources for the development of desired competence, the clarification of ideas presented in other parts of the course, the management of activities such as theatre parties, field trips, group projects, and so forth.

The laboratory periods provide opportunity for the student to obtain information that will aid him in identifying his own strengths and weaknesses—this, of course, under the guidance of his adviser. He receives and studies the significance of information gathered during freshman week—results on the college-aptitude, English, and health examinations. He records his voice; and he is helped in analyzing it. He takes tests to help him understand his ability to interpret data, his vocabulary level, his knowledge of facts about current affairs and the general culture, his pattern of beliefs about social issues. A resources-problems checklist helps him to sift out, cluster, and identify problems of major personal concern on which he may need help. Other tests—invoices and interest blanks—are filled out by the student according to his need. For instance, the Strong Vocational Interest Blank or the Kuder Preference Record may help a particular student clarify his feeling with respect to various occupations and professions. The two-hour laboratory period is also used, on occasion, for field trips to such places as social and welfare agencies, art galleries, newspaper offices, headquarters of various branches of government, schools for the blind and deaf, and other social or educational agencies.

The lecture-demonstration periods provide opportunity to present certain material effectively to large groups. One of the lecture periods, for example, is used to explain the factors of competence, describe how they were developed, suggest how they can be studied, revised, reduced, or expanded by each student. On this occasion the lecture sets the stage for smaller group discussions. Other lecture periods are given over to a discussion of effective study methods and the resources of the university for the improvement of study habits and skills; a discussion of the ability to communicate with others, with suggestions as to the resources of the university for the diagnosis and improvement of speech; a discussion of factors in social competence and the resources of the university for their analysis and improvement. A special effort is made in several lectures to motivate students to examine, individually and in discussion, their beliefs and controlling life values. Later, attention is given to analyzing the requirements of various occupations, particularly teaching. There is not, of course, a frozen calendar for these large lecture-demonstration groups. When it seems desirable, the large group is broken up for particular demonstrations and special types of activity.

PLACE OF EVALUATION IN THE PROGRAM

Since the major purpose of the total orientation program is to help students develop some competence in planning their affairs, it is natural that evaluative activity, like other activities in the course, is viewed in the light of what it can contribute to that major purpose. Evaluation in the orientation course has consequently certain characteristics. It is, for example, an integral part of the total program. It is continuous rather than periodic. It derives important evidence from informal associations between students and advisers and in the normal planning and learning activities of the course. Its results "flow into the remainder of the professional program."[3] And finally, evaluation "in this course and in succeeding courses has for the most part a common base—the Major Factors of Competency."[4]

[3] From a paper, "Evaluation as a Part of the Ohio State University College of Education Freshman Program," presented by L. L. Love at the conference on evaluation, Columbus, Ohio, 1942, p. 5.
[4] *Ibid.*, p. 5.

Space does not permit a detailed description of all the evaluative activity in the course. But we have attempted to describe
three important activities: the use of evaluative techniques in
helping the student understand his controlling life values; the
evaluative significance of a planning paper written by the student; and some of the ways in which the course as a whole is
appraised. Since the course and the evaluative procedures change
from year to year we have limited most of our discussion to the
appraisal procedure used during 1941 and 1942.

Appraising the individual's values

As the student begins to understand and accept the factors of
competence as a guide to becoming an effective teacher, he sees
that—as a person and teacher—he should be able to express in action a clearly formulated social and educational philosophy, to
contribute to school and community life, to help pupils clarify
their values, to interrelate school and community in teaching,
to increase pupils' understanding of the world in which they
live. Accordingly, among the more specific purposes of the
orientation program are the following:

. . . (1) to help you examine carefully your own beliefs about the
world in which you live and your part in it; (2) to assist you to look
critically at the things you now think are important in order to discover whether you have sound reasons for your allegiance to them;
(3) to help you see why you choose one value or one course of action
instead of others.[5]

The student is helped to identify his beliefs and feelings in a
variety of ways.

One avenue of approach in identifying controlling life values
and attitudes on social issues is through attitudes tests. Students
take the Scales of Beliefs tests developed by the Progressive Education Association.[6] These tests and several others in the orienta-

---

[5] Love, *Student Planning in College*, p. 85.
[6] For a comprehensive discussion of the development and use of these tests,
see Eugene R. Smith and Ralph W. Tyler, *Appraising and Recording Student
Progress* (New York: Harper & Brothers, 1942), Chapter III.

tion program are administered to students *en masse*. Recognizing the need for genuine student motivation and seriousness of purpose in test taking, the staff prepared a series of "test talks" which were mimeographed for distribution, study, and discussion. The one developed for the Scales of Beliefs is reproduced in part below. Seriousness of purpose is especially important in attitude testing, for the student can often color his answers to please the examiner.

Test Talks with Students

What are your attitudes about important social issues?

Some of your laboratory periods in Survey of Education 407 will be devoted during the first few weeks to taking a series of new and different tests designed to help you to know more about yourselves. Inasmuch as the tests will probably be different from any which you have ever taken before, you will be given these "Test Talks with Students" to read from time to time to aid you in understanding the purpose of the tests and how to take them.

Your grade in Survey of Education will not be affected by the results of these tests in any way. They are being given for an altogether different reason. They are being given to help you to get part of the answer to the important question now facing most of you, "Will I make a teacher?" or "How can I become an effective person?" Everything which you indicate about yourself as you take these tests will be reported to you individually by your adviser. Nothing will be held back for that would defeat the purpose of giving the tests. At considerable expense and with the expenditure of much effort, the College of Education is giving you these diagnostic tests which will enable you to find out more about yourselves, and thus enable you to be more effective in your planning.

The benefits which come from taking these tests do not come automatically. First of all, you will need to follow quite precisely the specific directions which accompany each test; second, you should make a conscientious effort to "do your best" and "be yourself" as you take the tests; third, you should make certain that you clearly understand the results of the tests as your adviser reports them to you; and fourth, you should very seriously interpret these results for yourself in terms of your goals and your purposes and trace the implications of the test findings for your own planning.

No one but you can take this fourth and most important step. Your adviser, of course, will help you very much, and you should insist on his making the meaning of the results plain to you, but you are the one who, in the last analysis, must see the significance of the results in terms of your own aims, and plan accordingly. After you have done this, your adviser will be glad to answer the question which we hope you will ask, "What can I do about this?" by suggesting things you can do, places you can go, publications you can read, and other resources you can use in striving to become a more effective person.

A short time after you take each test, your adviser will give to you an individual test-summary sheet which will contain your results on that test. Both he and the junior dean will keep copies of these test-summary sheets so that they can study the results and thus be of more help to you when you see them in individual interviews. Although your adviser will explain the meanings of the various scores on the tests to you in your conference section, you will probably find it profitable to talk over your test results individually with him.

The first test which you take, called Scales of Beliefs, gives you the opportunity to express your attitudes about important current problems. Kaleidoscopic changes have taken place in our world during the past year. Many of men's ideals and institutions have been swept away. People have changed their former patterns of thinking. The basic values of many have shifted. Just how have your own attitudes been affected by recent events? What are your present opinions about nationalism as a policy, about militarism, and about democracy as a form of government? How do you feel about labor and unemployment problems, about the treatment of other races and minority groups, and about government regulation and control? There are no "right" and "wrong" answers to this test, so there is no way by which you can prepare for this test. It is not possible, in fact, to study in advance for any of the tests which you will take in Survey of Education (with the exception, probably, of the midterm and final examinations in the course!).

The Scales of Beliefs is divided into two sections of 93 statements each. You will take one section of the test on one day and the other section at a later time. The test is very easy to take. All you do is to read each statement in turn and then indicate by a mark on a separate answer sheet whether you agree with the statement, whether you disagree with the statement, or whether you are uncertain about your attitude concerning the statement. Remember, there are no right or wrong answers (obviously you have a right to your own opinions), so feel free honestly to record your own convictions. At the time that the summary sheets for the Scales of Beliefs are returned, your adviser will probably be able to suggest ways of improving the consistency of your thinking.

When the tests have been scored the student compares his own responses with those of others. He can see from summary tables, in relation to the student body generally, whether he is characteristically conservative, liberal, uncertain, or consistent in what he believes about democracy, economic relations, labor and unemployment, race, nationalism, and militarism. He may find that he is quite liberal in his beliefs about economic relations and labor and unemployment, and quite conservative in his beliefs about race and nationalism. These facts in themselves will not tell him whether the present status of his beliefs is good or bad. To determine that is part of a broader problem of education. He can check his beliefs against pertinent facts that may be available, read books to discover theories and principles that have been derived by scholars, observe social, economic, and political situations first hand, and he can discuss his beliefs with fellow students and teachers. The test should, in fact, motivate him to do these things. Later he may retake the Scales of Beliefs and find out what changes have taken place in his responses, comparing previous scores with later scores. He may find that he has moved in the direction of liberalism, or that he has become more uncertain or inconsistent in his point of view. Again, the results will not be significant *per se*. Increased uncertainty could be interpreted as a mark of progress if his original beliefs had reflected a thoughtless acceptance of the traditional precepts from a limited environment. As a matter of fact, unwillingness to express certainty on profound and controversial issues is often a mark of intellectual maturity. On the other hand, prolonged confusion and inconsistency toward related social problems may indicate that the student lacks ability to resolve them satisfactorily. Continued and increased confusion may, moreover, lead on to feelings of inferiority, insecurity, and frustration. One would hesitate to encourage a student who responded in this way to continue preparation for teaching, and especially for teaching any of the social sciences to high school boys and girls.

Indirect evidence in identifying values is obtained through an analysis of the student's scores on the Cooperative Contemporary Affairs Test. The student can compare his scores with those of students generally. He may discover, for instance, that he does not know as much about what is going on in the world as the average college student. It becomes obvious to him that one who is going to help young people learn about their world, who is going to express in his own actions, and develop in his pupils, effective personal and community relationships, should be familiar with at least some major areas of current affairs. He may discover that, compared with other students, he knows more about business and politics and less about movies, the arts, and literature; and that this may be a reflection of underlying interests and values. What interpretation is valid may not become clear until after repeated conferences with his adviser and extensive exploratory experience. It may be that limited background or lack of convenient reading material accounted for his performance, rather than lack of interest or a pattern of values. In any event, the role of the adviser in helping the student interpret test data is an important one.

Another approach to the identification of values is through the Mooney Resources-Problems Checklist. The instrument has 290 items classified under the following topics: health and physical development; finances, living conditions, and present employment; social and recreational opportunities and activities; relationships with other people; personal temperament; courtship, sex, and marriage; relationships with home and family; religion and ethics; fitness for a life work; fitness for college work; and satisfaction with college offerings. Each item is phrased two ways: first, as a resource, or strength, which one might possess; and second, as a problem, or weakness, one might feel he has. Corresponding items are set opposite each other, and the student responds by checking or doublechecking the item as a resource or problem, or by checking an in-between column. The following is illustrative:

Have enough money for suit-able clothes	Re-sources	In be-tween	Prob-lems	Have too little money for suitable clothes
Keep the friends I make				Tend to lose friends I make
Like to take my friends home with me				Don't like to take my friends home with me

The fundamental purpose of the checklist is to reveal assets and liabilities believed to exist in a student's relation to his environment. Implications of the student's responses can be explored in discussions with his adviser. The following summary of the responses of one student suggests that he has come to place considerable value on adequacy of relations with others:

Case No. 106, with major problems in the area of
"Relationships with Other People"

[*Items doublechecked as problems*]

Usually dislike having other people around
Have no close friends
Slow in making friends
Dislike someone very much
Let people take advantage of me
Lack leadership ability
Am seldom given a position of responsibility
Too often lose my head in arguments
Get too many criticisms from others
Someone dislikes me very much

[*Items singlechecked as problems*]

Have no one who really understands me
Have no one to tell my troubles to

In addition to these items, this person marked thirty more items as problems. Over one-third of these were in the area of "social and recreational opportunities and activities," and support the kind of response listed above. He feels he does not fit in the group with which he lives. His parents have been separated or divorced. He is undecided about his occupation. He is uncertain

---

[7] Ross L. Mooney, "Report on the Experimental Use of a Resources-Problems Checklist in Freshman Education Survey, Fall 1941" (unpublished manuscript in the files of the College of Education, Ohio State University), p. 12.

about several items in personal temperament, religion, and fitness for college work. No areas of resources seem to support him especially well.

Responses analyzed in this way can reveal a pattern of strengths and weaknesses. Obviously, the student must be sincere in his answers to the checklist, and the pattern of his responses should be related to relevant data from other sources. One of these sources will be the observations of his adviser; this implies that the adviser must develop more than a passing acquaintance with his students.

Finally, the student is encouraged to keep a personal diary in which he records experience associated with pleasure, discouragement, defeat, punishment, reward, exhilaration, admiration, embarrassment, enthusiasm, comfort, or discomfort. The analysis of these types of response in relation to the situations in which they occur can provide clues to an understanding of the beliefs and values that one holds.

Thus, through a variety of evaluative techniques—diaries, attitude tests, current affairs tests, an analysis of personal resources and problems, interviews, and discussions—the student is led to an examination and understanding of the values he holds.

Central role of the planning paper

The second major activity we have selected for description is the preparation and appraisal of the student's planning paper. The chief purpose of the orientation program is to help students learn to plan intelligently and to begin putting their plans into action. In order to do this, the student must try to get clearly in mind his immediate and ultimate goals; he must analyze the goals to determine what each will require of him; he must examine himself carefully to determine his strengths and weaknesses in terms of these requirements. With these facts in mind, he must decide how best he can proceed from where he is to where he wants to go. It is not intended that planning with respect to his goals will crystalize, but rather that his evaluation will be continuous, that new insights will emerge, and that these in turn will have new implications for evaluation and planning. He is confronted with this problem of planning early in the course, with the understanding that he must prepare a tentative plan before the end of the quarter. This is the major written assignment of the course.

Under the guidance of his adviser, the student uses the knowledge he has gained about himself, his intellectual ability, his health, personality, and emotional adjustment, his adequacy of oral and written expression, and his interests, attitudes, and values, to face more intelligently the problem of reviewing his professional or occupational choice and to plan accordingly. For students who have difficulty in gaining a hold or a beginning point when confronted with such a very real problem as that involved in planning for the future, the staff has prepared some useful suggestions. The following questions, for example, have been helpful to many students:

1. Starting from "wants." What are your goals? What are you after? What do you want to be? Where do you want to go? How do you propose getting there?

2. Starting from "resources." What are your strong points? What do you regard as your special assets? In what ways are you planning to use them?

3. Starting from "difficulties." What weaknesses do you have? What problems are you facing? What worries you? What stands in your way? How do you expect to overcome these obstacles?

4. Starting from "present activities." What are you doing now? Why are you doing these things? What values are you getting from them? What are you planning to do to get the most out of your present activities?

5. Starting from "critical choices." What important decisions face you? Have you chosen a vocation? Have you chosen your major in college? What important considerations are involved in these decisions? How may they affect many aspects of your present and future life? What plans are you making to guarantee the wisdom and effectiveness of these decisions?[8]

The staff has also prepared suggestions to help the student survey the world of work in preparation for his task of matching his own potentialities with what he can find out about the de-

[8] Love, *Student Planning in College*, p. 16.

mands of various occupations. The following classification of jobs is given to the student to guide his considerations:

1. Work dealing primarily with people
   a. Dealing *directly* with people; by influencing, suggesting, directing, advising. In this category would fall professions (which of course also deal to a large extent with ideas) as medicine, ministry, law, personnel work, social service, and teaching. In business this type of activity finds its most important outlet in management and selling.
   b. Dealing *indirectly* with people, through promoting and forming policies for others to follow, influencing groups, public opinion, etc. Such activity takes the form of advertising, journalism, public relations, social investigations, etc.
2. Work dealing primarily with ideas
   Certain occupations such as education, law, politics, advertising, management consist of a combination of work with ideas and with people. Some more specifically concerned with ideas are invention, research, and many phases of pure science or engineering. Also included are the artistic and creative professions which primarily are the expression of ideas through such media as architecture, fine arts, music, creative literature, design, and the drama.
3. Work dealing primarily with things
   a. Working with the thing itself—producing, handling, shaping materials. This work leads to many phases of applied science such as agriculture, forestry, medical and scientific research, engineering and construction, factory production, development of natural resources, and transportation.
   b. Working with the symbols of things—dealing with things in the abstract. This work includes accounting, statistical analysis, certain forms of research, drafting and design, credit work, and actuarial insurance work.
   c. Work dealing with the commercial exchange and impersonal distribution of things. This work is essentially the "trading" field. Included are marketing through newspaper and direct-mail advertising, and marketing through retail department and chain stores. Purchasing and work in foreign and domestic trading companies are also included in this category.[9]

In approaching the decision with respect to his occupation or profession, the student is encouraged finally to ask himself the

[9] *Ibid.,* p. 113.

following questions in order to assure that he does not leave avoidable gaps in the consideration of this most important matter:

Have I studied myself carefully by means of:

1. Talks with counselors, teachers, and other persons who have studied me and my capabilities?

2. Tests which measured my mental and physical qualifications or which measured the special abilities needed in the occupations of my choice (or in the several occupations which I am considering)?

3. An examination of the qualities and abilities I have shown in academic areas?

4. An examination of the qualities and abilities I have shown in extracurricular activities?

5. Recreational likes and dislikes, abilities and disabilities?

6. A physical examination by a competent physician which covered everything which might affect my vocational plans?

7. Self-analysis charts and ratings of my personal qualities made by others?

8. Tryout work experiences?[10]

The life plan, or planning paper, presented a week before the close of the quarter for the analysis of the adviser and for discussion between student and adviser, is the most important single instrument of evaluation of the student's achievement in the orientation course. It is prepared in duplicate: the original kept by the student and the copy left with the adviser. The copy will eventually go to the junior dean's office where it becomes a part of the student's cumulative record and follows him from the lower division through the upper division and eventually to the placement office. The student's planning paper is supplemented by a report from the adviser.

On the following pages we have drawn together excerpts from a planning paper written by a student and from an evaluative summary written by his adviser. The present organization of the material, the topical headings, and the profile of test data are not taken from the original papers. The statements under the several headings are, however, taken directly from the student's and the adviser's writing and are, we believe, representative of it.

[10] *Ibid.*, p. 121.

Figure I
TEST PROFILE OF "JOHN SMITH"

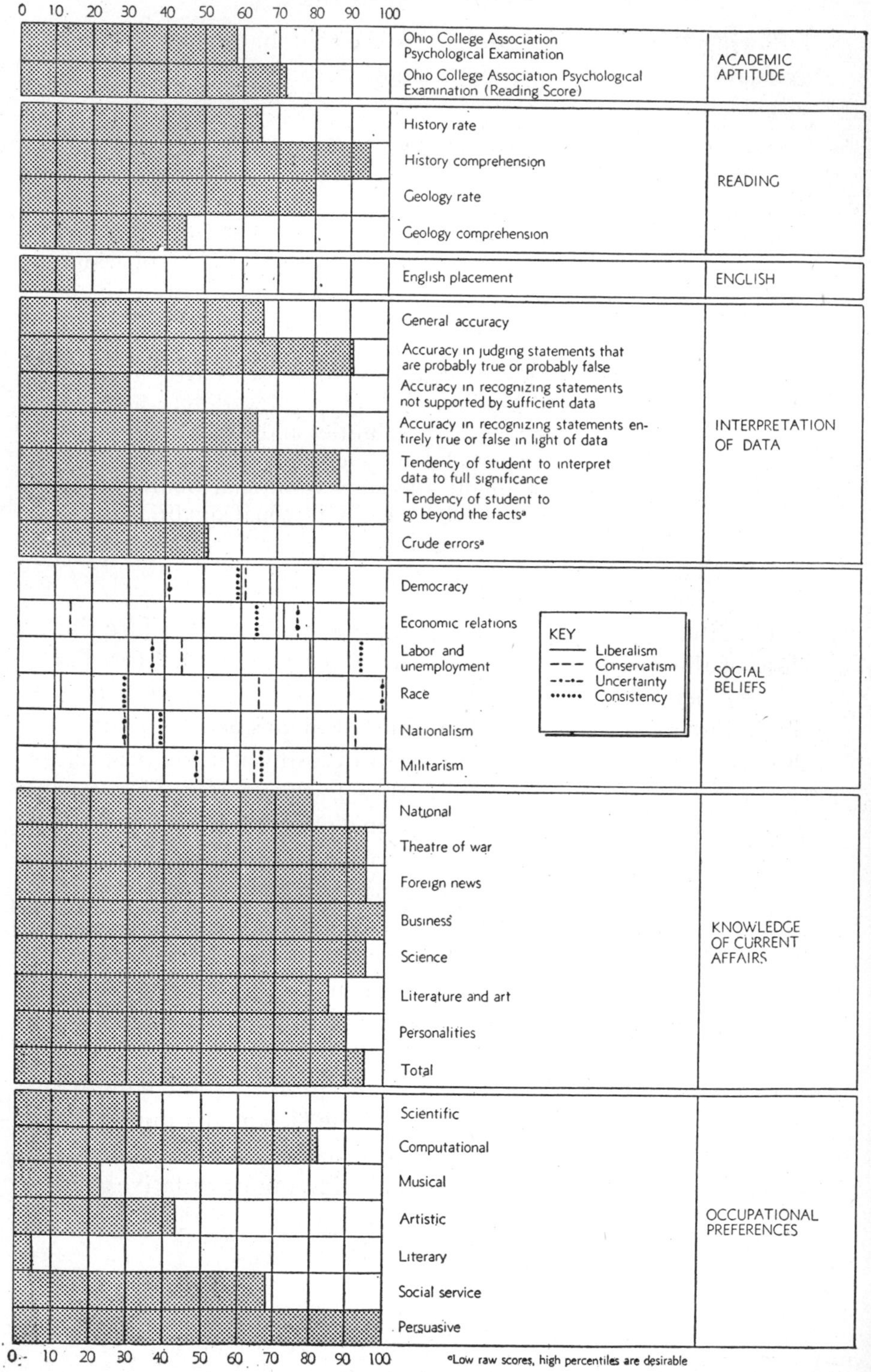

0 10 20 30 40 50 60 70 80 90 100		
Ohio College Association Psychological Examination		ACADEMIC APTITUDE
Ohio College Association Psychological Examination (Reading Score)		
History rate		READING
History comprehension		
Geology rate		
Geology comprehension		
English placement		ENGLISH
General accuracy		INTERPRETATION OF DATA
Accuracy in judging statements that are probably true or probably false		
Accuracy in recognizing statements not supported by sufficient data		
Accuracy in recognizing statements entirely true or false in light of data		
Tendency of student to interpret data to full significance		
Tendency of student to go beyond the facts[a]		
Crude errors[a]		
Democracy	KEY	SOCIAL BELIEFS
Economic relations	—— Liberalism	
Labor and unemployment	– – – Conservatism	
Race	-·-·- Uncertainty	
Nationalism	····· Consistency	
Militarism		
National		KNOWLEDGE OF CURRENT AFFAIRS
Theatre of war		
Foreign news		
Business		
Science		
Literature and art		
Personalities		
Total		
Scientific		OCCUPATIONAL PREFERENCES
Computational		
Musical		
Artistic		
Literary		
Social service		
Persuasive		
0 10 20 30 40 50 60 70 80 90 100		

[a]Low raw scores, high percentiles are desirable

PLANNING PAPER OF
STUDENT JOHN SMITH

SUMMARY MADE BY
HIS ADVISER

Potential Ability

My [score] on the OCA [Ohio College Association Psychological Examination] was at the 58th percentile. While this indicates I am no master mind . . . I am not inferior . . . when classed with . . . people . . . of my own category. I was a good student in high school . . . met requirements for the National Honor Society. . . . Why am I not doing better [slightly above C average]? I believe I can explain. . . . Out of school two years . . . out of study habit. I thought of being a doctor. But the field is overcrowded . . . competition is high . . . requirements exceedingly high. . . . I honestly believe I could have reached them. . . . The course is too long . . . finance tremendous. Necessitates my father working another ten years. He is eligible for retirement. Plan to major in mathematics. Second major in chemistry-physics combination. Will have but three more courses to qualify for general science major. Can do this in one or two summers. I heard Dr. ——— lecture on school administration. This type of work interests me greatly. Interests me so I am planning . . . to investigate this field as a possible one in which to work for a master's and possibly a doctor's degree. This could be listed as an ultimate goal.

Seems to be about average in academic intelligence. Although a member of the National Honor Society in high school, it seems likely he will have difficulty making grades higher than a C in college. He may have difficulty in attaining 2.25 point-hour ratio [slightly above C average] in his major field. He may want to consider more seriously the field of business. He had one year of night school, studying business administration and accounting. He liked the course but didn't like the school. On the Kuder preference record he was highest in persuasive preference —100th percentile. His second highest was in computational preferences, 80th percentile; next was social service, 70th percentile. All others were below average. Teaching was his first choice. . . . Medicine had been his second, but it is now eliminated and his third is business in which he is still interested. Evidence at the end of the quarter from the problem checklist shows he is not yet sure of his vocational choice.

Writing

However, my English is bad. I am difficient [sic] in this one field as indicated by my test-summary sheet. Incidentally, I was in the 15th percentile. To help remedy this fault I must take some more English courses. I have attempted this quarter to improve my speech and the use of English in general.

His lack of proficiency in this area and in the use of English is one of his biggest stumbling blocks. Makes glaring errors in the use of grammar and in the use of words. His percentile of 15 on the English placement test indicated extent of his proficiency. He has made a very real effort to improve. Planning paper was quite in contrast to his other papers in that it had few English errors. Still misspells many words. The following appeared in his planning paper: "benefitial," "speicilizing," "congradulated," "persuasuve," "difficient," "tenative," "fulle" [fully].

Speaking

Unusually able and willing to express himself orally. Contributed freely to conference group. Did such an excellent job instructing class on making out and filing winter schedule cards and of reporting happenings at the freshman council meeting that several of the students commented to me about it afterwards.

Reading

I must improve my reading rate as well as my comprehension of material because as my rate increased, my accuracy and comprehension dropped and vice versa.

In general, he reads faster and comprehends better than the average student. At 80th and 65th percentiles on rate and 45th and 95th percentiles in comprehension, accuracy on the geology and history reading tests respectively. The 71st percentile on reading part of the OCA. His leisure-time reading is in the field of current events.

Interpretation of Data

My interpretation of data shows that I tend to go beyond the facts. This is about the only bad habit I have, as is indicated in this test.

Seems to be about average in ability to think. His general accuracy on the interpretation of data test was at the 66th percentile, as was his ability to recognize obviously true or false statements. He was at the 91st percentile in interpreting probabilities, indicated by the data. In his accuracy in recognizing statements not supported by sufficient data and in his general tendency to ascribe more truth or falsity to statements than the data permit he is markedly below the average. He makes the average number of crude errors. Usually, the student is able and willing to think reflectively about various problems. His main fault is that he sometimes does it with insufficient data.

Social Attitudes

On the whole when my social attitudes test is looked at my percentiles are just a little below the 50th. This would tend to show that I am not radically inclined one way or the other. This, I believe, is a good indication for a teacher who will meet all types . . . of pupils . . . and parents.

In many ways this student is average and he is no different on the social acceptance scale except on consistency in which he is at the 60th percentile. Much more consistent and certain on problems of labor and unemployment, which would be natural in view of his employment experience. Very uncertain on racial issues. On this Scales of Beliefs test he was more conservative, although at the same time quite inconsistent, than in his statements in his paper on beliefs. In his paper he classified himself as a liberal. Seems to know how to arrive at beliefs intelligently but has not thought through all of these issues as yet. Class discussions and conferences revealed tolerance toward beliefs of others. Quite willing to express his own beliefs.

The profile includes only those data that can be readily interpreted in terms of percentile scores. There are, of course, many other aspects of growth about which the survey course and the teacher education program generally are concerned. Some aspects of social competence, for example, are suggested in the further excerpts reproduced below:

STUDENT	ADVISER
Some of the organizations I was active in in high school were: Latin Club, Science Club, Chemistry Club, Student Council, Library Councilor [sic], Hi-Y, "L" [literary] Society, Class Day Program, Monitor, and National Honor Society. I believe that I have a well rounded social background by belonging to these organizations as well as to the young people's group in the church. Besides these, I belong to a worldwide fraternal organization.	Has an excellent social adjustment. Although few dates . . . he seems to get along well with both sexes, including contemporaries and older and younger people. Very well liked by other students. . . . Exhibits considerable evidence of leadership and cooperation. Was elected freshman council representative from his conference group, receiving ten votes to a total of nine for other nominees. Reports indicate that he has contributed some leadership to the council. Is a steward in the church and first vice president of Epworth League. Tentative plans include the Math Club, Pershing Rifles, and perhaps a fraternity later on. Much more active in community than in high school group. Recognizes necessity for establishing himself academically before going too heavily for social contacts. Unusual poise and self-control. Willing to face reality. Quite stable and mature emotionally.

The planning paper from which these excerpts were taken is not among the best nor the poorest of those turned in by the students. Rather, the planning paper is typical in that it represents the kind of problem to which the students direct their attention. It is typical in that data in it are sometimes overlooked, sometimes merely described, sometimes interpreted, and sometimes used as a basis for planning. It is typical in showing that students have much to learn about appraisal, and the use of resources. The adviser's report is typical in much the same sense. It is typical of the insights and oversights that advisers have and make. For example, as one reviews the student's and the adviser's reports, several general observations seem appropriate. Both student and adviser tend to use data primarily to describe present status; they rarely suggest the implication of data for planning. In considering test scores the student refers almost exclusively to total scores; the diagnostic implications of part scores are passed over. In contrast, the adviser is more analytical in considering the test scores; moreover, he tends to bring in data from other sources—as in references to misspellings in papers and to oral reports in classes. The student has changed his choice of a vocation from medicine to teaching but he does not see the relevance of his low scholarship in mathematics and science to his selection of these subjects as a teaching major. His adviser sees the alternate possibility of business or selling as vocational choices, but he does not suggest the possibility of combining economics and accounting with social studies for a major field. Perhaps a profile, such as that reproduced on page 66, would have helped the student see more interrelatedness among the test data. In the student's paper, especially, there was relatively little mention of university resources that he could use in helping him overcome deficiencies.

Appraising aspects of the program

One line of evidence for the evaluation of the orientation program was provided by a special analysis of fifty-four planning papers written by the students in four advisory sections.[11] Answers were sought to such questions as: Has the student stated immediate and ultimate goals? If so, to what extent has he used

[11] Eleanor A. Gerding, "Analysis of the Planning of a Group of College of Education Freshmen" (a thesis presented for the degree of master of arts, Ohio State University, Columbus, Ohio, 1940).

evidence from tests and from other sources in analyzing his assets and liabilities in relation to these goals? Does he show that he understands these goals? What resources, campus and community, does he plan to use in achieving his immediate and ultimate goals? Does he recognize his assets and liabilities in carrying out these plans? Does he recognize that planning is a continuous process? Does he integrate all of these factors into what seems to be a reasonable plan for himself? A majority of the planning papers—63 to 98 percent—showed that students had stated immediate and ultimate goals, used subjective evidence in analyzing assets and liabilities (less than half had used test results), shown a fair understanding of goals stated, planned to use campus resources in achieving immediate goals and realized their own limitations in using them, recognized planning as a continuous process, and developed a reasonably well integrated program. There were, however, wide variations among the papers from different advisory sections. Nearly every student in one group used test data in planning while in another section the students ignored test data completely. When the results of this particular analysis were brought before the advisers and the student council for discussion, several changes were made in the program. Methods of reporting test results were revised. Advisers held meetings to increase their understanding of tests, and some advisers invited evaluation experts to discuss tests results with their advisory groups. Other results led to other changes. For example, more attention was given the relation of campus resources to students' ultimate goals. Further use of community resources was encouraged. Field trips were planned more carefully, in line with student needs.

The following year a special study of student judgments concerning the effectiveness of their advisers provided another source of evidence in evaluating the program.[12] The role of the advisers in the orientation program, like the role of the planning paper, is a major one. Students in the orientation course were asked to appraise the helpfulness of their advisers on fifty-

---

[12] Joseph E. McCabe, "A Student Evaluation of the College of Education Freshman Advisory Program" (a thesis presented for the degree of master of arts, Ohio State University, Columbus, Ohio, 1940).

six different advisory services. A five-point scale, ranging from "very great help" to "practically no help" was used. Thirty advisers were so rated by the students in their advisory sections. Some of the items on which advisers were rated generally high or generally low are of special interest. For example, students thought the advisers were very helpful in acquainting them with other members of the group and in seeing how they could utilize campus resources for the development of certain characteristics. They thought the advisers had been much less helpful with respect to such topics as planning leisure-time activities, learning to use the library, and utilizing community resources. Again they rated the advisers high for interpreting test results in understandable language, ability to make them feel that the testing program could contribute to their development, and for constructive discussion of the midterm examination; but they rated advisers relatively low for help in seeing how past experience can be used in achieving goals, and for help in getting a clear picture of their abilities. Students thought their advisers effective in identifying some of the things they should consider in planning and in actual help in planning; but relatively unsuccessful in bringing about changes in their purposes through criticism, in aiding them to judge the actions of others, and in pointing out concrete ways of improving their quality of thinking. Other ratings indicated that students generally rated their advisers unusually high. Students looked upon the adviser as a real friend, felt free to discuss almost all problems with him, found him accessible and prompt in meeting appointments, respectful of their contributions, and interested in their criticisms.

In addition to these general ratings, certain comparisons are noteworthy. For example, the mean ranking of advisers who were trained in the field of personnel was above the mean for all advisers in every one of the fifty-six items of the rating scale. The mean rating of the eight advisers whose schedules were most flexible was also above the mean for all advisers on every item in the scale. And finally, the mean rating of five advisers who, in the opinion of the director of the program, were most familiar with the course was compared with the mean rating of eight advisers identified as least familiar with it. Those most familiar with the program were rated more effective on fifty-one of the fifty-six items.

These ratings suggested to the staff at Ohio State University the desirability of special training for instructors who are to be counselors, of flexible schedules and ample free time, and of a familiarity with the program that is gained through participation in its development.

It is important that those who participate in the ongoing program, and especially those who have not taken part in its development, gain clear insights into its purposes and mechanics. Regular meetings of the advisers have been one source of such understanding in the orientation program. The meetings also serve an evaluative function. The advisers meet to familiarize themselves more thoroughly with the program as a whole, and more specifically with new activities as they develop from week to week. They meet to improve their own effectiveness as advisers. Naturally much of the discussion is in reference to individual students, and leads to an analysis of why the program is failing to meet the needs of these individuals and to suggestions for improving the services to them. Sometimes the discussion of many cases will point to a rather general weakness in the program and modifications can be made without further systematic appraisal. At other times the need for systematic appraisal will be suggested. One strength in the advisers' meetings as a source of useful evidence for evaluation lies in their regularity and purpose. Opinions expressed are not impromptu notions. They are based on much class and out-of-class contact with the students. Indeed, some evidence which each adviser can bring to these regular meetings comes from evaluative discussions, some planned and some spontaneous, which he has had with the students in his conference section as well as from a variety of informal observations and interviews with individuals.

CHANGES IN THE PROGRAM

Any program that is not static changes from year to year in the light of experience and shifting conditions. Keeping open channels of communication among students and advisers and administrators helps facilitate timely modifications. At Ohio State University changes have occurred along several fronts. Some tests have been dropped from the battery indicated on the student's profile; other tests have been added. A diary, once required, is now optional. But beyond these and other details there are two changes of larger implication.

In 1942, a new form was developed for the advisers' final evaluation of the status and progress of students in the orientation course. The advisers had been summarizing student progress in terms of the eighteen factors of competence. These factors, however, are much broader than the objectives of the orientation course. Many of them are the major responsibility of the upper division. For advisers to evaluate student progress toward goals that had not been a major concern of the program had proved difficult and frustrating. In the meantime, a committee had developed an annotated rating scale for the appraisal of students for admission to junior standing. This form called for ratings on traits and skills that were predominantly the responsibility of the lower division. Since the students' advisers in the orientation program remain their counselors during the freshman and sophomore years, it seemed appropriate for an appraisal of individual progress and status at the close of the orientation course to be made on this rating scale.

A second major change, or rather a trend, has been the placing of more and more responsibility for scoring tests, summarizing inventories, and interpreting results upon the students. There is less machine scoring and more student scoring. Students score their papers in the laboratory sections where advisers can aid them both in the mechanics and in the summarizing of results. Seeing the logic of the test, how the results add up, stopping to examine items on which answers are at variance with the key, all make for understanding and acceptance of results by the students. The instructional values of appraisal are thereby increased. And students are helped to develop the insights into evaluation processes that, as teachers, they will need to have.

Progress has been made toward the intelligent use of evaluative evidence in planning, but this still remains a very difficult problem in the course at Ohio State University and, indeed, in any course having similar objectives. For effective planning one needs to grasp clearly the complex interrelationships of data. Sources of help need to be clearly identifiable and readily available. Some of the university's sources of help have become more readily available to meet individual student needs, particularly the speech, writing, reading, and study clinics. But how a student can plan to use the resources of the history or political science department to reduce his inconsistencies and uncertainties in social beliefs is a subtler problem; the relationship between the particular student's need and the content of the course is less direct. Another barrier to the use of evaluative data in planning is found in the fact that students sometimes find it difficult to accept evidence of their strengths and weaknesses, and cannot face the implications for planning. Moreover, it is not easy for the advisers to help them, for there is a danger in forced or premature introspection. Frustrations may arise when a student is forced to consider evidence about himself before he is ready. Special consideration will be given to this problem later in the chapter.

EMPHASIS ON STUDENT MOTIVATION

The personnel program of the Teachers College, at the University of Nebraska, is concerned with the selection of students, orientation, departmental advising, counseling, placement, and follow-up. The orientation of freshmen is thus part of the personnel program. There is also, of course, the usual advisory work done by university instructors. At Ohio State University orientation was part of the instructional program, in the sense that the students' advisers were members of the teaching staff.

Major opportunity for the counselor to work with freshmen at Nebraska is provided in a two semester-hour course entitled "introduction to teaching." The activities of the course include class instruction devoted to orientation to the university, orientation to teaching, and an evaluation by the student of his own competence for teaching; individual clinical counseling based on cumulative case data—special aptitude tests, student questionnaires, and the like; and laboratory sections devoted primarily to improvement in reading and study habits.

As at Ohio State, the data submitted by the student at the time of admission to the university are available to the adviser in the orientation course. These data include the application for admission which, in addition to the usual identification data and a recounting of extracurricular activities, covers preference for school subjects, educational plans, and financial plans; a report from the high school principal, showing transcript of credits, the student's rank in his class, special interests, marked inabilities, whether or not he is recommended for university work, test scores, and a general statement of personality and character; a personality rating scale supplied by the high school principal or other staff member best qualified to furnish such information; the results of preregistration tests administered when the student comes to the university, including English usage, study skills, reading comprehension, mathematics, and a psychological examination. All the data are summarized and the test results entered on a profile chart for each student.

The student, under the guidance of the counselor, compares his goals with similar lists developed by other students and with lists published in various professional books; rates his personal characteristics and compares them with ratings by faculty members and other students; checks his estimate of his abilities and interests against evidence revealed by appropriate tests; if necessary, follows up the health examination by carrying out activities recommended for his improvement; checks progress in reading and study skills as indicated by standardized tests. In the laboratory section, he gets practice in the improvement of reading, study skills, and speech if he needs it. So that he may develop conviction as to the importance of what he is finding out about himself and see its relevance to his educational program, he is encouraged to visit schools, observe, and report on such elements as school organization, placement of responsibility, curriculum organization, student welfare, sources of family income, and community relationships. Class discussion, self-evaluation, field visitation, work in the laboratory, and individual counseling are closely coordinated. The last of these is especially emphasized. Through clinical counseling students are helped to keep the knowledge they are gaining about themselves in proper perspective.

CENTRAL ROLE OF SELF-INTEREST

Instructors in the orientation course believe that they have an unusual opportunity to demonstrate to the students the workings of a program geared to meet their needs. Most students begin their university work highly motivated to establish themselves academically. The instructors have found that, in the first discussion periods, students are aware that their ability to read, write, and express themselves orally is going to play a major role in academic success. Students know too, that health, study habits, and personality are going to be factors in success and happiness on the campus. And they are eager to consider first those factors that will contribute most directly to success in courses.

Capitalizing on this readiness, the instructors have found that the discussion almost always turns to the nature of reading, to ways of finding out how well one reads, and to ways of improving. The discussion moves rapidly to cover such elements as vocabulary, differentiating between main points and detail, the limits of the students' effectiveness in reading fiction, expository writing, and technical material as determined by his established reading habits and background. Students soon begin to ask about ways of determining their effectiveness. This leads to a discussion of the purpose of certain tests and eventually to the use of some of them—usually the Iowa Silent Reading and the ophthalmographic tests.

The genuine interest thus aroused in the purpose and outcome of testing leads the student to an interest in scoring the test, analyzing the responses, and interpreting the results. These procedures require new skills and insights of the student. The instructor, instead of using his time to perform these tasks, uses it to teach the students to do them. The student learns that there are prescribed ways of scoring and sees why they must be followed; he learns that certain groups of items in the test reveal types of strength and weakness, that with some tests classification of strengths and weaknesses is gained by multiple scoring, and that in others responses to specific items must be studied and classified in order to gain evidence concerning specific needs; he learns that such analyses have some value in showing strengths and weaknesses *per se* but that relative significance through comparison with the performance of other students is also useful. As additional tests are taken and analyzed, the student enters his test results on a profile chart. The interests of students in this procedure move from one skill and competence to another—reading, writing, speech, study habits, mathematics, knowledge of general culture, and acquaintance with contemporary affairs. They do not necessarily come in this sequence, but the interests of most members of the group usually do. The concentration of interest of the group makes for interstimulation that would not result from an entirely individualized program. Individual differences in motivation and understanding with respect to common and divergent problems are met through personal contact with the instructor.

By about the fifth or sixth week of the course, students usually begin to look beyond factors directly related to academic competence. Problems of social adjustment and professional choice become dominant. Some students begin to wonder if they should prepare to teach. Others question the appropriateness of their choices of majors and minors. Personal adjustment and interest inventories are used in the manner previously described. Students by this time look forward to scoring and analyzing their test responses. Some of these instruments, however, have highly complex scoring procedures that can be more accurately and appropriately scored by machine than by hand. The Strong Vocational Interest Blank is an example. In this case the instructor explains the way in which the test was developed, how the norms for occupational areas were derived, and how the test as a whole is scored. In order that the student may comprehend the meaning of a score on the blank, he scores the test by hand for the occupational area in which he believes he is most interested. The instructor then has the test scored for the other areas of vocational interest by machines and the results are entered on the profile chart by the student. Problems of vocational choice and social adjustment are considered further in individual conferences. With data from a variety of sources assembled, including an autobiography, the student has a conference with his instructor in which they discuss implications for the future. The student checks his judgments against those of the instructor and writes a planning paper in which he outlines an educational program by which to guide himself during the rest of his time at college.

As students begin to understand their needs, they begin to look to the resources of the university with some seriousness of purpose. Sometimes they fail to find an established phase of the university program that assumes responsibility for helping them with certain of their problems. This was formerly true of deficiencies in reading and speech, but remedial reading and speech laboratories are now in operation. Creating a greater sensitivity in the established program of the university to needs students discover still remains a difficult problem, however. One procedure for building this sensitivity has been especially fruitful. The counselor in the introductory course invites all of the teachers of a particular student to a conference. The student's profile of test data and other information are laid before them. The counselor relates his experience with the student, the tentative plans that have been made, and the types of help the student is seeking. He then gives the student's teachers opportunity to relate their experience with him. They discuss ways in which the program of the university, and their courses in particular, can make better use of his abilities and respond more fully to his needs. The procedure is not restricted to the discussion of particularly difficult cases. Clinics have been held for students outstanding in every way as well as for those who are deficient in one or more respects. The effect of the procedure in making the staff and program responsive to student needs has been heartening.

APPRAISALS OF THE PROGRAM

A variety of evidence has been gathered in attempts to evaluate the effectiveness of the orientation program at the Teachers College. Outcomes in the reading and speech laboratories have been studied. For example, the typical freshman at the conclusion of the reading improvement program is approximately three-fourths of a year in advance of arts college sophomores who have not been in that program. The greatest improvement, on the Iowa Silent Reading Test, has been found in the section on paragraph meaning, word meaning, paragraph organization, and location of information.

In the speech program, out of 264 freshmen in one entering class, 84—or 32 percent—were rated as needing corrective training.[13] The speech test consists of conversation, reading a paragraph from a textbook, and reading a list of sentences that incorporate most of the speech sounds.

Not more than fifteen students are placed in one laboratory section, those with similar difficulties working together whenever possible. Voice recordings are made. Members of the group write criticisms as each student's record is played, and these criticisms, along with ones by the instructor, are turned over to the student. The comments serve to sensitize him to his difficulties, and provide a basis for planning with the instructor ways of overcoming them. When a student thinks he has corrected one of his difficulties, he makes another recording. He attends the speech laboratory only so long as is necessary. At the close of the laboratory period for speech correction, students are classified into three groups: those whose difficulties have been corrected, those who should continue independent work, and those for whom continued work in the speech laboratory seems necessary. Of the 84 students in the speech laboratory during one semester, 70 percent were rated in the first group; 22 percent in the second group; 7 percent in the third. Approximately four-fifths of the students rated the work in speech improvement

[13] Ralph Bedell and Maurine Poague, "The Nebraska Speech Improvement Program for Prospective Teachers," *Educational Administration and Supervision*, XXVII (February 1941), 153.

very high in interest and value. Staff members who have been in charge of the speech laboratory believe that individual diagnosis is essential for each student, that instruction must be planned on the basis of the diagnosis, but that this instruction can be carried on effectively in groups. They recognize, of course, that a few students have defects sufficiently severe to demand individual assistance. A follow-up study at the end of each year in the university and then out into the field is being planned.

Student opinion concerning the orientation course has been obtained through a "teacher rating by student" blank, filled out anonymously. Most of the students believe the course is exceedingly practical, forces them to think more than most other courses do, and overlaps high school courses less than do other college courses. Interest is slightly greater than in other courses, the work is judged to be somewhat easier, and they like the course slightly better than the average course.

When senior students were asked to rate the values they had derived from various aspects of the university's personnel program, three-fourths of them considered their work in the freshman orientation course as among their most valuable experiences.

The evaluation of the orientation program is admittedly incomplete. The major emphasis thus far has been on appraising students' skills and interests and abilities. An extension of the evaluation to include such topics as students' values and caliber of thinking should be useful. Occasional mass readministration of some of the tests, and follow-up interviews with individual students, might also contribute useful evidence regarding the strengths and weaknesses of the program. At the present time, plans are being developed for gathering systematically the faculty's opinion with respect to the program.

BEGINNINGS OF AN ORIENTATION COURSE

At Southern Illinois Normal University, at Carbondale, a rather loosely knit program of orientation and guidance was in operation for several years. Ten to fifteen freshmen were assigned to each member of the instructional staff who would

PROGRESS REPORT TO STUDENT SPONSORS BY THE COMMITTEE ON EVALUATION OF THE ORIENTATION AND GUIDANCE PROGRAM

	Check (√)	[Comment]
A. Aims in the educational or "academic" life area	A.	A.
1. Facilitating registration procedures	1	1
2. Stimulating development of basic skills	2	2
a. adequate reading habits	a	a
b. acceptable standards of speech and writing	b	b
c. habits of logical or "straight" thinking	c	c
d. efficient time budgeting and study habits	d	d
e. intelligent library usage	e	e
3. Obtaining and using information on academic achievement and mental age levels	3	3
a. intelligence tests	a	a
b. English and reading tests	b	b
c. social science tests	c	c
d. natural science tests	d	d
4. Stimulating awareness of campus resources	4	4
a. recreation opportunities	a	a
b. cultural opportunities—concerts, etc.	b	b
c. school traditions and spirit	c	c
d. school regulations	d	d
e. extracurricular groups—their functions, how to get in, etc.	e	e
f. curricular offerings—how to read the catalog, certification requirements, etc.	f	f
g. campus geography and departmental organization	g	g
h. book rental system	h	h
i. health department facilities	i	i
j. local employment opportunities	j	j
B. Aims in regard to physical aspects of student living	B	B
1. Adequate housing and lighting	1	1
2. Information and helps in regard to cost of living	2	2
C. Aims in the vocational guidance area	C	C
1. Locating interests	1	1
2. Relating interests to abilities potentialities	2	2
3. Supplying source materials on vocational opportunities and trends	3	3

	D	D
D. Aims in the area of personal adjustment	D	D
1. Facilitating social-emotional orientation	1	1
a. early opportunities for development of social companionships with same and opposite sex	a	a
b. overcoming self-conscious feelings in regard to social status and personal adequacy	b	b
2. Improving habits of personal hygiene, dress, manners, etc.	2	2
3. Developing healthy insight into normal adult personality mechanism, stimulating self-knowledge	3	3
E. Stimulating the development of a healthy philosophy of life for the mature college student	E	E
We should be glad to receive any additional evaluations of the present freshman program which you would like to make, or any suggestions as to the procedures of our evaluation program. Please use the back of the checklist or an appended sheet.	Suggestions concerning additional aims, or observations resulting from counsel experiences.	

[Space for remarks]

. . . Following each aim listed in the . . . [outline] you will find two spaces, one in which we should like you to place a check if you have worked for the realization of that particular aim in your counseling activities, and the other in which we should appreciate some comments as to the kinds of activity you have carried on in the given checked area—and if possible an estimate of the proportion of your group with which you have carried on the given activity. Please add comments as to why you have "steered clear" of certain aims listed in the report.

assume responsibility for working with and advising them, individually and in groups, during freshman week and throughout the freshman and sophomore years. No specified amount of time was prescribed for individual or group meetings, and no official credit was given. In 1940-41, a committee was appointed to evaluate this freshman-sophomore program.

The first job tackled by the committee was to clarify the goals of the advisory program. The committee produced an outline of suggested aims, and transformed it to a checklist on which advisers could indicate the types of assistance they had tried to give. A copy of the checklist and an excerpt from the directions for responding to it are given on pages 82 and 83.[14]

The replies showed much variation in the extent to which different advisers had attempted to implement the different aims included in the list. By and large, considerable attention had been given to helping students budget their time and to stimulating greater awareness of recreational, cultural, and employment opportunities on the campus. Relatively little attention had been given to problems of personal adjustment. Many advisers expressed difficulty in using test data. Some of their comments will illustrate: "in favor of having this information but the results need to be analyzed and given to the . . . [adviser] in a form that is usable"; "of little value without a measure of interest and ambition"; "didn't know how to interpret the scores."[15] About half the advisers said they talked about vocational interests with the students, but only a fifth reported any definite attempts to relate interests and abilities, and none referred students to source materials on vocational opportunities or trends.

In addition to preparing the checklist the committee asked the following two questions:

1. Approximately how much time have you had to spend with each member of your freshman group (on the average) this quarter, *excluding* the time spent on class scheduling at the beginning of the quarter?

[14] *Report of Committee Activity—1940-41*, by the Committee on Evaluation of the Freshman-Sophomore Orientation and Guidance Program, Southern Illinois Normal University (mimeographed).

[15] *Ibid.*, p. 5.

2. Approximately how much time do you estimate a freshman sponsor should profitably spend with each freshman. . . ?[16]

It was found that the average estimate of time that should be spent was about two hours and that the average time actually spent was slightly less than one hour.

The total picture drawn from the adviser's opinions, and from the opinions of some students as well, was one of wide variation in the extent to which student needs were being served. For the advisers who were most concerned about students' problems the brief contacts they had were very inadequate. The committee, therefore, made the following recommendations:

1. It is proposed that at least an experimental attempt to conduct a freshman orientation course be tried out next year.

2. It is suggested that this course might well be called "introduction to education" rather than "freshman orientation."

3. It is suggested that as a minimum there be at least two meetings of the course per week—probably one large lecture section and one smaller section meeting.

4. It is suggested that the faculty sponsors *not* be expected to be section leaders, but rather that a smaller number of interested section leaders be secured on the basis of their interest in the program.

5. It is proposed that a chairman for the course be selected this year; that he be given the opportunity of workshop experience to organize the course plan.

6. It is suggested that the course be a two-quarter course with one quarter-hour credit in education for each quarter and that in general the first quarter focus on "orientation to college life and achievement of academic skills" and that the second quarter focus on "orientation to professional choice (with special reference to education as a profession)."

7. It is suggested that the course chairman be given a reduced teaching schedule in his department at the request of the personnel council.[17]

The suggestions were acted upon favorably and the course was initiated in the fall of 1941. In the new program, which was similar in intent to the Ohio State and Nebraska programs, advisers were assisted in their counseling by senior students who

[16] *Ibid.*

[17] *Ibid.*, p. 27. Note: The chairman of the committee left the college to assume new responsibilities shortly after these recommendations were made.

were enrolled in a seminar on personality and social adjustment. The seniors also assisted in the evaluation of the program by constructing and analyzing questionnaires and by interviewing the students. In addition to serving as a field experience for seniors in their seminar on personality and social adjustment, this arrangement provided needed help to advisers that is worthy of further exploration. Institutions that do not have the resources of graduate schools and the help of graduate assistants frequently feel unduly handicapped. It is true that seniors should not be given counseling responsibilities that go beyond their professional understanding and competence. On the other hand, college seniors will soon be holding full-time jobs in high schools, and the opportunity to have a kind of internship while still in college should prove valuable to them as well as helpful to the college advisers.

A large majority of the freshman students felt that the orientation course was very valuable and believed that it should be continued. The majority thought it should be a required course; a minority that the second quarter might be made elective. They were unanimous in the opinion that it should carry credit. The majority felt that it should carry two hours of credit each semester; a few that it should be a one-semester course carrying three hours' credit.

The opinions of the faculty advisers were divided. Three definitely felt that they would like to see the course repeated and would like to continue participation as advisers. One member definitely stated that he did not want to participate if the course were repeated, that the content was not heavy enough to carry credit, but that he would like to continue carrying advisory responsibilities with students. Two other members questioned the amount of credit on the ground that there was not as much solid work as was included in other courses. One member felt that the course should carry credit in sociology rather than in education. The new director of the program felt that there had been insufficient cooperative study and planning, and that the course would have been stronger the first year had the advisers planned together for a year in advance of initiating the program. There was, in fact, some lack of understanding among the advisers of various parts of the program and of the procedures involved; the opinions noted above reflect this lack of common viewpoint. Plans for closer cooperation are being worked out as the program continues.

The development of the "introduction to education" course at Carbondale is of special interest because of the way in which it grew out of revealed weaknesses in the existing program of freshman orientation and guidance. It shows, also, that such a program may encounter difficulties in growing to full stature when leadership is withdrawn at critical times, and that the advisory reponsibilities involved are not easily fulfilled by persons drawn from the instructional ranks. This does not mean, of course, that advisers should be drawn exclusively from the personnel division. It emphasizes, rather, the need for cooperative study by those who would help college students in their personal and professional orientation and planning. The project is interesting, finally, because seniors have been used in the advisory program with freshmen, both to the advantage of the seniors in their growth, and to the advantage of freshmen and staff members in expanding the advisory resources of the institution.

SELF-EVALUATION UNDER GUIDANCE

In the orientation and guidance programs we have described it is quite apparent that much of the evaluative activity centers around the individual student. An effort is made to transfer to the student much of the responsibility for appraising his progress. With the help of his adviser he analyzes his own strengths and weaknesses and the special skills needed in a teacher; he makes plans for improving his competence, drawing upon the resources of the college and the community; and he judges his progress toward the attainment of these goals.

This emphasis on self-evaluation raises several questions regarding the role of the learner, the teacher, the adviser, and the evaluation specialist in appraisal procedures. The emphasis on self-evaluation in the present chapter follows from one of the major goals of orientation programs, namely *to help the learner increase his ability to identify his own strengths and weaknesses and plan accordingly*. Perhaps this major goal of orientation courses should be expanded and incorporated within the major goals of all education. There would be good reason for so doing, for many of our important decisions in life are made by us, not for us. This is true for children in their out-of-school hours, for counselors and teachers in their professional responsibilities, and for adults generally as they deal with their life problems. There is an added reason for emphasis on self-evaluation in teacher education. Students preparing to teach have to learn about evaluation. In the process of identifying their own strengths and weaknesses, under the guidance of those who are capable of helping, they can develop insights into the appropriateness of techniques and the psychological effects of processes that they themselves will later need to employ.

The processes of evaluation are more likely to be in harmony with a democratic philosophy of human relations when the major responsibility for appraisal is carried by the learner than when it is placed on a teacher or expert. When the responsibility is carried by the specialist there is a tendency to administer tests *en masse* for convenience, to interpret the results for the students, to tell them in what ways they are strong and weak, and often to prescribe what steps they should take next. In so far as these procedures reduce the security and destroy the integrity of the student, they work in conflict with two very important goals of democratic education—the development of personal security and respect for individuality.

What processes of evaluation would be more desirable? It would seem fairly safe to assume that a decision will be accepted for its fullest value in planning next steps when the decision and the basis on which it is made are clear to the student. What are the antecedents of understanding, accepting, and acting on decisions? One's level of maturity, background of experience, emotional stability, and desire to know are probably all important and interrelated antecedents. These factors have been summed up in one word by those who have studied conditions under which children learn to read—readiness. And readiness is an important factor in self-evaluation, for if it is ignored self-evaluation may be as disturbing to the security and integrity of the student as appraisal by a second party. Readiness and the role of the learner, teacher, adviser, and evaluation expert are very much intertwined.

The teacher or adviser and the evaluation specialist assume responsibility for helping the learner increase his ability to discover and use data in coming to intelligent decisions. The nature of the help depends upon the needs of individual students. Many college students have had limited experiences of the type that motivate them to seek intelligent decisions about their future. To force them to face evaluative evidence of their strengths and weaknesses in the light of professional demands is to run the hazard that the evidence will be little understood or accepted. It may be important to plan with them some exploratory work experience. It may be necessary to lead them through a series of experiences which will help them verify their professional choice or gradually bring them to question its appropriateness. It may be that parents or friends are expecting, or even insisting, that they pursue a specific program. To make students face disillusioning evidence without considering ways of releasing such pressures would be highly frustrating to the students. It would be unfortunate to force on them self-evaluations that disturb their security and about which they feel they can do nothing. On the other hand, it would be unfortunate to delay bringing a student to face a problem if it meant that he was likely to put four years of effort and money into preparation for a profession only to find failure experiences so numerous as to make him continuously unhappy on the job. It is not an easy problem to resolve this dilemma.

The teacher and specialist can help the learner recognize his own limitations and lead him to an intelligent use of resource material and personnel, to a sensitivity to and intelligent use of the appraisals others will inevitably make of him in social, employer-employee, and other relationships. No individual, regardless of how expert he becomes in his own interpretation of data, will be able to derive all of the best answers. Part of the responsibility of instructors and evaluation experts is to acquaint students with the inadequacy of certain types of evaluative data and with the frailties of human interpretations. There follows naturally the additional responsibility of helping them to use wisely the help they can get from teachers and consultants. It may not be too much to hope that students who develop ability in self-evaluation under guidance may continue to make use of that ability after they leave college.

There is danger in developing undue sensitivity to the opinions of others. It would be well to remember the fable of the old man, his son, and the donkey. He tried to please everyone but he pleased no one and lost his donkey too. On the other hand, it is unrealistic to ignore what others think. Here again we have a problem of readiness. It seems reasonable to believe that readiness to face new data is probably conditioned by previous experience in self-appraisal. Having had some practice in developing plans and estimating one's likelihood of being able to carry them out, one is prepared for further planning at more complex levels. Having gained the feeling that there is a validity of relationship between one's plans and goals and what one already knows about himself, the student has a sense of security and direction that enables him to differentiate between useful and useless suggestions. It is a responsibility of education to help people appraise the validity of advice from others.

The ability of any one individual to interpret data is limited by his experience, his mental ability, and his emotional organization. This is true whether the data are about himself or others. Often data about himself relate to aspects of life in such a way as to make him respond emotionally to them. It is therefore highly important that the learner recognize the need for validating his highly personalized judgments against those of the teacher and expert who may interpret the evidence from a wider background of experience and in a less emotionalized way. It is also important that the learner not be forced to consider evidence and make decisions which by virtue of immaturity, limited background of experience, or emotional set he is incapable of understanding, accepting, or using constructively.

These implications may be summarized briefly for emphasis. The responsibility of the teacher and evaluation specialist is primarily one of guidance. They help the learner discover and use relevant data in reaching his decisions. They help him recognize his own strengths and limitations and lead him to seek the resources and insights of others. They help him become sensitive to the evaluations which other people—friends, teachers, employers—will inevitably make of him, so that he may use these judgments intelligently in his planning. They help to validate his own personal (and sometimes emotional) evaluations against judgments drawn more objectively from a wider background of experience. Thus, in orientation and guidance, the role of the teacher and evaluation specialist takes new meaning, becomes not so much a task of evaluating the student as of helping the student make the most thoroughly adequate and intelligent evaluation of himself. And this task, for the evaluation specialist, is added to his familiar role of appraising the effectiveness of the program.

When a student is motivated by genuine curiosity to appraise his status or progress, when he is seeking to improve his basis for planning next steps, when he wants the evidence because he believes it will be useful to him, when he looks upon instructors and experts as sources of help, some of the customary evaluation procedures may be inappropriate. For example, it is not likely that readiness to take a particular test will occur in all students simultaneously. It may not be desirable to wait to give a test until all students are ready; and it may be highly undesirable to make certain students wait on others who are not ready. At least one solution would be the testing laboratory as now in operation in some institutions. Students can take certain tests in these laboratories whenever they are ready. There will still be occasion, of course, for group administration of tests, as in selective admission programs at the time of enrollment, and in research projects.

Real motivation on the part of the learner to evaluate also opens up new possibilities for the scoring of tests and the summarizing of results. If the student is interested in the results for the value they will be to him in planning next steps, one important stimulus to dishonesty in scoring his own paper is absent. The same is true for dishonesty while taking the test. The instructional value of appraisal activities may be greatly increased when the student scores his own paper. He sees the magnitude of his strengths and weaknesses as he makes the check marks. He notes what his errors are. He classifies and analyzes them. These activities focus his attention on the content of the test, where it should be, but in so doing they may also help him bring more meaning to his interpretation of the numerical score. He will need help to develop these skills and insights. And this help is a function of the teacher and evaluation specialist. When the student knows that he will use test results for his own benefit and that the teacher and others are helpers rather than judges, an important factor contributing to the invalidity of attitude and interest and personality questionnaires is likewise minimized—namely, the tendency to answer in the way the student thinks he *ought*. Even with the best rapport and motivation, some students may be unwilling to face the evidence. They may for that reason prove unreliable in taking and scoring tests. Responsibility does not develop overnight. But those who remain irresponsible are exhibiting a trait that should raise grave doubt concerning their qualification for becoming teachers. Advisers and instructors cannot identify this trait unless they become well acquainted with their students. Neither can they identify it unless opportunity is provided for the trait to express itself.

Another outcome of self-evaluation as described here is to give the student a more important role in the channeling of information from the cumulative record to the instructional staff and vice versa. Adequate channeling of this information has been a major problem in centralized personnel offices. Most attempted solutions have gone around the student. But when the student wants, understands, and accepts the evidence and uses it in planning, he becomes quite naturally the channel through which most of the evaluative data can be carried to all who may help him.

In concluding the discussion of some of the ramifications of self-evaluation, we would like to re-emphasize a number of points: first, the growing interest in self-evaluation has derived from needs that cannot be readily ignored; second, our knowledge of the limits to which self-evaluation can successfully be carried is sketchy; and third, there is need for experimental studies of the potentialities of self-appraisal under guidance. There have been few experiments concerned with this problem. Most of them have compared naive student judgments with those of experts derived through technical evaluative processes. If we are to determine the possibilities of self-evaluation, we will need experiments concerned with the quality of appraisal students make before and after education aimed at developing this ability. And the results should then be compared with results of superimposed evaluation to determine the extent to which they are actually accepted and used by the learner.

Because of the heavy guidance function of orientation programs, the leadership of the personnel division is drawn upon extensively. At the same time, there is a tendency to place major responsibility for counseling on the shoulders of the instructional staff, in order that channels be immediately opened whereby the educational program of the institution may respond to student needs. Except for cases of serious maladjustment where counseling demands a highly technical type of training, the personnel division is rapidly recognizing that one of its major responsibilities is to develop effective working relationships with the instructional staff. Because of these close relationships, the orientation program needs to be undertaken cooperatively. If a student succeeds in the orientation course in developing a program through which he hopes to achieve personal and professional goals, and the other aspects of the institutional program are not geared to meet his needs, the result may be confusion, insecurity, and disappointment. Whether this result is due to unrealistic planning on the part of the student and his adviser, or whether it is due to needlessly inflexible attitudes and rules elsewhere in the institution is not the main question; for in either case the result is symptomatic of lack of cooperation and understanding. The experiences, evaluative procedures, and cumulative records, initiated in the orientation program should be the springboard for subsequent aspects of the institutional program. If this is to be achieved, the orientation program needs to be planned and developed so as to gain the interest, good will, and active support of all areas into which its results feed.

IV

General Education

GENERAL EDUCATION both precedes and follows the development of professional interest. It extends throughout the span of formal education from kindergarten to graduate school. At the college level, it may be conceived as a broad foundation upon which professional competence is built. Or it may be conceived as the broadening of professional development and perspective so that special skills and insights are seen in relation to general ones. In schools where selection for and orientation to the profession of teaching occur during the freshman year, general and professional education may proceed simultaneously, each reinforcing the other. In most colleges and universities, however, professional education does not begin formally until the junior year; the freshman and sophomore years are devoted to general education.

General education for prospective teachers is not essentially different from general education for all other college students, but it has a special significance. In the eyes of the public, the main business of the schools is the transmission of the culture— culture, that is, in the sociological sense of the word embracing the "activities, ideas, and purposes that a society has inherited from the past *and* has produced for itself."[1] This task imposes responsibilities on the schools to work for the attainment of certain outcomes: for example, "(1) the acquisition of basic skills; (2) the formation of habits; (3) the cultivation of interests, sensitivity, and appreciation; (4) the promotion of knowledge and understanding; (5) the inculcation of attitudes and ideals."[2] In whatever way these outcomes or goals are classified

[1] R. Freeman Butts, *The College Charts Its Course* (New York: McGraw-Hill Book Company, 1939), p. 422.
[2] Edmund E. Day, "Basic Responsibilities of General Education in America," *The Educational Record*, XVII. Supplement No. 10 (October 1936), 11.

the basic fact is that the schools face all of them continuously, from kindergarten through college. As one ascends the educational ladder he finds that these basic tasks of general education change in degree and complexity. At the college level and for prospective teachers, general education assumes special importance because teachers, more than other persons, have a responsibility for transmitting the culture to young people and for being themselves good specimens of the culture.

Because there has been so much debate during the past decade over the philosophy, organization, and content of general education, we shall review some of these basic concepts before describing attempts to evaluate several programs. Definitions and programs of general education vary widely among different colleges. MacLean and Bigelow,[3] after surveying the various practices which are labeled general education in a variety of colleges, found in them a common denominator—a search for unity, a reaction against the free elective system. Butts[4] also suggests that the general education movement is a reaction against free election. We can perhaps agree that general education is an attempt to unify the heretofore heterogeneous curriculum.

Various organizations of programs in general education may be observed. Some have tended to emphasize survey courses in which broad fields of knowledge are integrated or the wisdom of the race is condensed. Here the organizing principle is the subject matter. Others have tended to emphasize the importance of practical preparation for adult living—education for citizenship, consumer education, education for home and family responsibility, and so on. Here society is the integrating principle. Still others have been concerned mainly with the personal and social needs and interests of individuals, the development of personality, and the building of interests. Here the individual is the integrating principle, and subject matter is a means to an end.

[3] Karl W. Bigelow and Malcolm S. MacLean, "Dominant Trends in General Education," *General Education in the American College,* Thirty-eighth Yearbook, Part II, National Society for the Study of Education (Bloomington, Ill.: Public School Publishing Company, 1939), Chapter XVI, pp. 351-82.

[4] R. Freeman Butts, *op. cit.*

Probably all programs of general education have some common aims. The variations cited above arise partly from opposing conceptions of the way in which those aims can be attained most effectively. All such programs seek to produce more competent adult members of society—citizens with faith in democracy and knowledge to help solve problems of contemporary life. All of them seek to produce, directly or indirectly, more competent personalities—stabler, securer individuals possessing values that are personally satisfying and socially good. Educators, in other words, believe that personal and social competence are desirable objectives of general education. They believe that a good general education must be functional in that it must serve to develop such desirable competence.

Increasingly, general education is defined as a program of experience which enables a student to gain a broad perspective on individual and social problems, so that he approaches with clear understanding and insight his responsibilities as a worker, a future parent, citizen, and human being. It is concerned with students' personal, social, and emotional adjustments, attitudes, appreciations, just as much as with their acquisition of knowledge, or the truth.

A program of general education may be functional in one or all of three ways—in the selection of material to be studied, in the organization of material to be studied, and in the kinds of activity employed in learning. In the last analysis, of course, a program of education is functional only if it accomplishes the goals it has set for itself, and this index of accomplishment is best sought in the degree to which students have attained the goals of the program.

Evaluating a program of general education is not different from any other evaluative task. In Chapter I we described the process of evaluation as including five steps: determining objectives, clarifying these in terms of student behavior, identifying appropriate sources of evidence, applying suitable measuring devices, interpreting the results in the light of goals originally defined. One should not infer from a logical description that the process of evaluation follows a rigid sequence of events. The process may be initiated simultaneously on several fronts. Some attempt at the definition of objectives, however, is commonly undertaken in the early stages of an evaluation program. One reason, of course, is that whenever one attempts to measure something he is implying that certain goals are important; making explicit these implied goals can give better direction to the gathering of evidence.

DEFINITION OF OBJECTIVES

The task of defining objectives is one of making value judgments: judgments of right and wrong, good and bad, desirable and undesirable. Goal setting, in other words, is the business of philosophy. But it is not an armchair business. Objectives should be firmly grounded in facts. Educational programs are shaped in part by social forces and in part by the character of the students to be served. Objectives can, therefore, be based upon experimental data concerning the abilities, needs, and interests of students; the abilities, needs, and interests of the adults they are likely to become; and the demands of the society in which they live. Indeed, unless objectives are anchored to such data they may appear to be mere high-sounding words. Moreover, the manner in which objectives are developed is important, for means and ends are not unrelated.

The experience of several institutions in formulating objectives will illustrate some of the techniques and procedures that have been tried.

A SYSTEMATIC APPROACH

At the General College of the University of Minnesota, a committee on objectives was appointed in 1938 by the director to develop a statement of the goals for the college. The committee's first step was to ask each faculty member to prepare a description (one or two pages) of what he thought should characterize a student who had completed the two-year General College program. How, in other words, would he describe a generally educated person? These descriptions were analyzed by the committee and every characteristic mentioned by any staff member was noted. The resulting list of characteristics filled more than twenty mimeographed pages. This list was then submitted to every faculty member with instructions to pass judgment on the appropriateness of each item. In this way every person had a chance to see the specific characteristics or objectives which had been suggested by every other person, without knowing which faculty member had made the suggestion. The faculty checked their attitude toward the items in this tentative listing according to the following key: (++) indicating strong agreement with the goal, (+) indicating agreement, (0) indicating no attitude toward it, (?) indicating doubt as to the appropriateness of the goal, and (—) indicating disagreement. These symbols were weighted numerically by the committee, and an index of the group's acceptance of each goal was thereby obtained. The committee then discarded the rejected statements and organized the acceptable ones into an outline under four major headings: knowledge; skills and abilities; attitudes, interests, and appreciations; and philosophy. This outline was accepted by the faculty as representing the aims of general education.

With this statement of goals for the college as a whole, the committee then sought to obtain from each instructional area an indication of its own primary and secondary goals, in order to find out which areas were assuming major responsibility for guiding students toward the attainment of the several objectives. Accordingly, the coordinator of each department was asked to indicate with a (++) each of the items on the outline with which his department was directly concerned, those toward which the instruction in his department was specifically aimed; to indicate with a (+) those items which his department felt were important and toward the attainment of which his department hoped it would make at least some contribution but not a major one; and to indicate with a (0) those which were neither major nor minor aims of the instruction in his department. In this way an estimate of the relative contribution of the various departments toward the attainment of the college's goals was obtained.

Through these procedures the objectives not only of the

college as a whole but also of the various departments within the college were worked out. Total faculty participation was sought in the preparation of the original descriptions and in the ratings of the importance of the items which had been mentioned in these descriptions. Departmental participation was sought in determining the relative emphasis of different departments on the aims of the college as such.

The following excerpt illustrates the form of statement in which the objectives were finally phrased. Under the general heading of "Attitudes, Interests, and Appreciations," one section was developed as follows:

A student should become increasingly aware of certain desirable modes of thinking so that he:

1. may develop the objective or scientific point of view, an attitude of dispassionate inquiry, in which curiosity and a respect for facts combine with the willingness to weigh all available evidence;

2. is willing to evaluate critically;

3. is open-minded, believes in delayed or suspended judgment until the evidence is all in;

4. has respect for expert opinion and tolerance for ways of thought and behavior different from his own, not only for the geographically and temporally remote but also for the immediate contemporary issues;

5. wants to resist common fallacies of thought, quack nostrums, superstitions, etc.;

6. wants to resist unscrupulous propaganda of all kinds (including advertising);

7. conceives of education and learning as a continually ongoing process;

8. exhibits greater independence in thinking, using fewer "crutches" than before his general education.[5]

The process of developing this statement of objectives occupied the committee for approximately a year. Major responsibility rested with the committee, and the faculty as a whole registered their beliefs through relatively formal devices—an essay and paper-and-pencil ratings. The faculty were accustomed to working in this manner.

[5] *Curriculum Making in the General College: A Report on Problems and Progress of the General College*, prepared by the staff of the General College (Minneapolis: University of Minnesota, 1940), p. 27 (mimeographed).

A COMMITTEE APPROACH

At the State Teachers College in Oneonta, New York, an evaluation committee undertook to develop a statement of institutional goals. The committee itself phrased seven broad statements which it believed would be acceptable in general to the whole faculty. These seven statements were then distributed to each staff member and to students in the junior class. Both staff and students were asked to list under each objective some of the specific forms of behavior which might be considered evidence that the goal was being attained. These suggestions were summarized into a final statement in which the general goals were followed by specific indications of their meaning in terms of student behavior.

The following example[6] illustrates the form:

The student should have made progress in the understanding and appraisal of contemporary culture not only of this region but of the nation and the world, as evidenced by:
1. Activities such as
    a. leisure-time reading and use of library
    b. interest in current happenings via newspapers and radio
    c. attendance at lectures and concerts
2. Interests whether satisfied or not in such things as
    a. art and music trips
    b. visits to museums
    c. travel
3. Characteristics such as
    a. open-minded to differing points of view
    b. appreciation of regional lore
    c. flexibility in regard to change

The seven general objectives were formulated by the committee in a few days. The process of assimilating and organizing the details suggested by faculty members and junior students consumed several months.

AN INDIRECT APPROACH

A committee at Southern Illinois State Normal University sought to develop a frame of reference that would be useful for

[6] From an unpublished manuscript in the files of the State Teachers College, Oneonta, New York.

subsequent evaluation and curricular revision. The committee drew up a list of fourteen assumptions about the contemporary world. Each of the assumptions was then analyzed and expanded by a subcommittee prior to consideration by the general faculty. Following faculty acceptance, a statement of the functions of the college and its teachers, as implied by the frame of reference, was developed. When this was refined it was submitted to the general faculty for approval. Approximately seventy faculty members rated each point in the document and not more than five dissenting votes were registered for any single point. About two years were spent in developing the statement. The functions of the school implied by assumption number one in the frame of reference,[7] quoted below, will illustrate its quality:

I. Contemporary American education proceeds in and for a democratic society, although at a time when democracy is threatened both by weakness within itself and by hostile philosophies in other parts of the world. These conditions imply that the school must:

   1. Attempt to discover, to analyze, and to define the weaknesses and strengths of democracy, with a view to helping correct the former and increase the latter

   2. Train the young citizen to be politically keen minded so that he feels a responsibility for
     a. participating in all the functions of government
     b. helping attract the best qualified citizens into public office
     c. evaluating old and new legislation, and not leaving these evaluations to a few delegated or elected individuals

   3. Accept the challenge hurled at democracy by hostile philosophies by
     a. fostering democracy as a way of life
     b. allowing frank comparisons between democracy, and other ways of life

A parallel aspect of the frame of reference involved the listing of some assumptions about the learning process. These assumptions were developed by a small committee and supplemented by suggestions from the larger faculty. One assumption will serve to illustrate the nature of this document:

[7] Final report of Southern Illinois State Normal University to the Commission on Teacher Education, Appendix 19, p. 1.

The individual learns most effectively, uses most intelligently, retains longest those facts, techniques, and skills which serve a recognized purpose at the time of acquisition, and therefore have significance to the learner.[8]

Thus the total frame of reference included assumptions about the contemporary world and assumptions about how students learn. The assumptions about society were translated into functions of the college implied by them. The assumptions about learning will be of value when the staff considers the type of experience they offer students in trying to fulfill the school's functions. While the objectives of the college are not stated in terms of their manifestations in student behavior, the process of moving from "the functions of the teacher" to a behavioral statement of goals is fairly clear. For example, one of the functions of the institution was described as to "attempt to discover, to analyze, and to define the weaknesses and strengths of democracy. . . ." Rephrasing and amplifying this in terms of student behavior, we might say that the school seeks to produce students who: (1) are familiar with the historical roots of democracy, perhaps evidenced by familiarity with certain books; (2) can identify democratic and antidemocratic elements in contemporary American life; some sort of matching test might be devised to reveal this ability; and (3) can identify antidemocratic elements in their own personal and social behavior (tests of attitudes toward Negroes, labor unions, etc., might be used for this purpose). Obviously, other examples of behavior could be suggested. Our purpose here is merely to indicate one way in which goals stated in terms of student behavior can be developed from the document already accepted regarding the functions of the college. And unless this step is taken the process of having formulated general goals is not likely to have great influence upon the educational program.

A DISCUSSION APPROACH

At Western Michigan College of Education a large committee on general education undertook to arrive at a common under-

[8] *Ibid.*, Appendix 15, p. 2.

standing and agreement as to the meaning of general education preparatory to evaluating the current program and recommending changes. Through direct discussion and debate of objectives, three dominant conceptions of general education, each strongly held by different members of the group, were brought to the surface. Some conceived of general education as the acquisition of minimum competence in such basic skills as reading, writing, speaking, spelling, computing. Others conceived of general education as a broad integration of the cultural heritage—familiarity with science, humanities, social studies, and so on, and a mind disciplined in critical thinking and logic. Still others looked upon general education primarily in terms of meeting the personal and social needs of individuals, in terms of functional everyday knowledge. Having clarified these different conceptions, the group found itself in the position of trying to recommend changes in the program that would prove acceptable to the adherents of all three. No consensus on basic concepts and objectives was reached in the time period of the cooperative study. Nevertheless, new courses were added and other changes were made in the organization and content of the program.

We have described the procedures followed by several institutions seeking to clarify their objectives. We have not described the values on which these goals rest; that is a broader problem of philosophy. No matter what values objectives are based on, faculties face the problem of clarifying their goals, and of stating them so that they can be used as guideposts in gathering and interpreting evaluative data.

It is clear from the descriptions of activities in these four colleges that a variety of techniques can be used in the development of objectives—written descriptive essays, checklists, ratings, large group discussions, small committees, research data.[9] The manner of working together and the techniques selected should be appropriate to the background of the institution and the interests of the local staff. The choice of procedure should be made with careful regard for the extent to which it

[9] The interview as a technique for clarifying objectives is discussed in Chapter V.

is likely to promote genuine interest in the evaluation, and willingness to accept the conclusions and modify practices in the light of them. If developing objectives is conceived as a first step in evaluation, consideration should also be given to the likelihood that the manner of development and the form of the statement will lead readily to next steps in the evaluative process. Over and above these special cautions, it goes without saying, the procedures should be democratic.

SOURCES OF EVIDENCE

The problem of what constitutes evidence that students have made progress toward attaining the goals of general education may be partly solved by the way in which the goals have been described. In the examples of objectives developed at Minnesota and Oneonta, several lines of evidence were listed. This evidence was stated in terms of what a person would do who possessed the general characteristics called for by the goal—were stated, in other words, in terms of behavior. General objectives are usually, perhaps inevitably, phrased in words capable of many interpretations—characteristics such as respect for democracy, creativeness, or social sensitivity, for example. Hence these general objectives must be defined, and the most direct and feasible way of defining them is by indicating some of the specific activities, interests, and attitudes that they imply. A person who possesses social sensitivity is one who exhibits such-and-such specific behavior. This behavior is evidence of the attainment of the objective.

That a great variety of observations might be relevant to the appraisal of a program should be obvious. But clearly, some observations may be more direct than others, or more closely relevant to whatever hypotheses are being judged. As relevant evidence one might examine the opinions of professors, the content of courses, the opportunity for extracurricular experience, the nature of faculty-student association, as well as the scores of students on tests of information, attitudes, and so on. An attempt to group a variety of acceptable evidence on a rough scale of significance may, therefore, be useful.

The ultimate test of a program of general education, and the ultimate or crucial evaluation of the extent to which students have profited from it, lies in an examination of the out-of-school lives of former students. What are the indications of personal and social competence in the lives of former students? What activities, attitudes, interests, adjustments, and values characterize their lives as citizens, as workers, as parents, and as individuals? Do these characteristics distinguish them from their fellows who have not had similar educational opportunity? Do they distinguish them from their fellows who have had a different type of general education? How well do they measure up to goals toward which their general education was directed? How much of the information and knowledge for which they were so carefully tested in college have they retained? Techniques for gathering data relevant to these questions include follow-up questionnaires, interviews, surveys, and tests.[10] The problems of appraisal are especially difficult in this area, for one cannot assume that adult activities, interests, and attitudes are directly attributable to school experience. Such things may be more properly attributed to the total pattern of society and culture than to one segment of it. But a college is indeed an ivory tower of isolation if it is not even concerned with the extent to which understandings and insights are manifested in the adult behavior of its former students. While data from follow-up studies may not yield the most clearcut and readily interpretable evidence, they do certainly provide crucial testimony in the evalua-

[10] Good examples of these techniques are reproduced in the following publications:

Lawrence Babcock, *The U. S. College Graduate* (New York: Macmillan Company, 1941).

Ruth E. Eckert, *Outcomes of General Education* (Minneapolis: University of Minnesota Press, 1943).

Ruth E. Eckert and T. O. Marshall, *When Youth Leave School: Report of the Regents' Inquiry* (New York: McGraw-Hill Book Company, 1938).

Walter J. Greenleaf, *Economic Status of College Alumni*, Bulletin 1937, No. 10 (Washington: U. S. Office of Education, 1939).

Walter Isle, "The Stanford University Follow-up Inquiry," Ph.D. dissertation in the files of Stanford University.

C. Robert Pace, *They Went to College* (Minneapolis: University of Minnesota Press, 1941).

tion of general education. The ultimate test of any program is in the character of its product.

The next most crucial source of evidence, and one which is more simply interpreted than data from follow-up studies, is an examination of the status of students about to leave college. What level of achievement have they attained in college? How much progress does this represent from their initial status in college? Answers to these questions call for three kinds of data: a survey of the initial status of students, a survey of student status at the time of leaving school, and a comparison of initial and final status showing the extent and direction of growth. Such surveys and comparisons might be concerned with some of the following outcomes: knowledge and insight in various areas (science, humanities, art, social science, and so on), interests, attitudes, adjustments, plans for the future—the degree of concern, of course, being a reflection of the basic objectives of the educational program.

The next source of evidence, a step short of examining the product as he leaves college, is an analysis of the institution's program. This involves, first of all, such considerations as the following: What is the typical pattern of courses actually taken by students and what variations are there from this pattern? To what extent do students actually take advantage of such facilities as libraries, museums, music listening hours, gymnasiums? What kind of student is using these resources and how frequently? To what extent do students actually participate in student government and other organizations and clubs? Comparisons between the availability of resources and the extensiveness of their use provide significant data for evaluation. Perhaps a related problem in this same area would be an analysis of the relationship between the kind of students served and the kind of programs offered. Are the offerings and facilities appropriate for the types of ability, interest, and background which characterize the students?

A fourth major source of evaluative data might be the collection of opinions from staff and students as to the values they see in the program. What do students think about the content of their courses, the teaching methods, the readings, the examination practices? What values do they believe they are attaining from their college experience? What values do they attribute to extracurricular activities? What weaknesses do they find in their program? What suggestions for improvement? What attitudes do faculty members have toward the program? What values do they believe students get from it? How is the college regarded by other groups of people—by other educators, by the parents of the students, by citizens in the local community, by former students?

ILLUSTRATIVE PROGRAMS OF EVALUATION

After the above analysis of the problems of evaluation and the available sources of evidence we can now turn to an examination of several evaluation programs in action, noting their scope, the basic problems met, the techniques used, and the organization or working relationships involved.

COMPREHENSIVE STUDY OF A COLLEGE

Although Minnesota's General College is not specifically concerned with teacher education and was not part of the cooperative study of teacher education, the program of evaluation developed there is perhaps the most comprehensive and systematic attempt that has been made by a single institution to appraise the outcomes of general education; no broad discussion of the problems of evaluation in general education can afford to neglect the experience at Minnesota. It should be said at the outset that we are dealing here with an experimental college, located in a major research center, and with an evaluation program financed in part by the General Education Board and directed by a specialist in evaluation and educational research. After we have described the program, we shall consider its implications for other colleges—particularly colleges without special resources in money and research experts.

Scope

In scope the evaluation plan covered five major problems.[11]

[11] Full details will be found in Eckert, *op. cit.*

The first of these concerned the definition of objectives. The way in which this problem was approached has already been described. The second problem was a study of General College students and their experience in the university. This study resulted in descriptions of the abilities, backgrounds, interests, and attitudes of the students; their reasons for entrance; their length of stay; the pattern of courses pursued; their educational and vocational plans; and other similar factors. It was rightly assumed by the college that one cannot properly interpret evidence of the extent and direction of change in students except in relation to the character of the students themselves and to the nature of their college experience. The third major problem was an analysis of the changes occurring in students during their residence in the General College—changes in information, adjustment, attitudes, interests, plans for the future. The fourth problem was a follow-up study of the activities, interests, attitudes, and problems of former General College students—young adults who presumably should show some evidence in their everyday, out-of-school lives of having had a general education. The fifth and final problem was an attempt to survey student opinions of General College courses, their reactions to the total program, their estimates of the help received from the counseling service, from faculty advisers, and from other college resources.

Use of tests

With this overview of the scope of the evaluation program we can examine in detail some of the procedures followed in carrying it out. Information for the study of students and their General College experience came largely from the registrar's records and from a personal-data inventory which the students filled out upon entrance into the college. The study did not include any special technique beyond the analysis of these records.

The problem of appraising changes in students during their period of residence was more complicated. The basic feature of the General College program, introduced about the same time the evaluation project was begun, was the offering of four orientation courses: vocational orientation, home and family orientation, individual orientation, and socio-civic orientation. These courses formed the core of the program and were designed not only to assist students toward improved adjustments but also in acquiring a body of information centering around each of these four areas of need. One major problem for evaluation, therefore, was to determine the extent to which students acquired this important information. The problem called for the construction of appropriate tests in each of these new areas.

The procedure adopted in the construction of the tests made use of the talents of every member of the General College staff.[12] To begin, the evaluators prepared a list of criteria for the selection of items, basing these suggestions on extended faculty discussions during the preceding year. Then the instructor and research assistant in each orientation area canvassed the previous year's orientation examinations, and examinations in related subject-matter fields, for appropriate items to include in the new tests. Then, working singly or with the evaluators, the instructors and research assistants checked this tentative sampling of items against the objectives of the orientation courses and against the materials actually presented in class the previous year. New items were constructed to fill blind spots, sometimes by the instructors and assistants and often by the evaluators. Through this interplay of suggestion and criticism two comparable examinations in each area were assembled.

These examinations were then submitted to the whole faculty for criticism. Because the whole faculty had worked together in setting up the orientation areas it was felt desirable that the entire group should have an opportunity to pass judgment on examinations constructed for them. It was suggested that staff criticisms be grouped in three categories: (1) consonance of the tests with the expected outcomes of the orientation area; (2) specific criticisms of items; (3) suggestions for new items—especially

---

[12] The following paragraphs draw heavily upon a previous publication: Ruth E. Eckert and C. Robert Pace, "A Co-operative Appraisal," *Journal of Higher Education*, XIII (January 1942).

contributions from the individual's own teaching field to the orientation area.

The tentative battery of eight tests had included about 600 items. A sum total of nearly 1,200 specific criticisms were made by the twenty-five faculty members. These criticisms consisted chiefly of objections to technical vocabularies, suggestions for clearer wordings, and objections to the narrowly factual character of many items. With this wealth of reference the evaluators, working with the instructors and research assistants, eliminated many items, made new ones, and recast many others. Equally helpful were the many general reactions to the content of the tests, especially references to important understandings which had not been adequately sampled. The sources of these suggestions were often surprising. For example, some of the most penetrating and useful criticisms of the social-civic test were made by an instructor in biology, an instructor in physical science, and an instructor in English. An instructor in speech made especially pointed comments on the tests in individual orientation and vocational orientation. That so many useful suggestions were made by people of widely different backgrounds is, perhaps, the best evidence of the value of widespread faculty cooperation in test building. Not only did this cooperative procedure result in greatly improved tests, but it likewise made faculty members more keenly aware of the many problems involved in test construction and served to acquaint them more thoroughly with the content and purposes of the new orientation courses.

While a majority of the items in these tests were of the conventional multiple-choice type measuring relatively specific knowledge, the faculty did try to formulate some questions to measure more complex insights, and to experiment with different patterns. A few examples may be suggestive to others with similar problems of evaluation in general education. In the individual orientation test, several items of the following type were included. The student is asked to rate each explanation of the situation as either reasonable or unreasonable.

Mary and George had a quarrel when they met after the summer vacation. She accused him of not loving her any more. Later George discovered that Mary was going out with another man.

1. Mary clearly had a strong feeling of inferiority.
2. Mary was oversexed.
3. Mary was trying to escape from her conscience by finding in George the faults which really lay in herself.
4. Mary was probably suffering from a lot of repressed desires.

Henry started his freshman year at college with high academic ambitions, but he had made less than a C average for the year. By that time he had decided that honor students are "grinds" who get little satisfaction from their achievements.

1. This is a perfectly sensible conclusion.
2. Henry was kidding himself so that he wouldn't feel too badly.
3. Henry was trying to avoid feelings of being less able than the other students.
4. He was trying to escape by daydreaming.[13]

In the vocational orientation test, one group of items centered around the problem of interpreting data in choosing an occupation. A brief description of "John Jones" is given, including some ratings on various abilities. There follows a list of twenty occupations. The student is asked to rate each occupation as (1) a good choice for John since the job fits his pattern of abilities and interests, (2) an unsuitable choice, since the job would not give John a chance to use his abilities fully, or (3) an unsuitable choice, since the work demands aptitudes that John does not possess. This task calls for the ability to interpret data and apply the results to a specific case; it assumes a knowledge of at least some of the abilities required by twenty different occupations.

In the socio-civic orientation test one group of items, in matching form, was designed to find out what students know about appropriate sources of information and help in relation to several common and practical community problems. The student is asked to indicate where he would go to get help in the following problems:

[13] From mimeographed copies of the tests on file in the General College offices, University of Minnesota.

1. To get ragweed cut down in a vacant lot
2. To force a landlord to repair an incinerator which frequently smokes up your apartment
3. To help you collect a loan of $50 which you made to a business acquaintance
4. To protect your house against robbery while you are out of town on vacation
5. To protest against the licensing of a beer parlor in your neighborhood

A. City engineer

B. Board of public welfare

C. City attorney

D. City assessor

E. Police department

F. Fire department

G. Alderman

H. Conciliation court

In all of the test excerpts the subject matter tested is practical, useful, and relevant to the lives of the young people in the General College. The items are cast in simple, nontechnical vocabulary. These characteristics are particularly desirable in tests of general education.

Several standardized tests of knowledge in various fields were also used in the total evaluation project. Among these were the Cooperative English Test, the Cooperative Contemporary Affairs Test, the Wesley Test of Social Terms. The instruments were administered to all General College students in the fall and again in the spring. This complete coverage made possible a number of significant comparisons: between students who elected the orientation courses and those who did not; between students who received one or more quarter's instruction in the orientation courses and those who did not; between freshmen and sophomores; between freshmen who took the orientation courses and sophomores who had taken them the previous year.

But the General College was interested in more than just informational outcomes. To measure changes in student adjustments, interests, and attitudes, some published tests were selected and some tests were locally constructed for the evaluation program. The Minnesota Personality Scale by Darley and McNamara was designed to yield measures on five factors: morale, social adjustment, family relations, emotional susceptibility, and economic conservatism. The Bell Adjustment Inventory provided measures of four factors: social adjustment, emotional adjustment, family adjustment, and health. Since some of the factors measured by these two tests overlapped, it was possible to note the consistency of the results. To measure attitudes toward social, political, and economic issues, the Pace test of liberalism and conservatism was selected. Comparison could be made between the results on this test and those on the economic conservatism section of the Minnesota Personality Scale. A questionnaire on recreational interests was locally constructed by the evaluation staff, drawing items from a number of published questionnaires. A checklist of opinions concerning home and family life was constructed, primarily by members of the home economics department. With the exception of this last instrument, all of these measures of interests, attitudes, and adjustments were administered to the entire student body in the fall and again in the spring. The opinion checklist on home and family life was administered to all students in the fall, but only to those students who had taken the appropriate course in orientation in the spring.

Use of a follow-up questionnaire

Another major focus of the evaluation study was to survey the out-of-school activities, interests, and attitudes of former General College students. Prior to the evaluation study, the General College had undertaken a comprehensive follow-up survey of nearly 1,000 young adults who had attended other divisions of the university.[14] A fifty-two-page questionnaire had been carefully constructed for this survey; more than two-thirds of the items had been directly suggested by General College staff members. Faced with the problem of surveying its own former students, the General College naturally drew heavily upon the experience gained from this larger follow-up study. Staff members re-examined this questionnaire and checked all items which they believed would be most worth repeating. These suggestions, combined with new items submitted by the instructors and the evaluators, resulted in a sixteen-page questionnaire

[14] Pace *op. cit.* Fuller discussion of this study will be found in Chapter VII.

which was sent to more than 500 former General College students. As in the larger questionnaire, the items were grouped under four major headings: earning a living, home and family life, socio-civic affairs, and personal life. A fifth section was added, focused on students' experience in and attitude toward the General College. Because many items in the sixteen-page questionnaire were identical with ones included in the fifty-two-page questionnaire, it was possible to compare the out-of-school activities, interests, and attitudes of former General College students wth those of similar students who had attended other divisions of the university.

Use of student opinion

The problem of surveying student opinion toward various phases of the General College program was approached in several ways. One set of data was gathered from personal interviews with the students. Another set was gathered by means of a questionnaire. The student council wished to undertake some project and the director of the curriculum suggested, among other things, that they consider making a study of student opinion toward the General College program. This idea appealed to the council; the project was then tied in with the evaluation study. Members of the student council suggested questions for the survey. The evaluation staff assisted in rephrasing some of the questions and suggested a few of its own. The student council announced the survey, selected a sample to be studied from each General College course, distributed and collected the questionnaires, tabulated the results, and submitted a report to the evaluation staff. Items in the questionnaire were concerned with students' reasons for coming to the General College, the values they thought they were attaining, their opinion of the system of comprehensive examinations, the help received from faculty advisers and counselors, and opinions about the General College courses. The last topic was approached by asking the students to check all courses they had taken for at least one quarter during the current year, and then asking them to rank these courses both with regard to their interest in them and the value they attributed to them. They were further asked to indicate what courses they would like to take that they were not now taking, what present courses they wished they were not taking, and what kind of course they would like to see offered in the General College that is not now offered. On each of these questions they were asked to give reasons for their answers.

The active participation of General College students in this project undoubtedly contributed much to their understanding of the program, as well as heightening faculty sensitivity to the need for revision and improvement in various courses and other college services. Moreover, the fact that the study was initiated, carried out, and summarized by students gave the evaluation staff a degree of confidence in the integrity of students' replies which might not have been justified had the study been made by the faculty or the evaluation staff itself. It is probably true that the validity of measures of opinion is strongly conditioned by the degree of rapport between those who administer the test and those who respond to it. In this study, the administrators were the students themselves.

Summary

Needless to say, the total mass of data gathered and analyzed during the two years of the evaluation study was impressive. To describe the results of the study is beyond the scope of this book. But one might very appropriately ask about the relative value or significance of the different activities that were undertaken. In general, the answer could be phrased as follows: the activities that were most meaningful to the college were the ones that called for the most participation by the faculty; and the data that were most meaningful were the ones that were expressed in the least technical terms. For instance, the amount of faculty time spent on formulating objectives, criticizing test items, or suggesting questions for the follow-up study was not great, but the outcomes exceeded what was gained from the statistical analyses of the information tests. Straightforward facts, such as the proportion of students who changed vocational plans while in college or the proportion who took some active part in campus activities, were more useful to the staff than complex facts, such as differences between test scores. That is to say, in the opinion of the evaluator and others who observed the Minnesota experiment, the faculty developed most interest and gained the clearest insight regarding ways of improving the program when they were taking part in the evaluation. In fact, more extensive faculty and student participation might well have been sought. For example, there would be less need for extensive clerical staffs to score papers and analyze results if students and faculty had more responsibility for appraising their own progress. Thus, the most profitable activities in the Minnesota evaluation are the very ones that could be undertaken most readily by other colleges.

INFORMAL APPRAISAL OF STUDENT PROGRESS

Another highly interesting experiment and evaluation in general education—and this one at an institution which specializes in preparing teachers—has been undertaken at the State Teachers College in Troy, Alabama. Contrasts between Minnesota's General College and the State Teachers College at Troy are striking. The General College is an experimental school of approximately 1,000 students and part of one of the largest state universities in the country. At Troy, there were less than 100 students enrolled in the entire freshman class in 1942. At Minnesota, research and evaluation services are largely in the hands of specialists; these specialists in turn have available to them the services of many other specialists in the university, as well as suggestions from the General College faculty. Further, Minnesota has had extensive experience in the development of objective tests, checklists, questionnaires, and other paper-and-pencil means of appraisal. There is no comparable specialization, centralization, or experience at Troy.

The general education program at Troy is concentrated in the first two years. In the freshman year it includes courses in "the bio-social development of the individual" and "the arts in individual development." These are supplemented by a service course in English and a special interest course. There is likewise an active guidance program during the freshman year. All students at entrance take physical examinations, an academic ability test, an English test, and fill out a personal-data record. During the year there is a systematic program of faculty counseling, in addition to that offered by the personnel staff. For the sophomore year the general education core includes courses in "man and his physical environment," "regional and national socio-economic problems," and "the arts in contemporary society." These are supplemented by work in applied mathematics, physical and health education, and a special interest course. Attempts to evaluate the program systematically have centered chiefly upon the work of the freshman year.

The problem of evaluating student progress toward the several objectives of the program required the development of a unified system of records in relation to these objectives. While the objectives are not described here, their nature can be deduced from the titles of the freshman and sophomore courses. Moreover from 1938 to the present, a large faculty committee on evaluation has submitted charts of educational goals to the general faculty once a year or oftener; these statements have been discussed periodically and revised in the light of experience. A description of the cumulative-record system, and of the way in which various members of the staff contribute to it, may afford helpful suggestions to others.

Results of the intelligence, reading, English, and health examinations and the personal-data record, gathered at the time of the student's entrance into college, are placed in individual folders and kept in the central counseling office. During the fall term the freshman faculty prepare brief summaries of the initial status and adjustment of students with respect to those objectives that have to do with personal, social, and emotional factors. Throughout the year anecdotal records of student behavior in informal situations are collected. These observations are noted by all members of the freshman staff and are turned in periodically to the counseling office where they are distributed to the student's faculty adviser. At the end of each term, the adviser writes a brief summary of the anecdotal observations and this is filed in the student's record folder. At the end of the year, the freshman faculty judge student progress and development during the year. This judgment is formed by reviewing each student's entrance-test data, the description made of his initial status, and the anecdotal records and summaries made by various faculty members during the year. This over-all description is written by the student's adviser, but it is subject to the approval of the freshman staff. In addition to these descriptive records, ratings are made at the beginning and the end of the year on a specially prepared rating form which calls for judgments on a six-point scale with respect to the following areas: health, personal appearance, social adjustability, meeting situations, use of leisure time, study methods and habits, communication of ideas, personal economics. At the end of each quarter, students write summaries of their own progress. And during the year students keep a record of their participation in college activities.

Up to this point, the description of the Troy program has centered on what might be called personal or descriptive records. The use of objective tests of personality and adjustment is conspicuously absent. The faculty have preferred to depend upon their intimate association with students, and their extensive opportunities to observe them under a variety of conditions, to provide them with adequate bases for appraisal. In addition to these personal or descriptive records, however, there is a cumulative record card on which is summarized relatively impersonal and objective information, data more closely related to academic achievement. The information thus recorded includes: (1) objective tests of information, vocabulary, facts and principles; (2) simple essay tests, midterm or final examinations, situations tests, problem-solving tests, and so forth; (3) self-written reports of field trips, special projects, activities, and so forth; (4) ratings by teachers of various student reports and products such as oral reports, reports on the use of the library, art products, music performance, appreciation, degree of participation in various activities, and so on.

A copy of this record form is reproduced on page 121. Space is provided to describe the evidence on which ratings are based or, if the source of evidence is a test, to record the name of the test and the score. All ratings are recorded on a three-point scale: 3 indicating that the student's performance falls in approximately the top fourth of the class, 2 in the middle half, and 1 in the low fourth. At the end of a term or year, ratings can be summarized in a variety of ways—an average of the ratings for each course; an average of the ratings for each type of objective, cutting across course boundaries; an average of the ratings for each type of objective in each course. The merit of using a consistent rating scheme is that it permits this variety of combination. The variety of evidence and experience recorded can also be noted.

A small staff working intimately together and in close daily association with a relatively small number of students may tend to be overinfluenced in their appraisal of students, perhaps unconsciously, by personality characteristics. One of the reasons for separating personal and impersonal evidence of growth in the system of records was to minimize this tendency. Likewise, the practice of discussing an individual student's problems in faculty meetings, and the practice of submitting the summary appraisals of students for inspection by the freshman staff, probably serves as a check against individual bias in the final estimates.

It is evident from this description of the evaluation plan at Troy that even the most closely knit faculty needs some systematic guide to give direction to its observations of students and its appraisal of them. The description is pertinent as an illustration of how one staff sought to preserve the advantages of informal personal association and still provide some simple means of channeling and organizing the results of their observations in communicable and relatively objective fashion. The need for organizing observations led eventually to the development of a statement of goals which could serve as a unifying framework.

TROY STATE TEACHERS COLLEGE
INSTRUCTOR-COUNSELOR, INDIVIDUAL STUDENT RECORD OF
GENERAL EDUCATION EXPERIENCE[a]

Name _____ Quarter _____ 19___ Instructor _____

Rating 3 2 1	Evidence on which rating is based Describe experience, work completed, or test	Test Score	Median

[a] G. F. Stover, *Preparing Teachers for Newer School Programs*, Bulletin of the State Teachers College, Troy, Alabama, XXIX (October 1942), 148.

One phase of an evaluation program at Milwaukee State Teachers College may be described briefly. In 1938, Milwaukee introduced five "area" or survey courses in its program of general education—physical science, biological science, social science, humanities, and social and aesthetic experiences. Subsequently, the fifth area was dropped and much of its content incorporated in the areas of humanities and social science. After two years, the achievements of students who had taken this new area curriculum compared as follows with the achievements of matched students who took the traditional curriculum:[15]

| | Median Percentile Rank | |
| | Area | Control |
Tests	N = 41	N = 41
Cooperative General Science Test (total score)	75	55
Cooperative English Test (total score)	49	45
Cooperative General Culture Test (total score)	78	65
Social Studies (subscore)	66	62
Literature (subscore)	74	60
Fine Arts (subscore)	80	78
Science (subscore)	82	54
Mathematics (subscore)	64	54

It is recognized, of course, that only informational objectives are measured by these tests. But one should not minimize the importance of measuring the acquisition of facts and principles. In any new program it is highly important to make sure that the major strengths of the old are not lost in the new. From the standpoint of evaluation as measurement and research, it is probably desirable to have new and old programs of instruction operating simultaneously so that comparisons between the two can be made, as at Milwaukee.

EVALUATION IN A HUMANITIES COURSE

At the College of St. Catherine, a course called "introduction to the humanities" was first given in 1939-40, centering upon the arts—music, architecture, painting, sculpture, and literature. Plans for the course were left flexible to allow it to develop

---

[15] Final report of Milwaukee State Teachers College to the Commission on Teacher Education, p. 71.

around the interests and needs of students, for the dominant objective of the course was to influence their daily lives. Three methods were used to keep the course functional in this sense. Cultural events in the life of the students and of the local community provided starting points for many discussions—concerts, exhibits, plays, field trips. The discovery and study of principles and elements common to all the arts were repeatedly emphasized. And students wrote their reactions to and analyses of aesthetic experiences in their everyday life—for example, to a piece of sculpture, music, a painting, a building, a poem, and so on—and these "judgment cards" were written daily.

To evaluate the new course in its first year several approaches were tried. The students' daily "judgment cards" were of course a major source of evidence. The instructor noted the subjects about which students wrote comments during the course. Interests, expressed by the choice of subject, in the fall, winter, and spring terms were compared, not only for individual students but for the class as a whole. The likes and dislikes expressed on these cards and the reasons given for those preferences were also studied. The cards, in short, provided constantly accumulating evidence of what was happening to the tastes and judgments of the students. Doubtless the technique of studying so many cards will seem laborious to many. But in a field where attempts at measurement and evaluation have been as meager as they have in the arts—especially with regard to tastes and appreciations and judgments—the accumulation of a great deal of basic data, of firsthand observation and experience, must precede the development of more precise measuring scales.[16] Another evaluative device yielded data similar to that gathered from the judgment cards, but under more controlled conditions. On the first day of the course, twenty-six objects—advertisements, reproductions of paintings, sculpture, vases, and so forth—were shown to the students. The same twenty-six objects

[16] Several highly suggestive and promising techniques for measuring art appreciation and judgment are described in: Ray Faulkner, "Evaluation in a General Art Course," *Journal of Educational Psychology*, XXXI (October 1940), 481-506. See also Eugene R. Smith and Ralph W. Tyler, *Appraising and Recording Student Progress* (New York: Harper & Brothers, 1942), Chapter IV.

were shown again at the end of the course. At both times students wrote out their reactions to the objects and the reasons for their likes and dislikes. Comparison of these reports yielded evidence of growth. A third evaluative technique was the second giving of a voluntary-reading questionnaire (Progressive Education Association test 3.3) which students had taken during their freshman year. Comparison of the two sets of results showed some shifts in reading attitudes both in the group and in individuals.

Other evidence of evaluative significance was accumulated informally during the year. The instructor has summarized the evaluation as follows:

Some of the students voluntarily made remarks in private conferences about the enjoyment so-and-so was getting from the study of humanities, that so-and-so was dressing with more taste, that they thought they were all more observing because they were writing judgment cards. Inferences made from answers to a questionnaire given on the first day, from judgment cards as they came in, from comments made by individuals in class discussions, from conversations in informal conferences with particular girls and with groups gave further insight into student needs and interests, insight which was used in stimulating, guiding, and helping the individual as well as the group. In some cases, even quite early in the course, it was evident from such data that the student found her living enriched by the experiences offered by the humanities course.[17]

Although the familiar evaluative technique of final examinations covering knowledge of facts learned in the course was doubtless used, it is not mentioned in the report. Of special significance is the apparent recognition at St. Catherine's that the usual subject-matter examinations are incapable of measuring student progress toward all of the important objectives of the humanities course. And equally impressive is their readiness to try new methods of appraisal for the objectives that they do consider most important.

Out of the experience in teaching the course the first year, the instructor developed a new statement of objectives. In the

---

[17] Sister Mona, "An Experiment in the Humanities," *Proceedings of the Workshop in General Education,* University of Chicago, 1940, Volume II: Humanities (Chicago: Cooperative Study in General Education, 1941), p. 18.

beginning her objectives were frankly general and tentative; the revised version was specific and stated in terms of student behavior. It was clear and meaningful to the instructor because it grew out of the year's experience and from observation of what actually happened in the course.

A COLLEGE PROGRAM OF COOPERATIVE APPRAISAL

A comprehensive evaluation of Bennington College was carried out in 1939 to 1941 with the aid of grants from the Whitney Foundation and the General Education Board. As in the case of Minnesota, the Bennington evaluation had no relation to the Commission on Teacher Education. But we mention it here because it illustrates procedures that should be helpful to teachers colleges.

The Bennington evaluation was concerned with three major problems: first, a description of the students—their backgrounds, their reasons for attending college, and their readiness for college as indicated by interests, scholarship, ability, and performance on tests of information; second, an analysis of the program—its aims and assumptions, the range of studies taken by students, the nature and quality of the winter work program, and a study of how students spend their time. The third, the evaluation proper, considered such questions as these: Do students follow their interests, what achievement do they show in various fields of knowledge and in relation to their interests, what friendship patterns do they form that facilitate learning, what changes occur in their attitudes toward education, what success do they have outside of college (in subsequent work in other colleges and in their employment), and what opinions do students, graduates, faculty, and outsiders express regarding strengths and weaknesses of the Bennington College program?

Much attention was also given to cooperative procedures and effective ways of working together. Although an evaluator from outside directed and administered the project, the faculty recognized it as their own. At the outset, the nature of the enterprise and the relation of the evaluator to the college were definitely clarified by joint agreement on the following assumptions for carrying on the study. We have reproduced them here as illustrative of a most desirable first step to take in an evaluation program:

1. Evaluation of any program implies a set of values by which judgments are made.

2. The values of an educational institution are expressed in the instructional program.

3. Bennington College exists essentially for the contribution it can make to the development of students. The educational values must therefore be interpreted in terms of changes in students the program is designed to bring about.

4. With the desired changes in students agreed upon, the chief task of the evaluation study becomes that of collecting and summarizing the evidence that will show the extent to which the changes are taking place or the degree to which the objectives are attained.

5. Because Bennington attempts to establish habits of learning that will function throughout life, it is essential that the evaluation study be as much concerned with graduates and former students as with the present student group.

6. An evaluation program conducted in terms of these assumptions must be a cooperative undertaking of the entire Bennington community.[18]

PROJECTS EMBRACING SEVERAL SCHOOLS OR COLLEGES

Another major project is the Cooperative Study in General Education sponsored by the American Council on Education. The chief contributions of this study to evaluation have been twofold—the analysis and statement in terms of student behavior of many commonly held objectives of general education, and the development of measuring instruments in relation to many of these important goals. At the level of secondary education, but still pertinent for general education in the colleges, has been the eight-year study of the Progressive Education Association. The objectives developed in both the secondary school and college studies are classified under similar headings. The classi-

[18] From unpublished mimeographed material in the files of Bennington College, Bennington, Vermont. The *Journal of Educational Research*, **XXXIV** (April 1941), contains a brief description of the plan on pp. 633-34. It is expected that a full report of the Bennington evaluation, by Alvin C. Eurich and Catherine Evans will be published after the war.

fications are descriptive of types of behavior rather than areas of academic subject matter. The major objectives at the high school level are organized under the following headings:

1. The development of effective methods of thinking
2. The cultivation of useful work habits and study skills
3. The inculcation of social attitudes
4. The acquisition of a wide range of significant interests
5. The development of increased appreciation of music, art, literature, and other aesthetic experiences
6. The development of social sensitivity
7. The development of better personal-social adjustment
8. The acquisition of important information
9. The development of physical health
10. The development of a consistent philosophy of life[19]

Many of the tests developed in the eight-year study are also appropriate at the college level. The following list of some of the more widely used of these tests, together with their identifying numbers in the PEA records, may be useful to the reader:

Under the heading of effective methods of thinking:
    Interpretation of Data (2.52)
    Application of Principles of Logical Reasoning (5.12)
    Nature of Proof (5.22)
Under the headings of social sensitivity and attitudes:
    Social Problems (1.42)
    Application of Social Facts and Generalizations (1.5)
    Beliefs on Social Issues (4.21 and 4.31)
Under the heading of interests:
    Interest Index (8.2a)
Under the heading of personal-social adjustment:
    Interests and Activities (8.2b and 8.2c)
Under the heading of appreciation:
    Seven Modern Paintings (3.9)
    Finding Pairs of Pictures (3.10 and 3.11)

Smith and Tyler[20] have described the development of these and

---

[19] Wilford M. Aikin, *The Story of the Eight-Year Study* (New York: Harper & Brothers, 1942), pp. 89-90.

[20] Eugene R. Smith and Ralph W. Tyler, *Appraising and Recording Student Progress* (New York: Harper & Brothers, 1942).

other tests and the reader should refer to their book for fuller information.

At the college level, the staff and participants of the Cooperative Study in General Education have developed several evaluation instruments[21] related to important yet seldom measured objectives:

> Self-Inventory of Personal-Social Relationships
> General Goals of Life
> Religious Concepts
> Inventory of Social Understanding
> Health Inventories:
> > 1.1 Health Activities
> > 1.2 Health Information
> > 1.3 Health Interests
> > 1.4 Health Attitudes
> > 1.5 Analyzing Health Problems
> > 1.6 Judging Sources of Information in Health Problems
>
> Checklist of Wartime Problems
> Satisfactions Found in Reading Fiction
> Inventory in the Arts

An indication of the nature and potential usefulness of some of these tests can be gained from the following brief description of the Inventory of Social Understanding:

... Social science teachers wanted some means of discovering what conceptions of the social order students have acquired in their previous education, what they believe about society, and what they think they know about it. The primary purpose of the inventory is to determine the degree to which the student is capable of differentiating between what the facts are and what he wishes them to be.

The inventory is made up of 150 statements which are the kind of remark which the student has heard, has himself employed, and has reacted to. They are clichés, based upon a fairly wide variety of significant facts and preferences which are closely related to the cultural background of students.

For each statement the student has an opportunity to indicate

---

[21] Ralph W. Ogan, "The Cooperative Study in General Education," *The Educational Record*, XXIII (October 1942), 696.

whether he thinks it is a fact which is true or false, or a judgment with which he can only express agreement or disagreement, or a statement about which he can make no judgment at all.[22]

A very widely used source of evaluative instruments for measuring informational objectives in general education is the Cooperative Test Service of the American Council on Education. The tests on general culture, English, and contemporary affairs are perhaps the best known among the instruments prepared by this organization. General achievement tests for college students have also been developed in literature, foreign languages, sciences, mathematics, and social sciences.

For information regarding tests of interests, attitudes, adjustments, as well as achievement, skills, and aptitudes, the reader should consult Buros' *Mental Measurements Yearbook*.[23] Descriptions of thousands of tests, relevant data about them, and critical appraisals of their value by research experts, administrators, teachers, personnel officers, and others will be found in these yearbooks.

SOME BASIC PROBLEMS

Reviewing the experiences described in this chapter and the other evaluation projects referred to, what can we say in summary about procedures that seem important in the evaluation of general education? What are some of the important problems to consider as one attempts evaluation in this area?

It is clear, first of all, that at some point during the evaluation process each of the institutions described or mentioned here has faced the problem of developing fairly clear statements of objectives. While it is true that some concept of objectives or goals should be made explicit at the outset of any sequence of evaluative activities, it is not necessary for it to be formulated in detail or in terms of student behavior. To insist upon a formulation that is both comprehensive in scope and specific in application before proceeding to other activities in the evaluation program may result in never getting to the other activities. The staff at

[22] *Ibid.* p. 699.
[23] *The Mental Measurements Yearbook*, Highland Park, N.J.; edited annually by Oscar Krisen Buros.

Bennington College, after two years of comprehensive and highly worthwhile evaluation, had not developed detailed and specific statements of objectives for different departments and courses. In a report on the Bennington evaluation we find this comment:

The statements of the educational objectives or purposes of the college as a whole or of the divisional faculties now vary greatly in their adequacy as a basis for operation. In only two divisions . . . do the faculty now fully agree on the objectives. Furthermore few of the objectives are now defined in terms of what they mean from the standpoint of student behavior—broadly defined.[24]

Some faculties may profitably spend considerable time discussing objectives and formulating specific statements during the initial phases of an evaluation program, but other faculties may wish to proceed more rapidly from a general concept of goals to engaging in definite attempts at measurement or appraisal.

A faculty may begin by trying to agree on what it means by general education. What is general education? What is its essential function in the college, in society? Or, what are the basic facts and ideas about our culture which students should possess? Beginning in this way, one of two things is likely to happen. Either the faculty, after extended discussion, will reach a consensus or it will find that opposing viewpoints have become more clearly delineated and it is further than ever from agreement. Whatever the outcome, the process may be a long one and the debate may be vigorous. There is of course nothing inherently undesirable about long, vigorous debates. They may, indeed, be very stimulating and rewarding. The danger in debate over basic philosophies is semantic; arguments develop over words. It is, in short, the verbalism of the process that constitutes the danger.

It is our belief that a direct attack upon philosophy and underlying points of view is, in many cases, not the most effective method for initiating an evaluation of general education. For an individual teacher, or within a single department, the method

---

[24] From unpublished mimeographed material in the files of Bennington College, Bennington, Vermont.

is more likely to work; but as a total institutional approach involving relatively heterogeneous elements, it is less well adapted. For one thing, some expectation of change in the cur-riculum—the introduction of new courses, modification of re-quirements, fusion of related departments, and so on—accom-panies the decision to evaluate a program systematically, at least in the minds of many of the faculty concerned. Speculation about what these changes are likely to be, and attitudes devel-oped in relation to them, tend to make even more difficult the task of coming to a common understanding. The task becomes still more complicated if proposals worked out in committees are debated in detail by the general faculty.

It is best, in our opinion, not to conceive of evaluation as a sequence of steps each of which must be completed before the next is attempted. Many of the tasks that are involved in an evaluation can be carried forward together. Goals may be sug-gested and become clarified through attacking specific problems as well as through direct discussion of objectives. A faculty might begin by asking: What are the students now getting out of the present program of general education? It might begin, in other words, by focusing its attention upon outcomes of the program as these are revealed in students. This focus, of course, requires getting judgments as to what outcomes are being sought. But a consensus is not necessary. It is only necessary to know what outcomes different persons have in mind and to decide which of them will be studied first. The question then arises as to how one can best measure or judge the extent to which these outcomes are being realized. Existing tests that appear relevant may be used, or the group may try some other means of gather ing evidence. Interpreting this evidence will raise questions about the relevance of the data to the objectives; this, in turn, will help to clarify the objectives and enable the staff to select or develop better instruments. The problem of interpretation will also raise questions as to what opportunity students have been given in the program to make progress toward the objec-tives, or toward whatever outcomes were measured in the tests. Out of experience in trying to estimate outcomes, objectives may become clarified. And changes in a program may be brought about more readily by examining evidence of student attainment than by considering new proposals in the light of some abstract concept of the meaning and function of general education. This experimental and developmental approach to the formulation of objectives was illustrated most clearly in our accounts of activities at Bennington, at St. Catherine's in the humanities course, at Minnesota in the development of tests for the orientation courses, and at Troy.

The definition of goals enters into every program of evaluation, but it may be accomplished through a variety of techniques (through interviews, group discussions, questionnaires, ratings, research studies, and so forth) and at different times in the total program of evaluative activities. The appropriate time and technique depend largely upon the habits and dispositions of the local staff, and upon some of the conditions we have described here. And the questions of timing and technique will, of course, be considered in the larger framework of democratic procedures.

Another observation that we can make from our descriptions of and references to evaluation programs is that most of them have deliberately sought to accumulate evidence relevant to all or nearly all of the major objectives of the instructional program in general education. And a corollary to this observation is that a great variety of techniques has been employed in gathering this relevant evidence. Because of the special emphasis at Bennington upon student interests, the evaluation program included such devices as a time analysis, a locally constructed interest index, an analysis of friendship patterns. Because of the special emphasis at Minnesota upon social and emotional adjustments of students and upon core courses in four functional areas of life, the evaluation program included some personality and adjustment tests and locally constructed examinations specifically related to the informational outcomes in the four orientation courses. Because of the special concern at Troy, Alabama, with students' personal and social adjustments the evaluation program included the systematic collection of anecdotal records.

Where standard tests are available and are appropriate to the objectives under consideration there has been no hesitation in using them. At Bennington, for example, the Cooperative General Culture Test was used. At both Bennington and Minnesota the Cooperative Contemporary Affairs Test was used. The Bell Adjustment Inventory, Minnesota Personality Scale, Wesley Test of Social Terms, and the Cooperative English and Literary Acquaintance Tests have all been used in some of the evaluation programs. But, there has also been a development in the direction of constructing new instruments in specific relation to each major objective of instruction. This is best illustrated in the activity of the Cooperative Study in General Education and the eight-year study. As these new tests are published and made available to schools other than the ones for which they were originally constructed, the effect will be to increase the range of choice open to those who wish to purchase paper-and-pencil instruments. There will, doubtless, always be many highly important aspects of any local evaluation program for which the means of collecting data must be locally devised. And it is a moot question among many people as to whether the insights gained from local endeavor do not more than balance whatever lack of measuring precision may result from failure to use devices made by experts. In addition to the use of tests, all of the evaluation programs have made extensive use of ratings—student self-ratings on personal and social traits, student and faculty ratings on values in various courses or phases of the programs, ratings by former students on the worth of their school experiences, and many others. There has, in other words, been a serious attempt to honor in the evaluation program most of the basic objectives that are claimed.

The final observation we wish to make is that the primary focus of evaluative activities in general education has been upon the broad evaluation of instructional programs rather than upon specific self-appraisals of individual growth. Objectives have been institutional objectives, not goals that each student has developed for himself. Measuring instruments have been used to reveal the extent to which the program has been successful.

Obviously the effectiveness of the program is judged chiefly by the growth of individual students in it; the fact that evaluation has been focused on the program rather than on the student does not mean that no student self-evaluation has occurred or that the appraisals would have been any better if self-evaluations had occurred more frequently. Within the primary focus of program evaluation much student self-evaluation can and does occur. At Oneonta, students shared in the development of objectives. At Troy, students appraised their own personal and social development; and student-counselor joint appraisal, following a chart representing the educational aims of the institution, has been emphasized. At Bennington, students kept records of how they spent their time. At Minnesota, students judged the value of their various courses to them. At St. Catherine's, students wrote daily accounts of their reactions to aesthetic experience. Many students doubtless had developed genuine motivation for taking standardized tests; many more doubtless, profited from the knowledge of their test performance. But it is in the area of professional orientation courses, rather than in general education, that the focus of self-evaluation has been sharpest and most fully developed. Perhaps some strong vocational motivation, or at least some interest besides the rather nebulous desire to know more about oneself, one's fellows, and one's environment, is needed to give self-evaluative activities adequate impetus and sufficient stability to be the focus of an evaluation program. Or perhaps increased emphasis upon self-evaluation will characterize the next major development in the evaluation of general education.

V

Professional Education

W HAT ARE THE special responsibilities of professional education? What are the responsibilities it shares with other phases of the college's program? These are questions encountered when one considers the plan and scope of evaluation in professional education. They are, of course, questions which must be faced in considering the evaluation of any one phase of a total program, for aspects (and particularly major ones) do not ordinarily have sharp boundaries that set them apart from other elements that comprise the total.

General education does not stop at the end of the sophomore year and professional education begin in the junior year, not even in colleges and universities which are divided into lower and upper divisions. Special interests in teaching as a profession sometimes develop among high school students. Some high schools actually give such students opportunities for exploratory professional experience. In teachers colleges the program of professional education frequently begins in the freshman year. We have already suggested how colleges in which the professional courses do not begin until the junior year can take advantage of students' presence on the campus in the lower division to collect pertinent data on which to base selection for admission and to provide orientation to the profession. In fact, the first in a sequence of professional courses is frequently an orientation course. In a recent survey of first courses in education Jensen found that the aims and purposes upon which there was closest agreement among instructors were those concerned with:

(1) the introduction of the prospective teacher to his profession in such a way that he will see education "as a whole" from the very first, (2) the individual-guidance process for all students planning on

going into education, (3) providing the necessary experiences that will enable the student to make a reasoned selection of education as a life career, (4) acquainting the student with the personality qualifications necessary or desirable in teachers, (5) using the history of education in interpreting past, present, and possible future trends, (6) acquainting the student with the major objectives of education, and (7) examining the philosophic bases upon which the process of education is grounded.[1]

The emphases upon guidance, self-analysis, and upon the philosophy and social setting of education indicate a concern for many problems in common with orientation, counseling, and general education.

APPRAISING ASPECTS OF PROFESSIONAL EDUCATION

Our concern in the present chapter is with professional education—with the evaluation of elements of professional education as well as of the whole programs. We describe, first, evaluation in three aspects of professional education—a psychology course, a measurement of students' understanding of child growth and development, and a course in educational sociology. Then we describe the patterns of appraisal in four programs of professional education. Our accounts do not include evaluations of student teaching. We do not in any way suggest that student teaching is not an essential part of professional education; on the contrary, we regard it as so important that a special chapter is devoted to it. Of the descriptions of over-all appraisal, the first—at Milwaukee State Teachers College—proceeded mainly through the development of objective tests and scales. The second and third, respectively at the School of Education of the University of Texas and at Teachers College, Columbia University, combined various objective tests with student and faculty judgments and discussions. The fourth, at the School of Education at Stanford University, proceeded mainly through the col-

---

[1] Harry T. Jensen, "Selecting Aims and Purposes of the First Course in Education," *Educational Administration and Supervision*, XXVIII (September 1942), 401-13.

lection of opinion. From these descriptions ways in which different kinds of data can be effectively gathered and used should be suggested.

STUDENT JUDGMENT IN EVALUATING A PSYCHOLOGY COURSE

One element that is found in all professional programs of teacher education is a study of psychology. At the College of St. Catherine, a new course, an introduction to psychology with special emphasis upon human growth and development, was given in 1940-41. Offered for sophomores, the course was designed for but not limited to students who planned to become teachers. The work of the first quarter was focused chiefly on the study of infants and small children, and the second quarter centered about the study of adolescents. The more important formal means used in evaluating student progress included examinations to measure knowledge of facts and principles, term papers, case histories, and an autobiography. In addition, at the end of both the fall and winter quarters, a questionnaire was filled out by the students in which their reactions to various phases of the course as well as some of the understandings gained could be expressed. The questionnaire was intended primarily as an evaluation of the course rather than of student progress. Because the practice of giving questionnaires such as this is being followed in quite a few colleges, some analysis of its value and use may be helpful.

The questionnaire in the psychology course at St. Catherine's had two parts. Students' answers to the items in Part I could all be summarized under three headings: "yes," "in part," "no." We have reproduced the questions and indicated the proportion of students whose answers were classified as "yes." The items in Part II called for answers which could not be summarized under simple headings. We have consequently reproduced the questions without attempting to indicate how students responded to them.[2]

[2] "Supporting Documents," from the final report of the College of St. Catherine to the Commission on Teacher Education, pp. 11 ff.

| Percentage of students answering "yes" | | Questions in Part I |
(Fall term)	(Winter term)	
66	86	1. Did the content of the course start at the level for which you were prepared? If not, explain.
81	96	2. Have you found the subject matter interesting?
92	90	3. Do you consider the subject matter of this course a valuable addition to your knowledge?
46	66	4. Have the materials of this course either directly or indirectly thrown a light on your personal problems?
58	69	5. Has the course helped to make other educational experiences more meaningful?
48	73	6. Has the course assisted you to develop a more wholesome philosophy of life?
85	84	7. Has the course helped you to be more tolerant of other people?
60	61	8. Has the course opened up for you any new fields of interest?
82	90	9. Has the course increased your understanding of human nature?
92	89	10. Has the course increased your understanding of child growth and development?
68	75	11. Was the presentation interesting?
60	59	12. Were the discussion periods long enough?
39	42	13. Were the discussion periods valuable?
66	72	14. Has your observation in the pre-school increased your knowledge of child growth and development?

Questions in Part II

1. Approximately how many hours per week have you spent in studying for this course?

2. State in five or more brief sentences the insights or understandings you have gained or had strengthened as a result of this course. And which you feel will be of practical value.

3. List the books and/or periodical articles which you have found most helpful.

4. List the subjects touched upon in this class or in your reading which you would like, if time permitted, to pursue further.

5. Rate the following from 3 to 1 (3 being highest, 1 being lowest) as to their contribution to your understanding of human growth and development. If any of the following seem to be of equal value, give them the same rating: lectures, discussion periods, observation.

6. List the values which you feel you derived from the following: lectures, discussion periods, observation.

7. What suggestions would you make for improving this course?

8. Please make a general statement concerning the values of the course to you.

9. What subjects would you like to have treated during the next two quarters of this course?

In Part I questions 4 through 10 reflect some of the objectives of the course. Students' answers to these questions might be considered as evidence relative to the attainment of the objectives.

Much more significant evidence, however, would come from the students' examinations, term papers, and case histories. The other questions in Part I and most of the questions in Part II are designed to get student opinion on various aspects of the course—the lectures, discussion periods, observations, readings, and so forth. One may well ask what is the value of this. After all, is not the instructor a better judge of what materials are important and of how they can be presented than the student? If one had to give a "yes" or "no" answer to this question it would be "yes." But teaching is a two-way process. It involves a teacher and a learner. And learning is conditioned by motivation, by the meaningfulness of materials to the learner, by the learner's belief in the value and use of the materials to him, and by a host of other factors. Thus the opinions and beliefs of the students are important to know for they influence what will be learned and provide valuable clues to making the course more effective. Used for these purposes such questionnaires as we have described here can be valuable aids in the improvement of teaching. The good teacher will be sensitive to these matters. A questionnaire study can serve to sharpen this sensitivity and increase its range by providing a means for everyone to express his opinion.

A TEST TO MEASURE UNDERSTANDING OF CHILD GROWTH

The objective of understanding child growth and development is not peculiar to courses in psychology. It pervades all of teacher education. Especially in the preparation of elementary school teachers, the importance of understanding children is generally recognized. It should be no less a prerequisite to success in secondary school teaching for the problems of adolescents are as complex and in as great need of understanding as are the problems of young children.

Techniques for evaluating teachers' understanding of child growth and development have not kept pace with the growing importance attached to the objective. Emphasis in courses in child psychology, adolescent psychology, and human growth and development is being increasingly placed upon long-term records of an individual's development, upon the individual's particular pattern of growth, upon the relationship among various growth processes, and upon the importance of considering many aspects of the individual's experience in trying to interpret his behavior. In the actual school and classroom understanding must be applied to particular individuals. Yet many attempts to evaluate in this field are focused upon a knowledge of facts and principles and their general application to broad and oversimplified problems. And often the evaluation is dependent upon unsystematic observations summarized in a rating.

One technique of evaluation that appears to be soundly related to these emphases is well illustrated by a case-study instrument developed by Warren R. Baller[3] of the University of Nebraska during a year's study at the collaboration center operated by the Commission's division on child development and teacher personnel at the University of Chicago. The case-study instrument, based on the actual records of a boy referred to as Mickey Murphy, presents the kind of data that might be available about any boy in a junior high school. Because the test is built around the facts and procedures and recommendations in an actual case, the interpretations and outcomes are the ones which were really made and which actually happened.

More specifically, the structure of the case-study instrument is as follows: First, a considerable amount of information about the boy is presented. The student is then asked to express agreement, uncertainty, or disagreement with a series of propositions which are analyses or interpretations of the information. The student then indicates what he would do to increase the information and improve the procedures related to the case. Next, a large amount of additional information is given. Following this, three exercises are called for: (1) the student responds to a series of hypotheses or assumptions indicating whether he thinks each is definitely warranted by the data, tentatively supported by the data, contradicted by the data, or not supported by sufficient evidence to justify an opinion one way or the other; (2) the stu-

[3] Warren R. Baller, *The Case of Mickey Murphy* (Lincoln: University of Nebraska, 1943).

dent expresses agreement, uncertainty, or disagreement with a series of recommendations for improving the adjustment to the problems described in the case; and (3) the student indicates what information he would still like to have to come to a more satisfactory interpretation and where he would go to get this information. At this point still more information is given and the student responds again to the same series of hypotheses and recommendations described above. In short, three blocks of information are given and following each the student must make some judgments and some recommendations for acting; following the first two blocks he must also indicate what further information he feels he needs. The first set of data includes school records, anecdotes, and opinions that are usually found about pupils in many schools. The second block presents fuller details from the school records plus some information gathered by a visiting teacher. The third set of data gives information gathered through interviews and further study of previous school records by one of the teachers who was given special responsibility for studying Mickey's problems.

This structure is designed to furnish evidence on five major aspects of the student's competence in understanding child growth and development. First, when (with how many data) does the student consider that he is ready to take action in a given case? Second, does the student take into consideration enough of the conditions that might have significant bearing on the case? For example, data relative to the following conditions are given: child's relation to parents, to siblings, to peers, adjustment to teachers and other adults, achievement in school studies, physical development, mental development, interests and ambitions. Third, how sound is the student's selection of evidence to support his hypotheses? Fourth, does the student know where and how to secure additional information? And fifth, how relevant are the student's recommendations to the interpretations he has made of the data?

The use of the case-study instrument is by no means limited to the formal measurement of student understanding of child growth and development, for it can serve an instructional as well as an evaluative purpose. In many schools and classes where the instrument was used in preliminary form, it served as the basis for class discussion and study. The instructor and students engaged jointly in analyzing Mickey's problems, making recommendations, and considering the adequacy of different techniques of child study revealed in the case. The case study, then, can be a learning experience as well as an evaluative exercise. For its use as a test, scoring keys have been developed. College students, experienced teachers, and experts in psychology have taken the test and their responses have been studied to determine the best answers to the items. In several sections of the test, the degree of difference between the responses of experts and inexperienced students provided the basis for assigning weights to different responses. Some techniques for summarizing the scores are suggested by the author and others can be worked out by those who use the test. When we have available a whole series of case-study instruments, each based upon children of different ages and in different environments and with different types of major problem, we shall have made considerable progress toward the measurement of understandings which have heretofore not been tapped by many tests. And we shall, at the same time, have a wealth of highly important instructional material.

PATTERN FOR EVALUATION IN EDUCATIONAL SOCIOLOGY

In addition to a growing emphasis in professional education upon understanding human growth and development there is also a growing emphasis upon understanding the culture and society of which education is a part. And both of these emphases, with increasing frequency, are being implemented by direct contact as well as vicariously through books. Observation of children, experience in dealing with children, field trips to community centers, direct contact with the community, and so on, form one significant technique of gaining understanding. This study of the relationship between the schools and society is sometimes called educational sociology. At Stanford University in 1940-41 an undergraduate course in educational sociology was part of a required sequence of subjects in the curriculum of professional education. The instructor attended the Commission's Chicago workshop in the summer of 1940 and worked on plans for evaluating the course.

The plans were carried out in 1940-41 and described to the School of Education faculty at Stanford the following year as suggestive of how other instructors might proceed in examining their courses. The procedure can be described in four steps. First, each course should be examined to determine to which of the broad aims of the School of Education it makes a contribution. Second, the objectives of each course should be stated in terms of student behavior. Third, the specific experience and activity each course provides in the attempt to realize its objectives should be listed. And fourth, the kind and variety of evidence each course uses, or might use, in verifying student achievement of the objectives should be studied.

The specific objectives, experiences, and evaluation for the course in educational sociology were outlined as follows:[4]

Objectives—To prepare teachers who have competence in:
1. Defining the problem areas of educational sociology in terms of the critical issues or key questions for educational action
2. Knowing where and how to find the socio-economic facts pertaining to these critical issues and their solution
3. Building and employing a set of values in their interpretation of data and in their plans of action which are personally accepted, democratic, internally coherent, and consistent with current socio-economic conditions and trends
4. Formulating experimental ways of adapting their school's program to the critical issues in current socio-economic conditions and of better directing these socio-economic conditions and trends toward democratic ends
5. Acquiring skill in *group* attacks on common problems in educational sociology

Experiences—Readings, study, and discussion of:
1. The social bias of education
   The American democratic ideology
2. Whom should the school serve in a democracy?
   The distribution of schooling

[4] Daniel C. McNaughton, "An Evaluation of the Teacher Education Program of the Stanford School of Education" (unpublished dissertation for the Ed.D degree in the files of Stanford University, California, 1942), p 56.

3. How should the school serve in a democracy?
   The roles and aims of the school
4. Where should the school serve?
   Democracy and the economic system
   The youth problem
   Vocations
   Problems of consumers
   National defense and the schools
5. Optional topics for individual study
6. Extraclass activities
   Student discussion groups
   One group visit to a nearby extraschool agency with educational responsibility or influence

Evaluation—The following sources of evidence will be used in appraising student progress:

1. Five individual papers written specifically to show the student's development in aims 1, 2, and 3
2. Four papers composed by groups of students. Each student will receive the mark given to the group paper
3. A firsthand report on some nearby extraschool agency with educational responsibility of effect, which students will visit
4. Reports every three weeks from the group chairmen, describing unusual activity and contributions of members of the group during that time
5. A final examination, cooperatively planned, to supply whatever evidence is lacking when above activities have been completed

One device used but not listed in the source quoted from above, was an attitudes test related to objective number 3. Items for the instrument were drawn from tests 4.21 and 4.31 of the Progressive Education Association's eight-year study, and from Harper's test reproduced in the first yearbook of the John Dewey Society. The items were classified and scored to show attitude shifts under such headings as individualism versus cooperation, insight into the nature of current economic difficulties, a reasoned point of view versus prejudice in the classroom, and the meaning of democracy. Student responses at the beginning and the end of the term showed attitude shifts in the direction of a higher proportion of liberal opinions on all four of the categories, and changes that were statistically significant on three of the categories.

We have not reported the evaluation in educational sociology in detail; our chief concern has been to illustrate a pattern, a way of going about evaluation in any course. Evaluation of a course, and a teacher's evaluation of student progress in a course, are the commonest sort of appraisal. When such appraisal is deliberate, systematic, and planned it seems reasonable to believe that it will be more adequate and more useful to both students and teacher. The four questions suggested here provide a useful starting point in this regard: What does this course contribute to the broad objectives of the institution? What are the specific objectives of this course—what changes in the behavior of students is it designed to bring about? What opportunities does it provide for students to attain the objectives? And, what evidence is available for judging the extent to which students do attain the objectives?

APPRAISALS OF PROFESSIONAL EDUCATION PROGRAMS

Having reported briefly evaluations within segments of the total program of professional education, we turn next to descriptions of over-all evaluations.

AN APPRAISAL THROUGH OBJECTIVE TESTS

An experimental, integrated program of professional work at the Milwaukee State Teachers College had been in existence for several years when a systematic evaluation was begun in 1940. The program aims at a closer relationship between professional study and actual teaching experience. The professional work is not taken in separate courses but is integrated with practical experience through group meetings, conferences, readings, and study under the leadership of the supervisor and critic teacher with whom the student works in the practice school. Materials considered in these group meetings, conferences, readings, and so forth, grow primarily out of a variety of problems faced by the student in his observation and practice teaching. The evaluation of this program has been approached mainly through a series of paper-and-pencil tests.

Role of the evaluator

An evaluator from the University of Chicago was appointed on part time to give technical leadership to the project. This person worked in consultation with both the university and the Commission on Teacher Education. The first task undertaken by the evaluator was to gain familiarity with and make explicit the objectives of the integrated program. This was done primarily through interviews and discussions. The evaluator interviewed all of the instructors concerned, getting from them statements of the objectives they considered important. The evaluator likewise looked at the tests and other evaluative devices in use and read articles about the integrated program published by different faculty members to see what objectives might be implicit or explicit in those sources. Further ideas were gained from interviews with critic teachers, students, graduates, and superintendents. A composite statement was then prepared by the evaluator. Each of the nineteen objectives included in the statement was paralleled by one or more quotations from faculty interviews or publications showing that the objective was held important by some of the staff. A few examples of these objectives are quoted below:[5]

It is expected that a teacher will:
1. Believe in cooperation within the classroom, the profession, and the community
2. Believe in the desirability of meeting the needs of children and recognizing their interests
3. Be interested in working with children in large and small groups, and with a single child
4. Participate in cultural activities
5. Read both professional and nonprofessional books, magazines, and newspapers
6. Be able to locate information that is needed by a teacher

From these examples it is clear that the objectives, while not detailed, are fairly concrete and phrased in terms of student behavior—overt behavior or implied, as in the case of beliefs.

[5] Vivian V. Edmiston, "An Evaluation of the Integrated Professional Curriculum at Milwaukee State Teachers College" (unpublished dissertation for the Ph.D. degree in the files of the University of Chicago, 1943), pp. 35 ff.

Objectives were also thought of from another point of view, namely, the situations in which the expected behavior should occur. For example, teachers were expected to have certain beliefs and understandings and engage in certain activities with respect to classroom situations, broader professional relationships, and community situations. And further, these beliefs, understandings, and activities could be classified as pertaining to children, to professional colleagues, or to parents and laymen. These classifications proved suggestive in developing evaluative instruments.

The objectives were further classified and detailed in terms of student behavior through the development of a series of tests related to them. Small committees of supervisors were set up to work with the evaluator on the development of instruments. Each committee worked on the objective in which it was most interested. A brief description of the series of tests which was developed will indicate the scope of the project and the extent to which the objectives were detailed in the process of test building.

Description of tests

1. "Inventory of Activities." On the assumption that the kind and frequency of association with younger boys and girls and experience with many groups of people may be indicative of fitness for teaching, and that teachers should have many such contacts, a checklist of activities was constructed. One reads as follows:

> During this school year, I have had informal chats with boys or girls, at their suggestion, about their
> personal appearance
> relations with brothers and sisters
> relations with parents
> hobbies

Other items were included in the list as well as ample space for the student to record additional ones. He tells the approximate ages of the youngsters with whom he has had such contacts and the frequency of their occurrence. There are questions about leadership activities with young people's groups, college extra-curricular activities, work experiences, and so on. Two inventories were prepared—one dealing with activities of a student, and the other with activities of a teacher.

2. "Inventory of Reading." This form was also of the check-list type, with general categories of reading followed by spaces for the student to record what he had read. Under the general heading of professional books, there are subheadings on child development, the curriculum, educational philosophy, educational psychology, extracurricular activities, personality adjustment, history of education, techniques of teaching, tests and measurements. For each author or title the student lists, he checks appropriate columns to show how he read it (skimmed, started it, read through, studied thoroughly, used for reference) and why he read it (assigned, recommended by professor, recommended by friend, suggested by librarian, picked it up myself). Similar, but not identical, headings and questions are set up for nonprofessional books, professional magazines, nonprofessional magazines, and newspapers. The staff believed that this instrument could be used to gather evidence of the effectiveness of the program in widening the reading interests of students.

3. "Interest Index." The interest index consisted of 111 statements of activities related to the work of a teacher. For example, "to show a junior high school boy how to make a model airplane," "to read a current book on child psychology," "to call at the home of each kindergarten youngster," "to belong to a Little Theater group in the community." The student indicates on a five-point scale how well he would like to engage in each activity. The items are not listed in any apparent order, but they are keyed as contributing to one or more types or categories so that the student's responses can be analyzed in five different ways. One analysis will show the nature of the activities that interest the student—reading, planning, experimenting, working with materials, and so forth. Another classification will show the grade levels in which there is greatest interest. Another will show the size of group with which the student prefers working. A fourth classification is in terms of three headings—classroom

interests, professional interests, community interests. And the fifth classification is based on subject-matter divisions of the curriculum.

The plan of deriving multiple scores from a common body of test items has been followed in several of the instruments developed at Milwaukee. In this respect the scoring techniques for many of the Milwaukee tests followed a pattern used in several tests developed in connection with the eight-year study of the Progressive Education Association. The reasons for multiple scores have been phrased succinctly by Smith and Tyler in their recent book describing the construction of many of the PEA tests. They say:

. . . human behavior is ordinarily so complex that it cannot be adequately described or measured by a single term or a single dimension. Several aspects or dimensions are usually necessary to describe or measure a particular phase of human behavior. Hence, we did not conceive that a single score, a single category, or a single grade would serve to summarize the evaluation of any phase of the student's achievement. Rather, it was anticipated that multiple scores, categories, or descriptions would need to be developed.[6]

4. "Locating Information as a Teacher." Developing in students a knowledge of where to go for help in solving educational problems was another major objective of the Milwaukee program. The test constructed in relation to this purpose consists of thirty-eight situations or problems with five possible sources of information listed under each. For each source the student indicates whether it is a "likely," an "inefficient," or a "definitely poor" place to get the needed information or help. The first situation in the test illustrates the type of item:

Your fifth-grade class is studying the state of Wisconsin. You would like to have maps for each pupil to use.
1. A service station of a well known gas company
2. The catalogue of a school supply house
3. The state department of education
4. The Ditto Company (since your school has a Ditto)
5. The local office of the U. S. Forestry Service

[6] Eugene R. Smith and Ralph W. Tyler, *Appraising and Recording Student Progress* (New York: Harper & Brothers, 1942), p. 12.

5 and 6. "Factors in Working with a Class"; "Factors in Working with a Child." These tests are similar in form. In the first, three class situations are described, each followed by a list of about twenty activities. The student is asked to indicate whether each activity is "desirable," "of uncertain value," or "undesirable." Then, for each activity considered undesirable, the student indicates which factors from a given list have been either overly or insufficiently taken into account. The factors which the student must consider are as follows:

The extent, rate, and pattern of maturation determine whether an activity is appropriate or not for a given age
School activities should be planned with a view to developing desirable adults for our society
School activities should be planned with consideration for interests of students
Pleasantness facilitates learning
A class should be considered in terms of the individuals of which it is composed

In the second test, a larger number of situations is described and the given list of factors or principles to be considered includes eight items. Several ways of interpreting student responses to these instruments are provided for in the scoring. One can consider the items marked as desirable and not desirable. One can analyze the principles marked as applying or not applying to a given course of action. The test is designed as a measure of the student's ability to relate general principles of education to specific happenings in the classroom and specific dealings with individual children.

7. "Objective Attitudes in Personal Relations." Here again the test consists of descriptions of situations followed by lists of activities. The student must judge each activity as one to be "avoided," one about which he is "uncertain," or one that is "desirable." The following indicates the nature of the test:

A little refugee boy who had recently joined the first-grade group did not have any clay with which to model. While the teacher was getting some for him, a first-grade boy divided his clay with the refugee. While they were working together later in the period, the refugee boy leaned over and kissed the first-grade boy.

As the first-grade teacher, you should:

Have the refugee boy work by himself until he learns how to work with others

Not notice the incident

Explain to the refugee boy how we show friendship

Commend the refugee boy for showing his friendship

Reprimand the refugee boy, telling him pupils in your classes do not do that

In commenting on the test Miss Edmiston writes:

The device was an attempt to study attitudes that become apparent in human relations. The items following each of the described situations are classifiable as statements indicating that the person responding is one who:

1. swings completely over to the other person's point of view, even when there is some merit in his own position, or
2. views the matter objectively, trying to see both sides of the question, and trying to give due credit to the position of both the other person and himself, or
3. tries to personalize the situation as far as the other person is concerned, perhaps by imputing oversensitivity to him, or
4. takes the situation personally himself, perhaps feeling hurt about it, or
5. tries to avoid the real problem implied in the situation either by immediate or complete avoidance, or
6. favors punishment rather than re-education for correcting a situation

8. "Educational Attitudes." This test is similar to the scale of "Beliefs about School Life (Form 4.6 from the PEA eight-year study). There are two forms so that the student's responses can be scored for consistency. Five attitudes are considered: "freedom for communication and action," "expectation of the possibility of improvement," "recognition of the interests and needs of children," "cooperation for the good of the group," and "the recognition of equality." Items can also be classified in relation to the functioning of the teacher in the classroom, in the profession, and in the community. The following statements illustrate the type of item in the test: "A teacher should feel free to participate in a political campaign as much as does any other person in the community." "Of two teachers of equal profi-

ciency, preparation, and experience, the high school teacher should be paid more than the elementary school teacher." "A child should be left free to do art work in his own way, rather than in the way suggested by the teacher, if he wishes."

9. "Case-Study Instrument." This is designed to measure student understanding of child growth and development. The instrument is similar in form to the one developed by Baller that was described earlier in this chapter.

A problem in interpretation

The problem of interpreting the results of the nine tests that have just been described proved somewhat complex. None of the tests was summarized solely by a single score. Each yielded several scores depending on the number of categories into which the items were classified. There might be three, or more than a dozen scores for one test. Moreover, it will be recalled, the same item in a given test might be included in more than one category. Thus, the part scores were not always additive, yielding a total score, but were overlapping. The categories, and the classification of items in relation to them, were determined by the evaluator in consultation with advisers from the University of Chicago and several members of the Milwaukee staff. It is not apparent from an inspection of many of the tests just which items contribute to different categories, nor even what the categories are. This concealment is generally considered desirable, especially in tests of attitudes and interests, because it is believed to minimize the likelihood of students giving stereotyped responses. If a student with his adviser wishes to study his scores on a test, he has first of all to accept the various categories that have been set up and then look through the scoring key to discover which items are related to them. The process is somewhat analogous to translating a foreign language when one has to refer frequently to a dictionary. This problem is not peculiar to Milwaukee, for it arises in connection with the use and interpretation of many recently developed tests that yield multiple and overlapping scores. There is no easy resolution to the dilemma. On the one hand, it can be admitted that homogeneous single-score tests are not well suited to measuring the multiple dimensions of human behavior; on the other hand, it can be admitted that the interpretation and use of tests such as the ones developed at Milwaukee impose heavy demands upon the time and insight of staff and students—demands which they may be unprepared or unwilling to meet. At Milwaukee it was found necessary to hold a series of faculty meetings to discuss the interpretation of the test results; intensive work by small committees followed the general meetings. We need to recognize that local acceptance and use of any new evaluative device frequently depends on local understanding of its meaning. And the building of this understanding is one of the necessary steps in a program of evaluation. Progress toward this end has been made at Milwaukee.

Two further comments about the procedures used at Milwaukee seem to us important. For one thing, the cooperative arrangement between Milwaukee and the University of Chicago is suggestive of a relationship other colleges may wish to promote. Too frequently, colleges say they cannot carry on extensive evaluation because they do not have the resources. Making available the resources of large graduate schools can overcome this difficulty. By careful planning the ideas of a local faculty regarding the kind of evaluation that would be most useful to them can be harmonized with the requirements of a graduate school committee for work which they consider to be of Ph.D. quality. And the experience for the graduate student of providing helpful service to the local college and at the same time meeting requirements for advanced degrees can be a valuable one.

The method of arriving at objectives and of making them specific is likewise of special interest. From interviews and readings, the evaluator phrased a list of objectives. They were not the result of large faculty meetings, debates, compromises, and votes. Yet they were acceptable to the education faculty as a working basis for the evaluation project. Detailed statements of objectives were not developed by the general faculty. Detailed statements, in fact, were never developed as such, but rather as the result of small working committes studying a general objective of particular interest to them for the purpose of devising evaluative instruments. Thinking about general objectives, in other words, turned to specifics in the process of developing the format of tests, choosing test items, and interpreting results.

TESTS AND OPINIONS IN APPRAISING A NEW PROGRAM

A special pre-service program at Teachers College, Columbia University, was designed for recent graduates of liberal arts colleges who had had no teaching experience, but who wished to become teachers in the elementary and secondary schools. The professional program consisted of three parallel parts: a central seminar, a divisional seminar, and practice teaching—each of which ran throughout the year. The central seminar was intended to be a clearinghouse for educational theory and practice. It was the place where the larger relationships of education to society were studied, and these in turn related to student discussions in the divisional seminars and to their experience in practice teaching. The divisional seminars were designed to relate special fields of subject matter within the broader divisional field, and to study principles and methods of teaching that subject matter. There were seminars in six fields: humanities and language arts, social sciences, science and mathematics, art and music, home and community life, health and recreation, and elementary education. Practice teaching, of course, is self-explanatory. At Teachers College it meant participation and practice daily in its own laboratory schools and the schools of greater New York. Beyond these three professional phases of the program there was time allotted for students to pursue advanced courses in their special subject-matter field.

As in most experimental programs, modifications have been made from one year to the next. Our description of the evaluation activities in the program will be limited, therefore, to those undertaken during the year 1940-41. We shall describe more fully the purposes or goals of the program, the scope and variety of evaluative techniques used in relation to these goals, some of the procedures for working together tried by the staff and students, and some of the outcomes attained.

Statement of objectives

A committee on objectives worked throughout the first year of the new program, 1939-40, on the job of formulating a statement of goals or purposes for the education of prospective teachers. Frequent discussions within the committee and with the entire pre-service faculty associated with the experimental program resulted in acceptance of the following tentative objectives. The statements reproduced here are abbreviated from a much longer document produced by the committee on objectives:

1. Teachers should develop effective and well balanced personalities for the enrichment of their own living and for aiding others better to develop well balanced personalities for themselves

2. Teachers should become persons rich in firsthand experience and in broader understanding of the many aspects of our culture, in order better to advance the experience and understanding of others.

3. Teachers should obtain an expert understanding of the process of human living, growing, learning at all ages, and should become competent in acting upon this understanding in teaching situations.

4. Teachers should obtain an understanding of and practice in the democratic process in all areas of living and should become competent in guiding young people to utilize such democratic process in their own living.

5. Teachers should become expert in utilizing their enriched experiences in guiding the process of living, growing, and learning in young people.

6. Teachers should develop an adequate working philosophy of life and education.

7. Teachers should be stimulated to desire continuous professional growth.

8. Teachers should become scholars willing constantly to use the resources and methods of critical inquiry in the fields of human knowledge relevant to their responsibilities as individuals and as professional workers in teaching and guiding students to use similar resources and methods in facing their own problems of living.[7]

[7] E. S. Evenden and R. Freeman Butts, eds., *Columbia University Cooperative Program for the Pre-Service Education of Teachers* (New York: Bureau of Publications, Teachers College, Columbia University, 1942), pp. 29-33.

Staff members who had special responsibility for evaluating the new program took part in this formulation of objectives; and further, they developed a set of guiding principles for the evaluation activities as follows:

1. To use evaluative procedures that would elicit as much cooperative faculty participation as possible in judging the value of the program as a means of teacher education

2. To use evaluative procedures that would elicit as much student participation as possible in judging the value of the program to them as students, in judging their own progress in the achievement of the objectives, and in achieving skill in making evaluative judgments about their pupils in turn

3. To use evaluative procedures that would provide evidence for making judgments concerning the degree to which students were achieving the objectives

4. To use evaluative procedures that would be most valuable in the continuing process of guidance of students, beginning with their selection for admission to the program and continuing through placement

5. To use evaluative procedures that would provide evidence for making judgments concerning desirable changes in the instruction and organization of the program in order to make more likely the achievement of the objectives[8]

The techniques and sources of evidence drawn upon in the appraisal of the program were not limited to tests and materials provided by special evaluators. There were, for example, regular staff meetings and annual progress reports prepared by the staff. There were data and impressions gathered by the guidance division, the professors in special subject-matter fields, and the student-teaching staff. There were several faculty committees that made studies of different aspects of the program. None of this activity was unrelated to the work of the special evaluation staff but some of it was rather independent of their work. Our chief concern here is with the work of the special evaluation staff: with the techniques of appraisal they used in relation to the eight objectives and with their procedures in relation to the five guiding principles. We shall give each of these topics brief consideration in the following section.

[8] *Ibid.,* p. 87.

Relation between evaluation techniques and objectives

There was first of all a battery of standard tests. This was a major part of the evaluation program. Included in the battery were an intelligence test and a reading test; these provided data useful for the selection of students for admission to the program and valuable to the guidance division in their work with individual students. Two attitude or personality tests were likewise used: the Bell Adjustment Inventory and the Rundquist and Sletto Scales for the Survey of Opinion. In addition to their value for student selection and guidance, these tests, given both at the beginning and the end of the year, provided evidence with regard to the attainment of the objective of well balanced personality. The fifth unit in the battery of standard tests was the Cooperative General Culture Test. It, too, was given at the beginning and the end of the year and provided evidence on the attainment of an understanding of the culture, as well as information useful in guidance.

Several tests were used to appraise the growth of an educational point of view among the students. Among these were a test of educational concepts by Rivlin, a true-false test of educational philosophy by the staff of the central seminar, and a situations test to measure the application of theory to school practices by the evaluation staff. The first two of these instruments were given at the beginning and at the end of the year. All three were related to the objectives of understanding human growth and learning, understanding the democratic process, the ability to apply these understandings, and the development of a philosophy of life and education. At the end of the year students in the central seminar wrote papers analyzing their growth during the program in relation to all the objectives.

In the late fall and again in the spring each faculty member rated the status of all the students with whom he had had contact. There were twenty-eight factors listed on the scale and these were related to all of the eight objectives. Few, if any, staff members, however, were able to rate students on all twenty-eight items. A follow-up questionnaire to the previous year's graduates was also included in the evaluation program.

Some cooperative procedures and outcomes

The use of some of the tests in guidance implies, of course, some degree of faculty cooperation. Two illustrations may be given, however, of more extensive student and staff participation in evaluation. The first relates to the development of the situations test. The necessity of giving a final examination in the central seminar at midyear provided the faculty and the evaluation staff with an opportunity to work cooperatively with students. The question of what would constitute an appropriate evaluation of the semester's work was discussed with a special committee of students for three regular meetings. Out of these discussions the students' opinions crystallized into two main suggestions: first, that they write a paper indicating what changes they would make in their practice teaching arrangements and why; second, that they be given an opportunity to try to solve a number of problems commonly arising in classrooms and to give reasons for their suggested solutions which would reveal underlying points of view or concepts about education. That these suggestions indicated considerable student insight is evident from the fact that development of the ability to relate theory and practice was among the basic objectives of the special pre-service program. To proceed with the preparation of a test in accord with student suggestion, the evaluation staff constructed a few sample items which were presented to the faculty of the central seminar for approval in principle. After this approval had been secured a final examination of twenty-five situations was constructed. Many of the situations described in the test were selected almost verbatim from students' own statements of problems actually faced in practice teaching. Following each of these situations there were listed five actions or opinions which might be taken concerning them. The student was asked to indicate the major concept or controlling point of view which each of these actions reflected. The directions for the test, together with two sample situations, are given on the following page.[9]

---

[9] C. Robert Pace, "A Test Relating Educational Theory and Practice" (to be published in the *Journal of Educational Research*).

DIRECTIONS:

The actions of a teacher in a classroom reflect his philosophy of education. In this test you are given twenty-five situations with some characteristic actions, opinions, or judgments which might be taken concerning them. Each such action, opinion, or judgment may be a reflection of one of the following large controlling points of view:

It may reflect either an autocratic concept of education, or it may reflect a democratic concept of education.

It may reflect a concept of learning which emphasizes the importance of discipline and mastery of subject matter, or a concept of learning which emphasizes the importance of students' interests and problem-solving techniques.

It may reflect an organismic concept of human nature, or an atomistic, intellectualistic, or mental-faculty concept of human nature.

Before each activity, opinion, or judgment for each situation are three groups of letters:

ADN   MSN   OFN

You are to cross out the letter that represents your judgment as to the controlling concept involved, where

A indicates the controlling concept is *autocratic*

D indicates the controlling concept is *democratic*

N indicates that neither A nor D is involved

M indicates the controlling concept is *mastery* of subject or disciplinary

S indicates the controlling concept is *student interest*

N indicates that neither M nor S is involved

O indicates the controlling concept is *organismic*

F indicates the controlling concept is *mental-faculty* or atomistic

N indicates that neither O nor F is involved

You should cross out one letter in each group of three, and you should have a total of three letters crossed out for each activity, opinion, or judgment under each situation. Do not leave any group of items blank. . . .

Sample No. 1

The department of education prescribes a series of units in grammar. The teacher knows that her students do not like grammar. In introducing these units to her sixth-grade class she uses the following approach:

ADN MSN OFN   1. Today we study grammar. Get out your notebooks and we will do some exercises.

ADN MSN OFN   2. She gives them an objective test, has them score their own papers, and drills them on the correct answers.

ADN MSN OFN   3. She says that we are all in the same boat. For the next few days we have to study grammar. How shall we go about it?

ADN MSN OFN   4. She gives them some exercises to do at home and then in class she discusses their work with them.

ADN MSN OFN   5. She uses history, a subject they like, as an excuse for getting them to write a short essay. Then she discusses grammar in their essays with them and gets them to rewrite the essays.

Sample No. 2

A high school class was studying music appreciation. The young teacher was disturbed because the only kind of music the students seemed to like was swing music. After thinking about the problem she decided that:

ADN MSN OFN   1. She would take them to a symphony concert to hear some really good music.

ADN MSN OFN   2. She would tell them stories about the lives of some of the great composers.

ADN MSN OFN   3. She wouldn't play swing music for them any more because they hear enough of it outside the class anyway.

ADN MSN OFN   4. Some swing music was better than others and there was considerable opportunity for critical judgment within the single field of popular dance music.

ADN MSN OFN   5. She would continue to play swing for them but would also try to get them to notice the kinds of music played in motion pictures.

The concepts involved in the test—about society, the learning process, and psychology—had been discussed at length in the central seminar during the semester. Eighteen faculty members took the test and made comments on it, and their responses provided the data for developing the scoring key.[10] From the standpoint of cooperative procedure in evaluation several factors are important: the test was developed out of suggestions which came directly from students; the situations in the test came directly from experience students had had in their practice teaching; and faculty assistance was involved in the development of the test and scoring key. If one accepts the point of view that evaluation activity should promote understanding and insight, as well as provide an estimate of status or progress, it seems axiomatic to say that those who have an important stake in the outcome—students and staff alike—should play an important part in the process.

Another example of student and faculty participation in evaluation is seen in the students' writing of self-evaluation papers at the end of the course. This assignment was discussed at two meetings of the student planning committee. It was suggested that the students consider the objectives of the program, their initial status with respect to those objectives, and the progress made. After they took the retests on general culture and adjustment and attitudes in the spring, they were given the test

---

[10] The test was scored on the basis of the number of untenable positions chosen. An untenable position was defined as one seldom or never chosen as correct by the faculty judges.

booklets and answer sheets for both fall and spring tests to study and use in whatever way they wished in writing the self-evaluation paper. No outline was suggested for the paper, however, and each student was free to write it as he pleased. Members of the evaluation staff participated in these planning meetings along with members of the central-seminar panel.

Some of the outcomes of the evaluation can be reported in relation to this self-evaluation paper. A reading of the papers indicated that the typical student had given evidence of growth in relation to six of the eight objectives. The objectives cited most frequently were the one dealing with personality and the one dealing with understanding the culture. Evidence from the standard tests bears on these points. Students registered little change in their scores on the Bell Adjustment Inventory. On the Rundquist and Sletto scales (there are seven of these) both men and women revealed a decrease in feelings of inferiority and a marked shift toward liberalism in their attitudes toward economic issues; but changes on other scales in the test —morale, family, law, education, and general adjustment—were negligible except for a slightly more liberal response to the education scale. On the Cooperative General Culture Test students made high scores at both the beginning and the end of the year—percentiles mostly in the nineties on college sophomore norms. In view of this high level, the increase of ten and eight percentile points made by men and women respectively, on the section dealing with current social problems, suggests that the program was especially stimulating in this regard. Progress toward the objectives of understanding child development, gaining insight into the democratic process, and developing a philosophy of life and education was claimed by two-thirds to four-fifths of the students in their papers. These matters were measured to some extent in the situations test, and the conclusions from that test had been that students understood them quite well. On the true-false test constructed by the central-seminar panel students made significant gains during the year. Reports from the practice teaching staff suggested that students' ability to guide the process of living and learning in young people was likewise much improved during the year. The total picture gained from many sources was one of a group of students "well satisfied with and much stimulated by their year's experience."[11] Writing the self-evaluation paper, it may be added, was one of the most stimulating aspects of the evaluation program—at least the students believed it so.

In some respects it may be surprising that a large majority of students made no mention of the battery of standard tests in their self-evaluation papers. The majority made no reference to the shifts in their scores during the year in spite of the fact that they had recently had the chance to study their performance on the tests (presumably in preparation for writing the paper). Indeed, more than a few of those who did mention the tests expressed doubt as to their usefulness. These facts point to the need for even greater efforts to bring all the staff and students into the planning and carrying forward of evaluation. The examples of cooperative procedure we have described are suggestive of further steps that might profitably be taken to meet this need. A comprehensive evaluation program inevitably draws data from a variety of sources and with a variety of techniques. To make evident the essential unity in this variety is a task that demands the widest understanding among all who are involved in the evaluation program.

STUDENT REACTIONS IN AN EXPERIMENTAL PROGRAM

Our third description of an evaluative program in professional education comes from the School of Education at the University of Texas. A selected group of students, called the X group, took a two-year experimental program starting in 1939-40. A group of students beginning this new program a year later was called the Y group. The content of the experimental program during the junior year was focused one semester on understanding the American secondary school as an institution and the other semester on understanding the school's pupils—specifically adolescents. The senior year's activities cen-

[11] Evenden and Butts, *op. cit.*, p. 107.

tered on problems related to student teaching. Informal discussions, seminars, field trips, individual projects, characterized the instruction rather than the traditional lecture-and-discussion procedure typical of separate professional courses. Student participation in the course planning and in other affairs was emphasized.

Evaluation in the sense of making decisions or choosing among alternatives was engaged in continually through student planning activities and widespread student participation in many phases of the program. Beyond this, the main techniques of evaluation included the following: careful records of class activity kept by student secretaries; occasional questionnaires on activities engaged in and their estimated value; self-evaluation papers—that is, individual students' reports of what they had done during a semester or a year along with their appraisals of those activities; special discussions with staff members relative to the program and its operation. Most of the appraisal, it is clear, was subjective and informal rather than objective and systematic. There were, however, two examples of the latter sort of evaluation that may be described briefly.

An objective information test, developed cooperatively by staff members from four departments, was administered at the beginning and the end of one year: the senior year for the X group and the junior year for the Y group. Both groups registered definite gains. At the beginning and the end of the senior year members of the X group were also rated by four staff members with respect to several lines of progress classed under the headings of attitudes, personal traits, and teaching skills. The same staff members also rated a matched group of students following the nonexperimental program of student teaching. At both the beginning and the end of the year, and on each of the three categories of ratings, the students in the experimental group were judged superior to the control group.[12]

[12] Robert Hammock, "Student Teaching in the Programs of Prospective Secondary School Teachers in the United States" (unpublished dissertation for the Ph.D. degree in the files of the University of Texas, 1942).

Some student opinions

One important procedure for evaluating the program was the collection and analysis of students' judgments—individually as expressed in written reports or questionnaires, and collectively as revealed in the summation of individual responses or in special reports by student committees. The foreword to one of these questionnaires (given to the X group at the close of the first semester of the senior year) reflects the relationship prevailing between students and teachers as well as the frankly experimental quality of the program:

Foreword: The following assumptions seem basic to the presentation of this questionnaire:

1. It is the privilege and responsibility of all members of the group to participate in an evaluative examination of the way in which the course has operated.

2. Since the varied activities have been conducted largely on an individual basis, an individual presentation of data is necessary to a view of the total range of activities and their values.

3. The purpose of the questionnaire is not to assemble evidence in justification of any course grade, but to secure data to be used constructively in the continuous search for ways to improve the teacher-training program in all possible aspects.

4. The questions will be answered with the frankness that has characterized the expression of the class throughout the experiences of the experiment, without concern for the effect of responses upon any personal attitudes of fellow classmates and instructors.

5. The questionnaire itself should be regarded as a part of the class procedure and as such should be judged along with other course activities.[13]

The questionnaire had five main divisions dealing respectively with class meetings, contacts with schools, reading and study, conferences, and miscellaneous activities. The questions included may be illustrated from the following selected examples under the heading of "reading and study":

Has the time spent in reading in this course (exceeded, been less than, been equal to) that devoted to reading for the course (besides Education X) for which you have done the most reading?

[13] "Report of Second Year of Experimental Group in Education (Education X)." (unpublished manuscript in the files of the University of Texas). p. 51.

Have you generally taken notes on your readings?

Has the course provided for *use* of the readings you have done?

In what way might the reading and study activities of the course be improved?

    Open shelf of well selected books for Education X in the library

    Required basic bibliography

    Occasional book reviews

Name the three or four books or studies or monographs that you regard as your most profitable experiences in reading this term and give your reasons for selecting them. . . .[14]

One question was interestingly phrased to evoke general criticisms of the course:

If you were to sit in with a committee to plan the fall semester of work for Education Y next year, what one or two or three or more constructive suggestions would you make on the basis of this term's experiences?[15]

This question, in various forms and phrasings, was asked periodically of both X and Y groups. The recommendations and suggestions collected in response to it throw considerable light on some aspects of experimental programs in general. The following recommendations are typical and were made at various times by both X and Y groups:

More faculty participation; participation by more staff members

More attention to instructional plans; class periods more definite in purpose

More definite plans and goals; goals more sharply defined

More carefully selected basic material; more emphasis on reading

Initial and continuous and final evaluation; more frequently evaluation of progress

Individual guidance; more personal guidance

Less freedom

More careful check-up of achievement; more detailed evaluation instruments

[14] *Ibid.*, pp. 55-56.
[15] *Ibid.*, p. 60.

The students' recommendations for more definite plans, more carefully selected basic material, and less freedom are interesting in view of the fact that the X group, at least, was judged superior in attitudes, personal traits, and teaching skill to a matched control group whose program of instruction had been characterized by definite plans, basic readings, and less freedom in long-established courses. It is not unlikely that there is a feeling of insecurity among students that tends to accompany many experimental programs—reflected in the wish for more faculty participation, individual guidance, more careful check-up of achievement. It is possible, too, that in the initial reaction against traditional methods both staff and students may tend to hold excessive notions regarding freedom, participation, joint planning, and similar presumably desirable concepts. Freedom is difficult, especially when unfamiliar; it is easier to be told and to obey. On the other hand, it is significant that the aspects of the program which students valued most highly were the field trips, observations, class discussions, informal student-faculty relationship, and democratic participation.

Student opinions such as these are perhaps more conducive to speculation than to certainty. Several of the recommendations referred to evaluation practices. Through many years students have become accustomed to evaluation by an instructor based largely upon final examinations. When the environment, the familiar pattern of education, is changed this evaluation practice seems no longer adequate to the students. Thus both the evaluation practice and the new pattern of instruction are blamed for the student's uncertainty in the new environment. Perhaps, as evaluation practices are improved and integrated with the instructional program, the student's desire for less freedom and more definite assignments would fade away.

After two years of experimenting the Texas staff settled upon a broad organization and sequence for the junior year's course. The course has incorporated many of the features students had found most valuable during the two years of experimentation. Moreover, the fact that the organization and sequence of topics and experiences in the course have been agreed upon should help to remove some of the uncertainties reflected in the students' opinions cited above. It should also be possible to develop evaluation procedures more systematically in the new program.

A SYSTEMATIC USE OF FACULTY AND STUDENT JUDGMENTS

Unlike the evaluation projects at Milwaukee and Teachers College, the over-all evaluation of the education program at Stanford University—up to the present time—has relied for its evidence almost entirely upon faculty and student opinions. Two aspects of the Stanford evaluation are noteworthy: the thorough manner in which opinions were collected and analyzed, and the concern manifested for widespread faculty and, to a lesser extent, student participation in nearly all of the evaluative activities. It is always difficult to fix dates for the beginning and end of any process, and the evaluation activities at the Stanford School of Education are no exception to this generalization. Our own account spans the academic year of 1941-42. During that time, a special evaluator devoted the major part of his time to the appraisal.

Clarification of objectives among the faculty

The first major step undertaken by the evaluator was to interview every member of the School of Education faculty. Many of these interviews lasted more than two hours, for they were designed not only to acquaint the evaluator and staff member with each other, but to obtain from each faculty member his judgment regarding strong and weak points of the Stanford program, general objectives for the School of Education, and specific objectives for each of his courses. The evaluator's notes from the interviews were written up as answers to the following three general questions:

1. What, in your judgment, are the outstandingly strong points of the total School of Education program?
2. What phases of the total program of the School of Education should, in your opinion, be examined with a view to improvement?
3. What is your tentative statement of the desirable general objectives for the Stanford School of Education?[16]

[16] McNaughton, op. cit., p. 41.

There were also notes to be summarized specifically for each course. These were brought together as answers to the following three questions:

1. What are the objectives which you hope your students will accomplish in your course . . . ?
2. What experiences do you provide in your course in order to make possible the attainment of these objectives?
3. What methods of evaluation do you use to measure the attainment of these objectives?[17]

The objectives, experiences, and evaluation practices in the educational sociology course described earlier in this chapter are an example of one instructor's reply to these questions. These interview notes were examined, sometimes modified, and then approved by each faculty member concerned. From all these notes the evaluator then summarized in one list the faculty's opinions with respect to each of the three general questions—the strong points of the program, the weak points of the program, and the objectives of the program. It was found that some things which were listed as strong points were also listed as weak points. For example, one staff member said, "Faculty members have developed a pattern of thinking which has internal consistency and unity";[18] while another said that there was a "need for greater clarification and unanimity regarding aims and functions."[19] It was found, too, that the objectives of the college had been stated by the staff from two different points of view: one group emphasized the major functions which the college should serve; another group stressed the characteristics of educational workers that the college should aim to produce. The interviews had provided motivation for thinking about objectives, and had served to bring together the opinions of the various faculty members. What was now needed was to get the collective judgment of the faculty on the statements which they had made as individuals. Two questionnaires were developed to yield this collective judgment. Their development, use, and analysis was the second major task in the evaluation program.

[17] *Ibid.,* p. 454.
[18] *Ibid.,* p. 456.
[19] *Ibid.,* p. 460.

The first questionnaire was concerned with the strong and weak points of the Stanford program. Factors that had been mentioned by individual staff members as either strong or weak points were listed, but phrased neutrally as factors to be rated. The faculty ratings for each factor provided a consensus regarding its strength. For example, the factor, "the internal consistency and unity of the philosophy of the faculty," received a composite rating of 3.35 on a five-point scale in which 3.00 signified a judgment of "neither strong nor weak" and 5.00 signified "very strong." Another factor, "freedom of faculty members to do their own thinking and express their own opinions," received a composite rating of 4.75. It is clear that this latter factor was regarded as a very strong point in the Stanford program. The total questionnaire called for ratings on from two to ten items under each of twenty-six headings. A list of some of these headings may suggest the scope of the questions: the philosophy of the faculty, the resources of the university, student-faculty relationships, adaptability of program to student needs, realism of program, the evaluation of results, the follow-up of graduates, effectiveness of practice teaching experiences, changes produced in students.

The second rating scale was concerned with the objectives of the School of Education. The first section of this questionnaire called for ratings on the relative importance of four functions of the School of Education, namely research, service to schools, preparation of teachers, and preparation of administrators and other educational workers. The second section called for ratings of the importance of various activities within each of these major functions; for example, what kinds of research and what kinds of service to the schools are most important? The third section of the questionnaire was headed: "What are the patterns of education most suitable for the different fields of educational work?" The fields specified were those of school teaching, administration, curriculum, personnel and guidance, and research. The faculty indicated on a five-point scale their judgments of the value of sixteen different elements of training in the preparation of workers for these fields. A few examples of these elements are a broad general education, a period of practice teaching, a study of educational philosophy, a study of the history of education.

The fourth section of the questionnaire provided the main basis for polling the faculty's opinions regarding the objectives of the School of Education. The statements of objectives represented a summary and refinement of the opinions expressed by individual faculty members in interviews. Further refinement had followed general faculty discussions and discussions within the evaluation committee. In the questionnaire the staff was asked to indicate whether or not each objective was desirable and, if desirable, where the primary responsibility for its attainment should rest. Their responses[20] indicated that all of the objectives were regarded, almost unanimously, as desirable. One part of this section of the questionnaire is reproduced here.[21] Main headings under which the other objectives are classified are also shown.

What should be the general objectives for educating teachers and other educational workers?

In order to obtain a consensus as to which of these objectives are important and where the responsibility lies for their attainment, check each of the following objectives in the appropriate columns:

Column *a*. This is a desirable objective and one which is a responsibility of every faculty member in the School of Education.

Column *b*. This is a desirable objective for which primary responsibility should be as l sumed by professors in certain areas of the School of Education (educationa-hygiene, guidance, curriculum and instruction, practice teaching, etc.).

Column *c*. This is a desirable objective, for which primary responsibility should be assumed by some undergraduate division, school, or nonteaching department (general education courses, school of specialized field, student counselor, student organizations, etc.).

Column *d*. This is a desirable objective, for which primary responsibility should be assumed by the individual student.

Column *e*. Not a desirable objective.

A. Understanding of social and economic conditions
The School of Education endeavors to prepare educational workers who:

---

[20] Twenty-two staff members answered the questionnaire. The percentages responding in various ways are shown in the excerpt reproduced in the text. One staff member made no response to these particular statements.

[21] *Ibid.*, pp. 496-504.

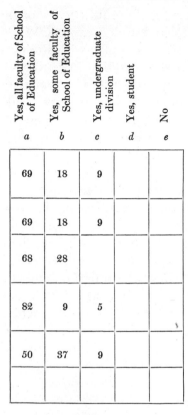

Yes, all faculty of School of Education	Yes, some faculty of School of Education	Yes, undergraduate division	Yes, student	No	
a	b	c	d	e	
69	18	9			1. Are aware of social and economic factors that bear upon society and are equipped for living in tune with these factors.
69	18	9			2. Arrive at intelligent, constructive conclusions about controversial issues.
68	28				3. Understand the environmental conditions which affect the work of educators. This involves patterns, trends, and changes.
82	9	5			4. Understand the responsibilities and opportunities presented by a democratic society.
50	37	9			5. Understand American culture, how it has developed, and what it might become
					6. Others.

B. Willingness and ability to undertake social improvement through education
C. Application of principles of human growth and development, and physical and mental health
D. Resourcefulness in using methods and materials to provide a stimulating learn-
E. ing environment
   Breadth and depth of background of experience
F. Ability to work with others
G. Ability in creative expression
H. Self-direction in professional and personal improvement
I . Possession of a desirable philosophy of life and education
J . Understanding of the operation and function of the school

Judgments of success among the students

The third and fourth major tasks in Stanford's evaluation procedure are related to the problem of getting judgments from students about the Stanford program and its objectives similar to the ones already gathered from the staff. Prior to the development of a questionnaire for students to fill out, a series of informal discussions was held with selected student groups. While the major purpose of these discussions was to plan with students for ways of arriving at student-faculty cooperation in setting up and evaluating learning procedures, the discussions themselves were evaluative in character for many comments were made concerning the effectiveness of the teacher education program. The conferences also served to prepare the students for more intelligent and mature reactions to the questionnaire which would soon be sent them.

The student questionnaire was developed to get answers to six main groups of questions: their purposes in coming to Stanford, the extent to which these purposes had changed, the efficacy of the program in helping them achieve their objectives, their opinions of desirable objectives for the School of Education, their suggestions for the improvement of the program, and the points they especially liked about the institution. Many items in the questionnaire were similar to those on which faculty opinion had previously been polled, so that comparisons between student and faculty judgments were possible. For example, one question was, "To what extent have the following factors contributed to the achievement of your purposes?" The fifteen factors listed were similar to the items in the faculty questionnaire on strong and weak points in the Stanford program—factors such as "the resources of the university (other than the School of Education)," "the contact with children, schools, and communities in the program," "the materials in the library," "the guidance of students by the faculty." In this way it was possible to see whether factors rated as strong points by the faculty were judged by students to have contributed significantly to the achievement of their purposes. Other parallels between student and faculty questionnaires were also provided.

The manner in which the student questionnaire was developed illustrates the attention paid throughout to cooperation and joint action among all persons concerned with the outcome. A tentative draft of the questionnaire was prepared by the evaluator. This was submitted to the evaluation committee for criticism. After revision in the light of their criticisms, it was submitted to the general faculty and again revised. Then it was critically examined by a student-faculty committee and revised a third time before it was finally mailed to all the School of Education majors.

Besides making these surveys of student and faculty opinion, the evaluator contributed one further service in developing the evaluation program at Stanford. He undertook to draw together and summarize data from other local investigations which had significance for the total evaluation of the college program. Among these were the Stanford follow-up inquiry reported later in this book, a master's study of student opinions on various aspects of the Stanford program, an evaluation of the effectiveness of two new unified courses basic in the program of teacher preparation, and evaluations made by various instructors of their own regular courses.

Interpreting the judgments

Data from these investigations as well as from the surveys of student and faculty opinions were drawn together around each of the ten major objectives of the program. For the objective stated as "understanding of social and economic conditions" the highlights of evidence related to it were as follows:

1. The faculty rated as good the students' mastery of materials and studies basic to sociology.

2. The course in educational sociology (in the judgment of the evaluator after studying the course materials) treats thoroughly the major principles and concepts of social life. Many other courses are directly concerned with developing understanding of social and economic conditions. Moreover, the faculty considers this objective a responsibility of the whole college, not just of a few courses or departments.

3. Students said that the program helped them develop an understanding of social and economic conditions.

4. The faculty rated as somewhat low the extent to which students were prepared to understand communities and community problems.

5. Graduates said that one of their hardest problems was adjusting to the community where they worked, and few activities they had engaged in at college gave them experiences that would have helped them face this problem more effectively.

6. Graduates suggested the need for more participation in community life in Palo Alto and the San Francisco Bay region.

7. Students did not credit contacts with children, schools, and communities as contributing much to the achievement of their purposes, and this was because they had relatively few such contacts.

In summarizing these and other evidences related to this objective McNaughton writes:

> In view of the evidence, the program of the School of Education attains the desired objective of an understanding of social and economic problems insofar as the study about society and economic factors, the nature of civic responsibilities, and the implications of these matters for education are concerned. The program seems, however, to fall somewhat short of developing the ability to discover and discharge social responsibilities, and to act with effectiveness in an actual community situation. The cause apparently is that provisions for continuous firsthand experiences have not been developed to as great an extent as the facilities for discussion, reading, writing and the organization of material around the more intellectualized aspects of social principles and philosophy.[22]

From the year's activities in evaluation that we have described here came two substantial achievements. First, the faculty succeeded in building an over-all picture of the objectives and the program of the School of Education. General objectives were formulated which were acceptable not only to the faculty but to the students. Specific objectives for each course were listed, specific experiences provided students in those courses were listed, and specific evaluation devices in use described. Second, evidence of the degree to which these objectives were being attained by students was marshalled from a variety of sources— from student and faculty judgments, from previous studies or surveys, from evaluations within specific courses. Out of the year's work likewise came plans for the continuation and expan-

[22] Ibid., p. 313.

sion of the evaluation program, and for attacking some of the weaknesses in the school's program revealed by the evaluation.

USE OF SUBJECTIVE AND OBJECTIVE DATA

The four programs of evaluation we have described illustrate different approaches to the problem of evaluating programs of professional education and illustrate the use of different types and sources of data. All the evaluation programs have been concerned with the development of objectives. And the sources of data used have included some that are primarily quantitative, as in standardized and locally made tests of student achievements, and some that are primarily qualitative, as in the collection of student and faculty judgments.

With regard to the development of objectives, the fact that appears most important is the close relationship between that process and the process of carrying forward attempts to evaluate the program. In the chapter on general education, we suggested that when the formulation of objectives was undertaken as an independent task the likelihood of moving on readily to evaluative tasks might be decreased. In the descriptions of what was done at Milwaukee and Stanford the relationship between objectives and evaluation was quite clear and direct. At Milwaukee, for example, the evaluator developed in a relatively short time, through interviews and readings, a statement of objectives that was acceptable as a working basis for a program of evaluation. These objectives were further defined through the process of developing tests to measure student attainment of them. At Stanford the evaluator got, through interviews, opinions from each staff member regarding the objectives of the program. He also got from them statements of the objectives for each of their courses, and at the same time an account of the experiences they provided to help students attain those objectives and the means of evaluation they were using to measure their attainment. Thus, from the outset, thinking about objectives was associated with thinking about how to measure their attainment. Moreover, when the staff was asked to rate the desirability of various objectives they were at the same time asked to indicate where they thought primary responsibility should rest for their attainment, and to judge different characteristics of the Stanford program as being either strengths or weaknesses. In all these examples, attempts to evaluate the program either accompanied or gave direction to the development of objectives. We believe this is a desirable procedure.

The variety of tests used in these evaluation programs may also be discussed briefly. To measure student achievement, both standardized and locally made tests were used, as well as local adaptations of standardized tests. Some of the tests have been of the familiar multiple-choice or true-false variety—as in the battery of standard tests used at Teachers College and the information test used at Texas. Others, probably the majority, have been of the situational type. Baller's case-study instrument is an outstanding example. Others are the Milwaukee tests and the instrument developed at Teachers College to measure the application of concepts to school practices. Whether standardized or locally made, it is probably fair to say that the situational test is growing in popularity. Doubtless some of this growth has been stimulated by the work of the evaluation staffs of the Progressive Education Association's eight-year study and the Cooperative Study of General Education. But basically it reflects a conscious desire to measure complex behavior and a conviction that it cannot be done adequately by simple-choice test items. The use of situations calling for a variety of responses rather than brief items calling for a single response gives to tests an appearance of greater validity, of closer correspondence to some of the objectives one is trying to measure. While this apparent validity is not thoroughly established, the trend toward greater emphasis upon tests which seek to measure the application of knowledge in situations that one can recognize as occurring in the professional lives of teachers is to be encouraged.

The use of subjective data was best illustrated in the evaluation program at Stanford. The systematic collection of faculty and student judgments as to how well the program was succeeding was a prominent feature of that appraisal. How valuable are judgments of this sort? The question would be more appropriately phrased as follows: "For what purposes are such judgments valuable?" Several purposes might be mentioned: to gain a quick overview of a total program, to reveal areas that should be attacked more objectively and systematically, to locate probable strengths and weaknesses. Another purpose, and one that can be served when both faculty and student judgments are collected, is to reveal divergences between the beliefs of faculty and students. This, of course, would suggest the need for a more objective analysis of the reasons for the divergence. For example, if the faculty thinks the personnel and advisory program is good but the students think it is poor, the fact that this difference of opinion exists is important. Students are the receivers of the service. If they do not think what they are getting is helpful, it is likely that the service is not fulfilling the functions it is supposed to fulfill. If they do not think the advice is helpful, they are not likely to follow it. In the same way, if a learner thinks a particular subject is neither worth while nor useful to him he is not likely to learn it very well. The attitude of the learner conditions the effectiveness of the instruction. The late Dean M. E. Haggerty of the University of Minnesota once wrote that the "effective curriculum" of a college was not what the instructors taught but what the students learned.

Surveying student opinion regarding the value of various experiences gives one clues to the effectiveness of the experience. But ordinarily, one would not rest satisfied with a wholly subjective evaluation. To find out how well students had learned any subject matter, a test of knowledge and skills would provide much more trustworthy evidence than a collection of opinions. In other words, what students actually reveal in achievement, insight, changed beliefs, concepts, appreciations, and so on is much better evidence that a program is succeeding than their, or the faculty's, opinion on these matters is. We shall have more to say on this topic in the chapter on follow-up studies. The point we wish to make here is simply that in the evaluation of many goals in education, the collection of opinions is no substitute for the collection of objective data. It may well be a very useful first step, serving to reveal areas that should be examined more closely and to evoke genuine interest and concern in the evaluation by drawing a great many people into the process. It may also be, for some goals of education, the only technique of evaluation that is appropriate or feasible. For example, no evaluation of a professional education program is complete until we find out how well the knowledge and insight students have gained are applied in actual practice. Paper-and-pencil tests of the application of knowledge are more properly called tests of the ability to recognize applications. Real application of knowledge is something that, in the last analysis, can be observed only directly in student behavior. The judgments of competent observers can be brought to bear upon this problem.

VI

Student Teaching

EVALUATION OF what students learn in courses of professional and general education is not complete until we have determined how well they can use their knowledge and insight in their own teaching. The building of closer relationships between theory and practice has been increasingly a major objective of programs of teacher education. In the last chapter the emphasis upon observation of children and adolescents, upon understanding human growth and development, upon observation in the community and the study of educational sociology, and upon field experience of various sorts all testified to the concern of educators for this integration of theory and practice. The fact that observations and field experiences are being knit more closely to professional courses provides opportunity to study this integration of theory and practice as the professional program proceeds. It is at the time of student teaching, however, that the best opportunities to evaluate the application of theory to practice ordinarily occur.

Student-teaching programs, of course, vary greatly from institution to institution. There are variations in the place where practice teaching is done—in a campus school, in local public schools, in out-of-town schools. There are variations in the time when the practice teaching comes—in the last part of the year prior to certification, in the junior year, or it may be distributed over a two- or even a four-year period. There are differences in the variety of teaching situations in which the student obtains practice—it may be confined to a single grade in a single school or distributed among several grades in different schools. These different types of arrangement for student teaching influence the scope of any program set up to evaluate the experience. It is not uncommon today to find students doing their practice teaching under conditions closely resembling a full-time job, living in the community, and participating in the total school program. Nevertheless, before one passes judgment upon the student teacher he needs to make sure how extensively the particular situation has provided opportunities for the student teacher to reveal in action the skills and insights which his educational program has sought to develop.

The following anecdote illustrates, with almost startling frankness, the importance of looking into this matter. Certain students were discussing their student-teaching experience. One of them said:

When I went to the high school in which I was to do my student teaching, I first went to the principal. He told me I was very fortunate in my assignment, that Miss X, under whom I was to do my teaching, was considered one of the most efficient English teachers in the city. I found her very efficient. She had her course outlined in great detail, and knew just what the students would be discussing during any fifteen minutes of the class period. After several days of observation, I was told to take the class the next day. I was given a copy of the regular teacher's outline. I studied her plans that night and I studied the necessary materials, but I knew that there were certain points in the outline that I would not be able to cover as intended by her. I thought of some new materials related to the topic up for discussion and was sure the students would be interested in them. Also, there were some problems that I wanted to get the students talking about. So I made some modifications in the plan. The next day, things went better than I had expected. It must have been pretty good for Miss X seemed to think so. Nevertheless, at the first opportunity after the class was over, she said, "That really was a pretty good job, but I have been developing my plans for these courses during these many years. I have them just about as I want them. Some of your new ideas look pretty good, but I would much rather you followed my plan. I am going to retire in a year or two. I don't want to change my plans, and I don't want to retire with a guilty conscience."

This student had little opportunity to reveal in action the competence toward which his previous general and professional education had been directed. His ability in teaching could not be broadly observed or appraised in this situation. His ability to adapt tactfully to a fixed situation could be observed, perhaps, but one could not see how well he worked with others in identifying pupil needs, or in developing a program, or in preparing materials. The competence of a teacher and the effectiveness of his general and professional education cannot be evaluated adequately without a knowledge of the opportunities that existed in student teaching for that competence to express itself. ⌐

As we describe various techniques that are being used for the evaluation of student teaching we shall comment further on the opportunities for significant experience which different programs afford. A critical discussion of techniques and problems of evaluation will follow the descriptions of evaluation practices in some of the institutions associated in the Commission's program.

DEVELOPMENT AND USE OF A GUIDE TO OBSERVATION

From the program of evaluation in student teaching at Ohio State University we have selected one element for rather thorough discussion—the development and use of the Ohio Teaching Record.[1] Probably no program of student teaching is, or can be, evaluated by a single device, but the Record represents one very important technique of evaluation—the planned observation of behavior—and the experiences and suggestions of faculty, students, supervisors, and public school teachers have contributed to its development. Describing its evolution and use, to the exclusion of other evaluative devices, should not be taken to suggest that student teaching at Ohio State University is evaluated solely by means of the Record.

PLACE OF OBSERVATION IN THE PROGRAM

Before examining in detail the development and use of the Record it may be helpful to review briefly the program of evaluation of individual student growth that precedes the period of

[1] Sources of information for this section: Louis Raths, "The Revised Ohio Teaching Record," *Educational Research Bulletin*, XX (December 1941), 241-48. William John Jones, "Improving Teaching in Ohio through the Experimental Use of a Cooperatively Developed Anecdotal Observational Record" (unpublished dissertation for the Ph.D. degree in the files of Ohio State University, Columbus, Ohio, 1941).

student teaching because the use of the Record is clearly influenced by that program. The reader will recall from the description of the orientation course for freshmen that the student under the guidance of his faculty adviser has appraised his potential abilities, skill in oral and written expression and in reading, his knowledge of contemporary affairs and general cultural matters, his attitudes and beliefs, social competence, quality of thinking, emotional stability. He has explored the resources of the university and has studied the significance of what he has learned about himself in relation to the factors of competence which are the goals of professional education. He has described the results of this study in a planning paper. With the help of his adviser he has made a tentative plan for his professional education program. And his progress has been summarized in terms of factors of competence for his own record and for the cumulative record in the dean's office.

Just prior to the beginning of the sophomore year a month's field experience in a public school has provided for some students another focus of evaluation.[2] During this field experience, which occurs in September, he has studied a school and its community, kept a log of his activity, and an anecdotal record of his observation. Questionnaires filled out by the student and the principal of the school where he worked revealed the type and quality of the experience. In a seminar at the university following the September experience the student has analyzed what he has seen and done in terms of a philosophy of education and a psychology of teaching and learning. This process of experience and analysis is calculated to broaden his understanding of the competence required of teachers and to reveal more clearly his own needs in this respect.

The faculty member who served as a student's adviser in the freshman orientation course has continued to counsel with him during the sophomore year. At the end of the sophomore year the adviser prepares a report on each of his advisees for the consideration of the committee on junior standing. This report

[2] A. J. Klein, ed., *Adventures in the Reconstruction of Education* (Columbus: Ohio State University College of Education, 1941), pp. 105-6.

consists of a series of ratings, with annotations, on those objectives for which the lower division is primarily responsible.

It is important to see the continuous evaluation program just described as an antecedent to evaluation in student teaching because throughout there has been a synthesizing framework—the factors of competence. Within this framework the program has taken shape and the evaluation has been carried forward. The student and his adviser have shared much of the responsibility for evaluating progress. The evaluation expert has contributed to the development of the evaluation program by helping to construct tests, rating scales, and other evaluative instruments and by giving special counsel regarding the interpretation and uses of evaluative data. In short, prior to student teaching, the student's awareness of the factors of competence has been sharpened and he has had considerable experience in self-evaluation under faculty guidance. With this background it is not surprising that the Ohio Teaching Record serves not only as a device for evaluating the effectiveness of student teaching but serves with equal if not greater importance as a device for promoting effective learning. It may be said to represent an extension at the level of student teaching of the type of combined learning and evaluating that has characterized the student's experience prior to his practice teaching.

EVOLUTION OF THE OHIO TEACHING RECORD

In October 1939, faculty supervisors, student teachers, and some sixty cooperating teachers in the Columbus schools began to explore together the problem of evaluating teachers' effectiveness. They set for themselves the task of identifying a great many activities in the classroom which might reveal the teacher's competence. They described literally hundreds of situations in which, they believed, the quality of competence in fulfilling instructional responsibilities would be observable. As these descriptions were studied they were classified under a number of headings, or as relevant to a number of important questions. What procedures were employed to stimulate thinking and planning on the part of students? Did the teacher identify some of the needs of different pupils and how did he try to meet these needs? What mechanics of teaching were used? Were the processes of teaching (for pupils, the processes of learning) democratic? What effects did the teacher's personality have upon the teaching-learning situation? To a considerable extent, of course, these questions implied a point of view regarding what constituted good teaching. As a matter of fact, the faculty at Ohio State had been discussing for several years the formulation of a statement on competence for teaching, although the first publication of such a statement did not occur until 1940. Under each of these questions or headings described above a series of specific activities and facts was listed. The result was the first edition of the Ohio Teaching Record, called at that time the "Observational Record."

To date, there have been two revisions of the instrument. In the summer of 1940, participants in the Ohio workshop in teacher education made suggestions leading to a revision known as the Ohio Teaching Record, experimental edition. This form was used in studying the work of regular teachers in fourteen school systems during the academic year 1940-41. Suggestions growing out of this experience and out of its use with student teachers led to a new form, the Ohio Teaching Record, revised edition.

Over-all changes

The observational guide itself is a booklet containing forms on which an observer in the classroom can record by checks and brief anecdotes what he saw and thought with respect to several major topics. This one-sentence description of the guide, however, does not suggest the rather marked differences that are apparent when one compares the three editions that have so far been published and used. There have been changes in the major topics or questions which direct the attention of the observer as he uses the Record. There have been changes in the way in which anecdotes are recorded. There have been changes in the way in which the observer's judgments are expressed. And there have been changes in the way in which the observations and judgments are summarized. These changes reflect convictions regarding the format and usefulness of the Record which are of importance to those interested in using it or developing their own techniques of classroom observation.

In the first edition the major questions have already been noted. Briefly, they were concerned with the procedures employed, the mechanics of teaching, meeting pupil needs, democratic aspects of teaching-learning situations, and the personality of the teacher. In the second edition these headings were the same except that the one on procedures employed was made more specific and became two topics: procedures relative to pupil-teacher planning, and objectives guiding the teaching process. In the third edition two new headings were introduced: "What was done to promote better school-community relations?" and "What evidence was there of specialized training in this area?" Also, in the third edition, the first four questions formed a sequence that can be summarized as materials, purposes, methods, and effectiveness and served to focus attention more clearly on what was originally included under the two headings of procedures employed and mechanics of teaching. Finally, sections on the teacher's personality and on pupil-teacher planning, which had appeared in the first and second revisions respectively were eliminated. These topics were accounted for in the final revision under other headings. The list of major headings in the latest revision is as follows:

1. Materials
2. Purposes
3. Methods
4. Effectiveness
5. Pupil Problems
6. Community
7. Democracy
8. Special Area

Thus, by the time of the third edition the number of guiding questions had increased from five to eight and had, in general, been organized more effectively.

Changes in the provision for recording anecdotes and judgments are, perhaps, even more significant than changes in the major topics. In general, the changes in recording anecdotes were from fragments listed under specific items to broad descriptions under general headings, from the atomistic to the organic. And the changes with respect to recording judgments were from the writing of specific on-the-spot reactions to the withholding of judgments until teacher and observer could discuss the record together. We have reproduced on pages 188-91 the major topic of meeting pupil needs as it appeared in three successive revisions so as to illustrate more clearly the importance of these changes in form.

In each revision, space is provided for recording anecdotes. In the first form the observer was instructed to insert the anecdote under the item for which it was significant. This proved impractical, for striking incidents were frequently significant with respect to more than one item. Recording fragments of an anecdote under several different items tended to obscure the wholeness of the event. This problem was overcome in the second revision by providing space at the bottom of the page for recording the anecdotes. The observer was then instructed to code the anecdote so as to indicate the specific pupil needs to which it was relevant. In the latest revision specific items are eliminated as such and the statements of need—now called problems—are grouped according to eight types. The observer is not asked to code the anecdote in relation to these types.

In the first two revisions the observer was instructed to indicate, in the columns to the right, his opinion of the effectiveness with which the teacher met pupil needs with respect to the specific items listed. In actual practice it was discovered that both students and mature teachers found the Record a much more helpful basis for discussion between them and their supervisors when judgments had been reserved until there had been an opportunity to discuss the observation. In the early editions there was a tendency on the part of some observers to record their judgments but not the evidence for them and when this happened the value of the subsequent discussion was markedly reduced. For these two reasons the recording of judgments by simple check marks was eliminated from the final revision and space was provided for summarizing ways in which teachers had helped students on their problems with criticisms, suggestions, and comments.

Changes in directions

The most significant changes are those that have been made in the directions for using the Record. These reveal some basic points of view about evaluation, especially in relation to learning. Evaluation has been traditionally a process in which instruments of appraisal are used *on* someone. From the beginning, the Ohio Observational Record was conceived as an instrument to be used *with* teachers and student teachers. Changes and additions made from one revision to the next reflect some of the difficulties experienced by supervisors in changing from a "using on" to a "using with" procedure.

In the form in which it was first used, the Record carried only one sentence that might be considered a general direction: "This Record is not a rating device, but a means of reporting what went on during the period of observation." In the experimental edition the general directions were more extensive. The observer was instructed that his record should provide a verbal snapshot of the teacher in action, that judgments and interpretations were to be made, but that in every case the data to support such judgments were vital, that on these recorded data the worthwhileness of the whole record depended. A short paragraph was given to the definition and description of an anecdote. This was followed by another paragraph which reiterated the importance of writing a description of the incident or situation which served as the basis for any check marks characterizing the quality of the teaching. Directions for a follow-up interview were also introduced, stating that the observation should not be considered complete until the observer had had an interview with the teacher. Information gained from the interview was to be made part of the record.

OHIO OBSERVATIONAL RECORD

(*Original edition*)

MEETING PUPIL NEEDS

Directions: Indicate your judgments on this form about the extent to which pupil needs were being met during the period of observation. Place checks in Column 1 beside the pupil needs which you feel were being met. If a situation arose where a need could have been met but wasn't, place a check in Column 2. Space is provided beneath each need to write in anecdotal notes to give meaning to each check mark. It is desirable to indicate *how* each need which was checked was met or could have been met.

	Met This Need (1)	Missed a Chance (2)
1. Need for activity		
2. Need for aesthetic satisfaction or developing appreciations		
3. Need for assurance of "growing up"		
4. Need for consumer information		
5. Need for creative experience		
6. Need for cultivating leisure-time activities		
7. Need for intelligent self-direction		
8. Need for physical and mental health		
9. Need for satisfying curiosity		
10. Need for security		
11. Need for self-assurance		
12. Need for social participation		
13. Need for social recognition		
14. Need for variety of personal interests		
15. Need for vocational orientation		
16. Need for world view and working philosophy		

THE OHIO TEACHING RECORD

(*Experimental edition*)

SECTION III: MEETING PUPIL NEEDS

Directions: Indicate your judgments on this page concerning the evident needs of pupils which were met or which were not met during the period of observation. Place a check ($\sqrt{}$) in Column 1 beside the pupil needs which you feel were being *effectively met;* place a check in Column 2 beside the pupil needs which you feel were being *ineffectively met;* and place a check in Column 3 beside the pupil needs which could have been met but which were not because the teacher *missed a chance* to use or change a situation in order to do so. As in other sections space is provided for the anecdotal notations which furnish evidence for your judgments. Add any other needs which you believe were provided for.

PUPIL NEEDS	Effectively Met	Ineffectively Met	Missed a Chance		PUPIL NEEDS	Effectively Met	Ineffectively Met	Missed a Chance
Need for:	(1)	(2)	(3)			(1)	(2)	(3)
1. Activity								
2. Aesthetic satisfaction or developing appreciations					17. Understanding one's world and seeing relationships in it			
3. Assurance of "growing up"					18. Orientation to the classroom situation			
4. Consumer information					19. "Belonging" to a group			
5. Creative experience					20. Attention			
6. Cultivating leisure-time activities					21. Genuine "success experiences"			
7. Intelligent self-direction					22. Solving personal problems			
8. Physical and mental health					23. Opportunity for expression in a variety of nonverbal media			
9. Satisfying curiosity					24. Functional information			
10. Security					25. Carrying through a purposeful activity completely			
11. Self-assurance					26. Knowledge of status and progress			
12. Social participation					27. Others:			
13. Social recognition					28.			
14. Variety of personal interests								
15. Vocational orientation								
16. Developing a working philosophy								

Need Numbers

ANECDOTAL EVIDENCE
(What was done to meet these needs?)

[Space for remarks]

THE OHIO TEACHING RECORD

(*Revised edition*)

PART V. HOW DID THE TEACHER HELP STUDENTS WITH THEIR OWN PERSONAL PROBLEMS?

Sec. 1. *Problems Relating to Health and Physical Development:* physical handicap; poor posture; over or under size; skin disorders; sleepiness; undernourishment; retarded growth; colds; weak eyes; poor hearing; unsuitable clothing; lack of cleanliness; headaches; disinterest in physical activities; bad teeth; sickness; gland disorders; bad eating habits; etc., etc.

Sec. 2. *Problems Relating to Personal Temperament:* nervousness; irritability; temper; moodiness; impulsiveness; dogmatisms; fears; forgetfulness; daydreaming; crying; complaining; confusion of desires; lack of confidence; lack of aims; lack of sense of humor; lack of imagination and creativity; etc., etc.

Sec. 3. *Problems Relating to Social Dispositions:* unfriendliness; jealousy; overaggressiveness; boastfulness; vulgarity; tactlessness; pugnacity; argumentativeness; cheating; lying; showing off; lack of manners; shyness; oversensitivity to criticism; irresponsibility; peculiarities; lack of taste in dress; inability in dancing, games, or other social skills; lack of interest in same or opposite sex; overinterest in same or opposite sex; sex irregularities; bad reputation; confusions on "right" and "wrong"; etc., etc.

Sec. 4. *Problems Relating to Home and Family:* foreign family; minority race; poor family; broken home; only child; more able brother or sister; irresponsible parents; family discord; over- or underdiscipline; delinquency; parents drinking; rebellion against parents; fear of someone in family; member of family in penal or psychopathic institution; schism in parent-school relations, etc., etc.

Sec. 5. *Problems Relating to Vocations, Work, and Money:* naive vocational aims; lack of vocational aims; lack of self-analysis on vocational abilities; confusions in selection of courses to prepare for vocation; lack of work experience; too many or too few home duties; need for part-time job; too much outside work; desire to quit school to work; little sense of value of money; insufficient money for school lunches, books, clothes; etc., etc.

Sec. 6. *Problems Relating to School Activities and Situations:* weakness in written or oral expression; restiveness in class; failure to concentrate; dilatoriness; fear of speaking up in class; failure in library use; overconcern for examinations; slow reading; failure in subjects; emotionalized reaction to grades; dissatisfaction with grade placement; poor place to study; too much home work; difficulty in understanding textbooks; antagonism to teacher; conflicting schedule; inability in use of numbers; confusion in a new school environment; etc., etc.

Sec. 7. *Problems Relating to Leisure-Time Activities:* inability in sports; indifference to natural phenomena; naivete in music; failure to develop use of hands in handicraft; lack of good hobbies; poor choice of movies; immature use of radio; poor reading habits; playing in streets and alleys; overallegiance to gang; lack of companions of own age; no time for play; lack of big-muscle diversions; etc., etc.

Sec. 8. *Problems Relating to Understanding of the Community, the Culture, the Universe:* ignorance of community facilities; prejudice against community groups; lack of sense of historical significance of community; naive beliefs in virtue of war; race hatred; ignorance of economic forces; puzzlement about origins of humanity, function of religion, the after life, the will of God; disregard for law; failure to sense proprietorship in public property; distorted philosophy toward WPA and other social agencies; overpatriotism; crusading impulse; confusion of democratic rights with license; etc., etc.

Observation 1

1. What personal problems were touched upon? How were they handled? What did *both* teacher and students *say* and *do*?

2. What criticisms, sugggestions or comments do you have? Defend your comments

---

Observation 2

1. What personal problems were touched upon? How were they handled? What did *both* teacher and students *say* and *do*?

2. What criticisms, suggestions or comments do you have? Defend your comments.

Observation 3

1. What personal problems were touched upon? How were they handled? What did *both* teacher and students *say* and *do*?

2. What criticisms, suggestions or comments do you have? Defend your comments.

The latest revision includes extensive instructions to the observer. Approximately 4,000 words are given over to the general
directions, organized under the following headings:

Introduction to the use of the Record
Recording observations
Using the Record form
Cautions to be observed in using the Record

In "Introduction to the use of the Record," the observer is
informed about the purposes for which the booklet was developed, the philosophy it represents, and the uses which are
consistent with that philosophy. It is not assumed that all teachers should be alike or that all programs of professional education
should be alike. The major purpose of the booklet, it is stated,
is to provide a description of the ways in which a teacher functions as evidence that will warrant judgments of the teacher's
effectiveness. The evidence to be recorded is to be considered
as only one of a variety of sources from which teacher and supervisor together can identify the strengths and weaknesses of the
instructional program and plan accordingly. It is assumed, however, that the observer is looking for instructional practices in
which democracy is exemplified in the daily activity of both
teachers and students. It is assumed that the observer is looking
for emphasis upon valuing, planning, thinking, problem solving.
It is assumed that the observer is interested in finding evidence
of concern for the personal problems of individuals and for cooperative patterns of behavior.

Under "Recording observations," some of the problems of
observing and recording are described. The observer is reminded that what he sees is conditioned by his experience, by
what he has been sensitized to look for. If, out of his background
of thinking and experience, he has formulated a clear concept
of good teaching, what he sees will be in relation to that pattern.
If he has no concept of good teaching his various observations
and judgments will be unrelated and of less value to the teacher
observed. The observer is instructed to record only those things
heard and seen which are significant. "If what is seen or heard
can be acted upon in a way to illuminate good teaching or to

improve teaching, then it is significant and should be recorded."
What is written in the book "should be a basis for discussion
with the teacher and, if acted upon, should improve the quality
of teaching or reassure the teacher of the soundness of her practices. It follows, then, that the most competent recording of
observations will be a product of those who have an hypothesis
of what constitutes teaching and what constitutes learning."
The observer is further instructed that the items in the Record
are illustrative, suggestive, sensitizing in nature, but that he
should not feel bound down by them.

In "Using the Record form," a great many suggestions are
made. The most common use of the Record is by supervisors as
they observe student teachers or regular teachers. Teachers
should be observed for several full class periods and the observations should come at different times of day. Where agreeable
with the teacher, anecdotes can be written during the observation periods. Recording the observation as soon as possible is
important; the judgment or value placed on the incident need
not be recorded immediately. Ordinarily it is best to record the
judgment during the interview which follows the observation.
In some schools where the Record has been used, staff supervisor, cooperating teacher, and student teacher recorded their
observations independently and formulated their judgments in
joint conference later. In other schools, student teachers and
teachers in service have observed each other. The Record can
also be used by students in professional education courses preceding student teaching; observing and recording can help them
clarify their professional goals and motivate their learning.

The section headed "Cautions to be observed in using the
Record" re-emphasizes some of the major problems described
above.

BASIS FOR SUMMARIZING OBSERVATIONS

In all three forms of the Record space is provided at the end
for the observations to be summarized. These summaries are
made following the major headings that have guided the observation. The latest revision, however, provides for two bases

of summarization: one in terms of the outline for observation and the other in terms of the factors of competence in teaching as developed and stated by the staff of the College of Education. One basis for summary is in terms of the things a teacher does. It is a guide for observing and describing what the teacher does in fulfilling his responsibilities: what he does with materials, methods, students' problems, community relationships, and so forth. The observer and teacher then generalize from these specifics in the follow-up conference. This method is particularly well suited to the interests and habits of the teachers in service and supervisors who were largely influential in the development of the Ohio Teaching Record. The other basis for summary, the factors of competence, is idealistic—as all statements of goals tend to be. It represents the best thinking of the college staff. It was developed as a framework within which to examine the undergraduate program for the preparation of teachers. It states the goals toward which progress of individuals in the program is to be evaluated.

Both bases of summary have been written into the latest revision of the Record for several reasons. Teachers are learners. They and their supervisors move with more assurance and security when they generalize from their own experience than when they try to follow the generalizations of others. As they study their experience their goals are modified, perhaps expanded. This is an inductive process. Forced to consider prematurely the generalizations of others, especially of college professors, teachers sometimes label them theoretical, impractical. Yet teachers need not lift themselves by their bootstraps alone when other resources are available. Deductive processes of reasoning are also useful. The use of goals (the factors of competence) as criteria for summarizing observations is such a deductive process. It can help to clarify the user's concept of good teaching, to see better the daily activities in relation to a broad philosophy. It is not expected that both methods of summary will always be used. But it is possible that both pre-service and in-service groups will gain valuable insights by attempting to review their work in these two ways.

In concluding this description of the Ohio Teaching Record we wish to emphasize again the point that an observational guide is not a test. Like a rating scale, its reliability and value depend heavily upon how well those who use it understand the words and sentences that are designed to direct the observer or rater. Building these understandings is the first prerequisite to the successful use of any observational record. Recognition of these hazards and limitations has led many people to shy away from the use of observational records. But instead of having this effect it should lead people to increase their efforts to develop competence in observation. In evaluating behavior as complex as student teaching the considered judgments of trained observers, based upon a series of well planned and carefully recorded observations, are the most refined and appropriate technique of evaluation yet available.

AN ADAPTATION OF THE OHIO GUIDE

At Furman University an observational record was developed that stemmed in part from the Ohio Teaching Record. The modification and adaptation of this instrument made at Furman are suggestive of ways in which techniques elaborately developed elsewhere can be used in new environments. And the fact that they adapted rather than adopted the Ohio Record has particular importance.

Prior to the academic year 1940-41, student teachers at Furman were evaluated mainly by means of a rating scale. The supervisor was asked to estimate the efficiency of the student teacher on each of six factors. They were (1) preparation—mastery of subject matter and planning of teaching procedure; (2) teaching technique—skill in the use of methods and materials of instruction; (3) pupil response—degree of participation in class activities; (4) classroom morale—attitude of pupils toward teacher and toward each other; (5) classroom routine—arrangement of room, equipment, materials, use of time; (6) professional attitudes—ability to work harmoniously with other teachers, supervisors, administrators, loyalty to the best interests of the school. The following sample of one of these factors illustrates the form of the rating scale.

PUPIL RESPONSE: DEGREE OF PARTICIPATION IN CLASS ACTIVITIES

Poor	Fair	Average	Good	Excellent
Pupils hostile, careless, indifferent toward work; being held down to hated tasks		Pupils agreeable; doing required work willingly; making occasional voluntary contributions		Pupils eager, absorbingly interested; putting forth best effort to achieve worthwhile goals

The supervisor was also asked to indicate on the rating scale the method of obtaining information regarding the student teacher's work—through conference with the student teacher, conference with the regular classroom teacher, observation of the student teacher at work, acquaintance in college class. And space was provided at the end for the supervisor to write a short paragraph for the placement files which would help a school superintendent estimate the student's general abilities as a prospective teacher.

One of the members of the Furman education faculty attended the Commission's workshop on teacher education in the summer of 1940, in Chicago, to study problems of evaluation; in the fall of 1940 she was made chairman of a committee to revise procedures for the evaluation of student teaching at Furman. At the workshop the group studying evaluation spent several sessions on the development and use of the observational record at Ohio State University.

Before the first meeting of the Furman committee a copy of the old rating form and a list of questions for discussion were sent to each member. At the meeting criticisms were made of the plan then in use and many ideas for improvement were offered. The chairman was designated to incorporate these ideas into an anecdotal observation form. She was also instructed to draw up a new form to use in summarizing the student's effectiveness as a teacher for the placement office. In passing, it should be noted that the committee consisted of representative teachers and supervisors from the Greenville and Parker district schools, where Furman students did their practice teaching, and of staff members from the university. Moreover, after some

progress had been made in the development of evaluation forms
student teachers were also invited to participate. In drawing up
the observational form the chairman incorporated ideas from
the old rating scale and from the observational record as it had
been developed by the staff at Ohio State University at that time.
The major divisions of this new anecdotal observation record
were as follows:

1. Meeting pupils needs: aids boys and girls in attaining maximum
growth in ability to face and solve problems of living and to make
a satisfactory adjustment to themselves and to others
2. Democratic procedure: promotes democracy as a way of life
in the classroom
3. Pupil response: ability and growth of teacher manifested in
the reaction and achievement of pupils
4. Functional mastery of subject matter: utilizes academic and
experiential resources to enrich the life of the pupils
5. Teaching technique: shows skill in use of methods, materials,
and special learning aids
6. Classroom morale: secures respect and cooperation of pupils
7. Classroom routine: is efficient in planning and managing details of work
8. Teaching personality: exhibits characteristics of personality
that will influence pupils and promote their growth
9. Professional attitude: realizes responsibilities as a member of
the teaching profession and utilizes various means of professional
growth
10. Community relationships: understands the strategic position
of the school and teacher in the community and interrelates school
and community in teaching

When these headings are compared with the major headings
of the observational record at Ohio State University, reported
on page 184, it is clear that the committee at Furman was concerned about some qualities of teaching that had not been included in the Ohio form. In some respects as a matter of fact,
the record at Furman is more like later revisions of the Ohio
Teaching Record than the first edition, although only the first
edition was in existence when the Furman staff developed their
instrument. The similarity and difference between Furman's
record and the various forms of the Ohio record are again ap-

parent in a comparison of the section on meeting pupil needs, reproduced on page 199, with the corresponding section of the Ohio Teaching Record, reproduced on pages 188-91.

It is apparent that the faculty at Furman University did not adopt outright the Ohio record; rather, they adapted ideas gained from it to their own purposes and program. They considered the strengths and weaknesses of the procedure they had been using. They studied procedures developed elsewhere. They clarified their own concepts of good teaching. Some of the items in the observational record from Ohio State seemed to them unimportant; some seemed to break teaching up into too much detail. They found that they were concerned with some aspects of teaching that had not been included in it. In other words, the instrument developed by another college staff did not entirely meet their needs. Their own instrument, developed cooperatively, was more intelligible to them. They had a sense of ownership in it. Students who participated in the discussions out of which it grew gained clearer understanding of what their supervisors and cooperating teachers considered good teaching and of the types of opportunity they might expect in their student teaching. Similar gains in understanding came to the public school teachers who participated in its development. The common understandings and points of view that need to be built if any observational guide or rating scale is to be used appropriately and effectively cannot be built in a day. One cannot shortcut this requirement by the easy adoption of an instrument that someone else has developed. This is not to say that one institution should never adopt, without modification, an instrument developed elsewhere. Nor is it to say that one should not use the best instrument available, wherever it happens to have been developed. It is to say, however, that no instrument of this type—observational guides, rating scales—can be employed wisely without first a great deal of discussion which leads to understanding and acceptance of its purposes, contents, and uses.

In general, the Furman record is used for the same purposes and in the same ways as the Ohio record. In addition, the major

Form I. ANECDOTAL OBSERVATION RECORD

Directions: In the column on the right check the attitudes and practices observed in the student teacher's work as follows:

Student_____

Supervisor_____

School_____

+ for favorable attitude or effective work

− for unfavorable attitude or ineffective work

Grade_____

+ − for conflicting evidence

0 for lack of evidence

Subjects_____

Write in anecdotal evidence for items checked, and write in additional illustrations of competence in teaching.

I. MEETING PUPIL NEEDS: Aids boys and girls in attaining maximum growth in ability to face and solve problems of living and to make a satisfactory adjustment to themselves and to others.

a. Recognizes and as far as possible, provides for the fundamental general needs: such as, the need for activity, healthful routine, feeling of belonging, social recognition, success experiences, self-direction, creative expression, aesthetic appreciation, functional information, and carrying out purposes._____	
b. Understands the special needs and problems of the particular class._____	
c. Recognizes individual differences in learning ability, interests, background, temperament, health, work habits, and degrees of maturity._____	
d. Creates an atmosphere of security, warmth, and friendliness in the classroom and in relationship with individual pupils._____	
e. Shows a genuine interest in the best all-round development of pupils._____	
f. Interprets problems of conduct in terms of their basic factors and causes rather than in terms of symptoms._____	
g. Makes and uses records concerning pupils in determining their needs, planning work, and guiding the learning process._____	
h. Provides for individual differences by grouping within the class, differentiating assignments, evaluating work in relation to ability, helping improve specific skills needed, making study of problem cases._____	
i. _____	

divisions or headings of the Furman record are used as points around which to write summary evaluations of students for the placement office files. Two forms have been prepared for these summaries. One consists of the headings of the anecdotal record set up as a graphic rating scale; the other uses the same headings but leaves space under each for the staff member to write a descriptive appraisal. In both cases, the use of identical headings enables the faculty to draw readily upon the data that have accumulated on the observational record. At present, each instructor can use whichever method of summary he prefers. A few use both methods.

AN ANALYSIS OF STUDENT PROBLEMS

At Teachers College, Columbia, the possibilities of using students' statements of activities, problems, and needs faced in their practice teaching as a basis for evaluation were explored. Each week students reported, on a specially prepared form, their experience with reference to the following four factors: (1) the nature of their practice teaching activity for every day in the week, (2) the problems they met, (3) the worth of the various activities, and (4) where they felt additional help and preparation were needed. This information, plus a chronological record of the problems discussed in the college seminars, provided the data for an investigation.[3] Some analyses made from these data will be described briefly, for they illustrate the extent to which relatively simple procedures can often yield highly meaningful results.

It is important at the outset to recall the setting at Teachers College in which the evaluation took place. In the previous chapter the nature of the special fifth-year program was described. It consisted of three parts: student teaching, a central seminar, and divisional seminars. The weekly reports of student teaching were conceived as an aid to coordinating the program

[3] John Chester Junek, "A Partial Evaluation of the Special Pre-Service Program at Teachers College, Columbia University, Through an Analysis of Problems Reported by Student Teachers" (an unpublished manuscript in the files of the Commission on Teacher Education).

so that problems met in the field could be dealt with in the college seminars.

As the weekly reports from students were turned in it became apparent that they could be classified and analyzed in various ways. The why and wherefore of the scheme of classification is, perhaps, not of general interest but a brief account can be given to suggest the nature of the analysis. There were three levels of classification. First, each problem or need or question was classified with reference to its functional purpose—the major topic it was concerned with. Among the twenty-three headings of this sort that were used the following are typical: planning, method, group management, individual guidance. The second classification was designed to show the state or context in which the problem was regarded by the student—the aspect of the total situation that the student seemed to be stressing or emphasizing. There were nine of these headings as follows:[4]

Children
Organization (classroom)
Learning process
Subject matter or course of study
Philosophy
Standards (values held by the teacher)
Theory and techniques
Administration (total for school)
Professional experience (student's own)
Self

The third classification further sorted the statements with reference to the following three factors:[5]

1. *Causation*. Did the student see and state a cause for the problem, question, or need reported? If so, did he place the cause in:
    a. Himself and his background
    b. Children and their background
    c. His critic teacher
    d. The subject-matter and room organization
    e. Administration and school organization
    f. Practice teaching
    g. Pre-service program

[4] *Ibid.*, p. 7.
[5] *Ibid.*, p. 8.

2. *Educational outlook or attitude expressed.* What attitude toward the educational process is reflected in the stated problems, questions, and needs? Is the student's attitude:

    a. Autocratic, as in

        "I think 'progressive' techniques are the bunk. It is only when I clamp down on the children in the traditional way that they behave."

    b. Cooperative, as in

        "How can I help and protect younger, more timid children from a child who is a bully without having them develop a running-to-the-teacher-for-help attitude?"

    c. A kind of "giving out process," as in

        "My field is English. Should I answer the children when they ask me a question about history or should I refer them to the other teacher?"

3. *Kind of problem, question, or need.* What type of response did the question demand?

    a. Was it a request for directions, particular books, information; the type of reply classed as *fact?*

    b. Did it call for reflective *thought* of a relative and interrelated nature?

One example will illustrate how the classification system was applied at the first two levels. A student says, "I need any help I can get in planning lessons." This statement was put under the heading of "planning." It also fell under two subheadings for it revealed an "emphasis on self" and an "emphasis on theory and technique."

How were these data used? Tabulations which were made each week showed that during the first four weeks there was an increase in the number of students stating problems, the number of problems stated by the students, and the number of problem areas into which the statements fell. In the following weeks the numbers decreased sharply. What might be the explanation of this fact? Further tabulations showed that the nature of students' problems and questions during the first four weeks centered chiefly in the major areas of method, group management, and individual guidance—with emphases upon children, standards of group behavior, and how to deal with individual children. An examination of the college seminar minutes for the corresponding period showed that the central seminar and three of the divisional seminars had discussed two of the areas most persistently questioned by students, but that by and large prob-lems when discussed were treated generally and in the abstract, and that for the most part the seminars were concerned with problems in their own area. In other words, the comparison sug-gested that the teaching problems and needs faced by the stu-dents were not in very many instances being discussed to the students' satisfaction in the college seminars. This knowledge could be used by the faculty in planning closer integration among the various aspects of the program.

Thus, through the single device of asking students to write each week a few statements describing the problems and needs they were facing in their student teaching, data were gathered which enabled the staff to plan closer integration among the three parts of the program. Other uses were made of the data which we have not described here. For example they were analyzed to reveal student progress toward the attainment of objectives, and to reveal the chronology of professional growth. The virtue of this simple device and the extent to which it will yield valid data for evaluation depend on the fulfillment of several conditions. Perhaps the most important condition is that problems, questions, and needs must be stated by students gen-uinely conscious of a difficulty. In other words, the students must write honestly and sincerely about the problems facing them as they see those problems. Whether they will do this is dependent to a considerable extent upon their finding that the problems and difficulties they write about are satisfactorily discussed in the college classes. If the reports are not used the most important motivation for writing them is removed. They become an arti-ficial assignment and their validity becomes questionable.

EVALUATION IN A STUDENT-TEACHING CENTER

The evaluation of student teachers in vocational agriculture at Michigan State College[6] is particularly interesting for several

[6] Material for this report on apprentice teaching in vocational agriculture at Michigan State College has been drawn from "Apprenticeship Experiences for

reasons. For one, it introduces some techniques beyond the observational methods we have already described. We have selected two of them for description: the use of student diaries or logs, and the use of an activity chart which is a checklist of activities classified under the major objectives of the student-teaching program. Other techniques are of course used in the total program but either their application is specific to the field of vocational agriculture or they involve techniques which have been described in the reports of other colleges. Emphasis upon student-teaching centers which give the student opportunity for a wide variety of experience, emphasis upon self-evaluation, and emphasis upon evaluation as an integral part of instruction are all also apparent in the Michigan State College program.

DEVELOPMENT OF A NEW PROGRAM

Prior to 1940-41, the student teachers in vocational agriculture were transported daily by bus to and from three teaching centers located within a radius of thirty-three miles of East Lansing. They spent half of every day there throughout three months. During this period the on-campus courses of each student comprised approximately one-half of his load. A course in special methods preceded the term of student teaching. Meanwhile among staff members, supervisors, and student teachers in the centers the belief had arisen that this arrangement limited the experience of the student teachers too much to the high school classroom, divorced teaching from the study of methods, consumed too much time in transportation, and fell far short of bringing the student to a comprehensive understanding of the teacher's responsibilities and opportunities in an agricultural community. These weaknesses in the program were not identified through any systematic survey or follow-up program of ap-

Prospective Teachers of Vocational Agriculture," prepared by the teacher education staff in vocational agriculture at Michigan State College and issued by the state board of control for vocational education, Lansing, Michigan; and a report to the Commission on Teacher Education by George P. Deyoe, who devoted his full time—September 1, 1941 to June 1, 1942—to the coordination and appraisal of the apprenticeship program with the joint support of Michigan State College, the state board of control for vocational education, the Michigan cooperative study of teacher education, and the Commission on Teacher Education.

praisal. No detailed goals had been stated, no careful analysis of opportunities or activities had been made. Nevertheless, there had been accumulated by those concerned a series of impressions, from observation, interviews, in-service contacts after employment, and other informal procedures, that the student teachers were not having the opportunity and experience which the faculty believed they should have. These impressions were sufficiently strong and clear to make the faculty at Michigan State College and the state board of control for vocational agriculture decide during 1940-41 to reorganize the student-teaching arrangements. Rather than postpone any revision of this program until a systematic appraisal of the existing one could be made, the staff decided to go ahead with the revision in the light of their best judgment and to provide for continuous evaluation as part of the new setup.

The new program was initiated the following fall, its main features being: (1) that the student would live for one term of approximately twelve weeks in the community in which he was to do his practice teaching; (2) that during this time he would participate as widely as possible in the activities of the regular teacher of vocational agriculture; (3) that this experience would be accompanied by and closely related to instruction and study in the methods of teaching vocational agriculture; (4) that supervision and instruction in methods would be provided by staff members of Michigan State College and the supervising teacher (the latter is both the regularly employed teacher of vocational agriculture in the teaching center and a member of the staff at the college); and (5) that students from the various teaching centers would return to the campus each Saturday for a seminar in methods and materials under the direction of the college faculty. These seminars would be organized mainly around the problems brought in by the student teachers. Thus, with the exception of the Saturday seminar, students would be urged to spend their full time, including evenings and weekends, in the community in which they were doing their teaching.

The faculty saw a special function for evaluation in this new setting. They felt that students could be motivated to the fullest participation by broad appraisal. And they felt that one focus for the evaluation should be the extent to which the student finds, avails himself of, and profits from the breadth of experience provided by off-campus teaching.

From objectives to a checklist of activities

Prior to the student's teaching experience, he has been helped, in professional courses, to formulate objectives. Usually these objectives were thought of and phrased in terms of understanding he believed he should acquire. As he begins practice teaching he is encouraged to reformulate these goals in terms which imply the development of "doing ability" rather than of understanding. The faculty and supervising teachers have also developed a statement of the major objectives of the student-teaching program. The first topic in this statement is phrased as follows:

1. Orienting oneself to a going program
   Objectives
      a. To become familiar, upon entering a department, with sources of information of importance
      b. To develop a favorable attitude toward the importance of keeping a record of such information as will be helpful to an ongoing department with possible changes in teachers
      c. To become able to recognize the stage of development of the pupils upon the entrance of the student teacher into the department
   Illustrative activities
      a. Study written records available
      b. Hold conference with the supervising teacher relative to the broad aspects of the total program
      c. Study the instructional materials used and developed by the pupils previous to the student teacher's training period

Coupled with the statement of objectives is a list of suggested activities through which progress toward their attainment might be made. It was a very simple step to transform these statements of objectives and activities into a checklist on which the student could record each week during the quarter many of the things he had done. The checklist would suggest to the student the range of activities he might try to engage in and, as he filled it out from week to week he could note various gaps in his experience. Moreover, if certain activities were seldom or never engaged in by any of the students in a particular teaching center, that fact might be suggestive of the quality of the teaching center. Various interpretations of the data would be discussed in regular conferences between the student and the cooperating teacher. Students and supervisors both participated in the development of the checklist and in discussions to determine how it might be used. Considerable leeway was left to the students in the actual use to be made of it. Some students, for example, merely checked the activities they engaged in each week. Others not only checked the activities they engaged in but did so by using symbols to indicate the extent of their participation or to indicate their judgment of its value to them.

The range of specific activities included in the checklist is illustrated by the following sixteen headings under which the items are grouped. The sixteen headings correspond to the topics around which the objectives of the student-teaching program were developed:

1. Orienting oneself to a going program
2. Developing and carrying out a program of self-improvement as a teacher
3. Organizing the room, equipment, and references
4. Managing the class
5. Studying individual pupils
6. Developing and supervising the farm practice programs
7. Teaching the classes
8. Conducting activities of the Future Farmers of America
9. Developing and conducting a young-farmer program
10. Developing and conducting an adult-farmer program
11. Evaluating the program of instruction
12. Making and using records and reports
13. Guiding and counseling
14. Participating in professional or whole-school experiences and extracurricular activities
15. Utilizing opportunities for community contacts and experiences
16. Planning a total program for vocational agriculture

The form of the checklist is illustrated further by the following examples of the activities in four of these major headings:

Student Teaching Period by Weeks

	1	2	3	4	5	6	7	8	9	10	11	12

5. STUDYING INDIVIDUAL PUPILS
   a. Study available records on individuals.....
   b. Make use of opportunities for informal contacts with pupils......................
   c. Assist in training pupils to care for their own possessions..........................
   d. Assist pupils with individual interests and problems...........................
   e. Make complete case studies.............
   [Space for others to be written in]

7. TEACHING THE CLASSES
   a. Study the existing course of study........
   b. Organize and use bulletin board material..
   c. Arrange supplementary materials and exhibits......................................
   d. Teach or demonstrate for part of a lesson...
   e. Prepare visual aids related to instruction...
   f. Plan and teach a complete lesson ....
   g. Plan and execute a field excursion........
   h. Plan and teach a complete instructional unit
   i. Analyze the strengths and weaknesses of the existing course of study................
   j. Make long-time plans for an improved course of study.....................

11. EVALUATING THE PROGRAM OF INSTRUCTION
   a. Participate in grading and interpreting tests
   b. Visit home farms of boys in classes to secure tangible outcomes of your own instruction..
   c. Visit former pupils to determine evidences of strong and weak points of the program of instruction..........................
   d. Develop an evaluation instrument that is suitable to measure the result in a given activity............................
   e. Guide a group of pupils in setting a goal in relation to a specific problem area........
   f. Appraise total progress of one or more pupils

5. UTILIZING OPPORTUNITIES FOR COMMUNITY CONTACTS AND EXPERIENCES
   a. Make church and Sunday school contacts..
   b. Attend PTA meetings.................
   c. Attend community meetings.... ....
   d. Assist in school fairs..................
   e. Associate with representatives of agricultural service agencies.................
   f. Participate in individual conferences with parents............................
   g. Assist in interpreting the school program to the community, through articles, talks, etc..

It is not expected that a student will do all the things suggested in the checklist, but it is believed that the student's experience should be rich and varied. Periodic discussion between the student and cooperating teacher, based on the checklist, can facilitate the intelligent planning of further activity for the student.

Use of student diaries

As a further aid to self-evaluation and planning, each student is encouraged to keep a diary of his activities. This personal record of activities, reactions, successes, disappointments, and interpretations, provides another basis for discussion with supervisors and cooperating teachers. Actually the record should probably be called a log rather than a diary, for its contents are not as intensely personal as the word "diary" might suggest and they are limited to professional experience. We have reproduced excerpts from the log of one student as an illustration of the potential evaluative significance of such documents. The diary of T. S. during each day in his first, fourth, and last week in the student-teaching center is given and his notes for selected days between the fourth and last weeks are likewise included. It is worth studying for what it reveals about his activities, changes in sensitivity, strengths and weaknesses, and about the quality of opportunity that is provided him in the teaching center.

For reasons that will be obvious to the reader, names of places and people are fictitious. The name of the supervising teacher is indicated as Mr. Y. Staff members from Michigan State College and the state board are indicated as such instead of by name.

The first week

Tuesday   March 31, 1942

Became acquainted with Midtown. Ate lunch at the Coffee Shop —very quiet; waiter and waitress not too anxious to please. Population 600. . . . Think I'm going to enjoy myself very much; looking forward to it all.

Wednesday   April 1, 1942

After a little orientation by Mr. Y [the supervising teacher] we began an inventory of available material. Watched students oiling harnesses; noticed that they seem very interested in their work. Things were not too orderly but everyone seemed to have something to do; boys in office, not working, talked about worthwhile things. Very enthused. 4-H club meeting in afternoon; about 30 attended; orderly. Met Mr. Z, county agricultural agent; very interesting personality. Saw movie. Sang in church choir this evening.

Thursday   April 2, 1942

Continued harness oiling; also inventory of materials. Attended regional FFA [Future Farmers of America] speech contest. Sincerely believe S should have received first place; received second. S has straightened out a couple of speech defects and although he did not place first he has gotten a *tremendous amount* out of the contest.

Friday   April 3, 1942

Class with Mr. Y this morning. Got the low-down on the Midtown setup. Drove to East Lansing in afternoon; took care of business there.

Saturday   April 4, 1942

First class with Mr. X from Michigan State College this morning; sure a jolly personality; got bit of ag. ed. history. Took care of business with college.

Sunday   April 5, 1942

Went to church today; large attendance. Took care of correspondence which has been piling up.

Monday   April 6, 1942

Beginning to learn names of boys. Met Mrs. Y at Lansing at 2:40.

The fourth week

Monday   April 20, 1942

Went to farm on judging trip where the class took a class of Jersey cows apart. Surprising to see that some of the outstanding judges placed the bottom cow first—they later confessed knowing her show record. The class was outstanding in that the top and bottom animals were rather easily picked. Observed heifers which were offered for sale. In the afternoon John [another student teacher] and I took the sophomore class out. We gave them the same class. M and N did well and gave good reasons but they have had a great deal of 4-H training; the other boys were just starting out but learned a great deal. There were no disciplinary problems and there was a great deal of interest shown.

Tuesday   April 21, 1942

The junior and senior classes again went on a judging trip; this time to N's and the farm across the road. I had charge of dairy. We learned some good lessons but the cattle which we worked with were very poor quality. Class also judged beef and horses. N disappointed in stallion which was shown us. As a point of interest we looked at a Pinto horse and its mother—much different from the draft horse. A few boys take judging work seriously, the others merely go.

Had a new experience this afternoon of operating a motion picture machine. It's really not hard at all. Get a great kick out of watching the grade-school teachers in action. After the movie Bill, John [other student teachers] and I went to price lumber for H. H is going to build a brooder house to be used later for a laying house. I arranged a farm visit with Mr. R who has brown Swiss cattle; then drove to an Ayrshire breeder where a field trip for Thursday was arranged. I again officiated, everything went off fine.

Wednesday   April 22, 1942

I was given charge of the dairy field trip to Mr. R's. Had a good class of aged dairy cows. Once again we had a good top and bottom. The boys were exceptionally attentive and there were no disciplinary problems. C and D, although usually very quiet, were especially attentive and showed a great deal of interest. All boys called upon gave good sets of reasons. Tested soil for F during noon hour. Listened to and observed sophomore class. Am to begin a teaching unit in swine production tomorrow.

Thursday   April 23, 1942

Awoke feeling fine, looking forward to one o'clock when I was to take the sophomore class under my wing for two days. Completed lesson plans last night and made final last-minute-detail plans in the morning. Opened up unit with Mr. X, John and Bill listening to procedure. Was very pleased with the results: the boys showed an unusual amount of interest in the feeder-pig unit; they helped remarkably well with the discussion; the outline developed very well. I sincerely believe they got a lot out of the day's work. Gave individual reports to boys who are normally a bit backward; this worked out very well. Also called upon N and M to explain some charts which they had made for last fall's fair—these were on feeding mixtures. One mistake which I made was the absence of a bit of humor after the announcement which concerned registration of city boys for farm labor. All in all it was very successful, and I feel right proud of myself.

Friday   April 24, 1942

Today I again took the tenth-grade class and we completed the unit on swine. Once again class interest was high. They decided to make a chart showing the diseases of swine and also their symptoms and cure. Gave class reports to three more fellows; they accepted the responsibility very well. The only boy giving much of a problem didn't care much to work; he leaned back in his chair quite often; he did however take part very freely in the class discussion. Both days of instruction were very fine and I know now that I can be a teacher, a really good one, if I try.

John begins his unit on poultry next week. I helped him arrange pictures for poultry identification in the afternoon. . . .

Saturday   April 25, 1942

Attended regular Saturday class in East Lansing today. Discussed pooling of experiences, George Dean and Smith-Hughes Acts. At one o'clock we went to a discussion on general problems of graduating seniors. Got low-down of community affairs at the local shoe store while getting shoes repaired.

Sunday   April 26, 1942

Attended church this morning. Studied material to be covered in the lesson plans of next week.

Selected days

Thursday   May 14, 1942

This morning I had a conference with E. He has an "all A" average and is much interested in mathematics and engineering. Don't know just what to advise him finally to do; somehow I think his mind is already made up—not to take agriculture; my conscience will probably force me to confirm this in him. . . .

After dinner we went on a field trip to weigh pigs and study swine management. We visited three farms and saw many very good practices used by the boys. In the evening Bill and I went to M to help him with his gilt. . . . She had 12 pigs. They were just a little small and showed a mineral deficiency. Then at 11:00 his mother asked us to have a cup of coffee and some meat and bread. They are certainly swell people—common, yes, but none better. I helped them milk and it didn't take very long with the three of us—Mr. and Mrs. and myself. Mr. X was out in the afternoon and we chatted about FFA; he also went on the field trip with us.

Thursday   **May 21, 1942**

Observed instruction in advanced class. They were filling out the farm survey under the direction of Mr. Y. During the period Mr. V and Mr. W [of the state department] arrived. They observed classes and I interviewed S. He said he liked this year's student teachers very much. N is definitely going into farming. . . . We also arranged a schedule for the tenth, eleventh, and twelfth grades. At noon we were taken to the farm shop by Mr. V and Mr. W, who were inspecting. . . . They brought out that the present shop, although good, was poorly arranged; they asked that it be changed. This was a very interesting experience. Then Mr. W discussed course building and the program of work of FFA.

Sang in church choir which is preparing to sing for the high school seniors on Sunday. Attended piano recital which was very good.

Monday   **May 25, 1942**

Worked in the department this morning. There is a great deal of cleaning to do and it sure accumulates during the year. We are making a visual aid file; it is to be constructed by hanging the charts on nails. Continued work in the department in the afternoon.

B wants us to ring his pigs. We went out at 4:30. Mr. D stopped and what a surprise! Why, he is a second Mr. M. The whole thing is very sad as the mother died a year ago. The daughter who is in the eighth grade does the cooking. Mr. D has to clean the house and do the breakfast dishes. They have 120 acres. It's just too much for one man to handle. We helped him milk and he was very appreciative. This is a farm visit long to be remembered.

Thursday   **May 28, 1942**

Was in school during the morning discussing very general problems; then at about 10 o'clock drove to the park for the school picnic. The teachers do not pull together and one would think they had met only a couple of days ago; yet they have supposedly worked together for an entire year. The superintendent was late and some teachers didn't even show up. The kids had a great time and the ball game was very good. Many took boat and canoe rides. N was all alone; L was also alone. This to me indicates a definite type of personality. The boys are not accepted by the rest of the group. A school board member's son was rather noisy and made at least one ninth-grade boy seem unwelcome. He is a good catcher but he knows it! The boy who pitched seems to have but one interest; this is in things of a physical nature; he is a good ball player. All in all the picnic proved a very good day for student observation.

The last week

Wednesday   June 3, 1942

. . . During the morning we enjoyed a discussion of the more general phases of teaching; such things as discipline and general evaluation were discussed. Bill and I spent the entire afternoon in the farm shop working on bulletin boxes. We made four altogether. Tonight we drove to Lansing to the ag. ed. banquet. It was a bit late in getting started but I had time to meet and talk to most of the fellows. . . . Mr. T gave a most excellent talk along the line of one year's teaching. The dean also gave a very fine inspirational talk. . . . On the way home Mr. Y talked to us about the supervised farming planning book, the Cook notebook, and finally about the condition of M's home.

Thursday   June 4, 1942

Continued work on course outlines today and especially this morning. We are making copies of some of the better ones. Also we are working on the breakdown of course topics furnished by Mr. W. Mr. W came at about 9:30. We discussed the summer program and general topics with him. It is a very good idea to keep a time record during the summer months to give to your superintendent. We got the file headings in the afternoon and typed general material. Dr. U [college staff] came at about 4 o'clock bringing with him boys who will be here next fall. They were given a general orientation by Mr. Y and we showed them our rooms.

Again Bill and I worked on our boxes and then in the evening went to the FFA wiener roast. After a swim we had the wiener roast and got a few words with the boys again. There was not too much in the way of organization but for a summer meeting it went off well. Of course there were a few boys whose main interest was not the FFA party; planning might have helped in this respect.

Friday   June 5, 1942

This morning I finished the bulletin boxes. Then during the remainder of the day I worked on my notebook and copied some notebook information. We feel that these notebooks will be very helpful when we're out on our own teaching. In the evening Mr. Y and I visited T, a part-time boy. T has 50 percent interest in 25 colonies of bees, 2 Holstein calves, and some hogs. His parents are very talkative, and seem to be fine people. Then we went to G's but G was at camp. His mother looked like a typical Hollander; his father has rheumatism. G has a good program and is this year's vice president of FFA. All was closed when we attended Lamp night for graduating seniors.

Saturday   June 6, 1942

Today in special-methods class we discussed professional ethics, personnel, and general topics of interest in 406. I got a complete set of bulletins for my files. Studied Lansing slum conditions for a while in the afternoon.

Sunday   June 7, 1942

Communion at church. Had dinner at the Co-op at MSC. Mr. O, registrar and former ag. teacher, was guest. Baccalaureate in afternoon: a very inspirational, boiled-down, excellent address. Attended sing in the evening.

Monday   June 8, 1942

During the morning John and I typed and worked on our notebooks. Then during the afternoon we went on a visiting tour. The first stop was at K's. He had left the farm to work in a hamburger stand; he gets 40 cents per hour, eight and a half hours per day plus meals; feels he is making more than he could at home. His mother was hopeful that he might return home. From there we drove to M's. He has 8 pigs left out of the original 12. The pigs were never too strong and the sow didn't give much milk. There is, however, a certain amount of filth around the place that is due to very poor management. We advised him to clean the place up and to get them on grass. Finally we got over to J's. His mother seemed very interested and talkative about her son's quietness and bashfulness. She recognizes that he has a very definite weakness in this respect. Then we went out in the field to see him and his dad. General problems such as war, weeds, and weather were discussed. Finally J showed us his cow and posed for a picture. From here we went to H's. He talked with us briefly about the draft and his future. Then we found P and talked briefly to him. Home contacts are fun, in fact the best part of teaching. This will be our last opportunity to say goodbye to the boys contacted; very hard to leave them.

Tuesday   June 9, 1942

Visited A, B, and S today. First we stopped at A's. Mr. Y has financed a gilt for the boy but has it in his name as yet. The hog had mange so A and I gave it a treatment with lime sulphur. We soaked the hog down. The problem is one of feed since they have no corn or oats in stock. Yet they have 25 little pigs and 4 sows. Mr. Y recommended they buy buttermilk and then feed a mix of two-thirds corn and one-third oats. He further recommended the building of a creep. They are very low financially, yet they have a five-year lease on the farm and may pull through O.K.

Then to S. He has 16 acres of soybeans in the process of being put in and hopes to buy a dual-purpose dairy-beef animal. We spoke to his father about driving to the sale on Thursday. He is going to let Mr. Y take along his trailer. S has brothers older and younger; the older one would make a good part-time boy. S is very good in books and may make MSC or perhaps a state farmer in the FFA. S seems very interested in FFA.

Then we drove to B's. The dad usually works in a factory but is now laid off temporarily. They had in mind dual-purpose livestock but prices have changed that. Instead they figure on feeder pigs for B to take to the fat stock show. Spent the afternoon in the department winding up questions in mind.

Had dinner at the Y's—a most excellent meal and fine talk during and afterward. His sons seem very active and full of pep.

It is clear that the diary, in and of itself, does not constitute an evaluation of the student's strengths and weaknesses, nor the progress that he has made, but it does give a revealing description of what he did. It is quite clear, for example, that during the first week the student was concerned mainly with orientation to the environment in which he was going to do his student teaching. The brevity of the entries is obvious and there is very little said about the significance of what he saw and did. Aside from a comment that the boys were interested in their work, that one boy had straightened out some speech defects, and that several people were very interesting or jolly, the record of the first week is confined almost entirely to a listing of activities.

In the diary of the fourth week, many more entries of evaluative significance can be found. The student comments on several reactions of the boys in his class—they were attentive, interested, quiet, and so forth. There is evidence that he was doing some planning for group discussions, individual reports, and projects. There is also evidence that he was getting out into the community and beginning to utilize community resources in his instruction.

The very interesting notes from between the fourth and last week and those of the last week can hardly be interpreted completely in the absence of the full text for the entire period. A consecutive reading of all of the daily entries, however, reveals over the entire period an increased sensitivity to the possibilities of an educational program that includes not only the high school students but the young farmers and the adults as well. There is revealed a sensitivity to the need for careful preparation of group discussions, an awareness of individual differences, the utilization of reading materials, charts, visual aids, community resources, and a knowledge of home environment. The student shows increased interest in the socio-economic level of the home, the family relationships, and a knowledge about the farm on which the family lives. He becomes interested in two boys who are not accepted by the group, in the guidance of boys with respect to their vocational plans, and in the problems of students and their fathers on the farm.

Some of the interpretations which we have suggested above may appear to go beyond the data. In practice, however, any generalization would be checked by the supervising teacher who had observed the student, and any interpretation would be discussed jointly by the supervisor and the student. Our aim here has been simply to suggest some of the values this type of diary evidence may have for evaluation.

One may wonder about the significance of such entries in the log as "looking forward to it all," "all in all it was very successful, and I feel right proud of myself," or "I know now that I can be a teacher, a really good one, if I try." Do they ring true, or are they planted for effect? The significance of these and many other expressions in the diary is not clear solely from the written statement of them. The supervising teacher, in planning with the student, observing him teach, seeing him in action in the field, and in conversation with him as they ride to and from their field work should become sufficiently acquainted with him to make defensible interpretations. The diary record can promote this acquaintance.

EVALUATION AS PART OF TEACHING AND LEARNING

We have described here only a portion of the total evaluation program. We have not described the use of tests, rating scales, and other familiar techniques. In a sense the heart of the evaluation program is found in the frequent and informal conferences between the supervisors and student teachers. It is here that the evidences of progress suggested in the diaries, the checklists, and other sources are brought in focus. While a regular time is set aside for these conferences they are by no means confined to any specific time. The student teacher works with his supervisor in the classroom, on the farm, spends much time with him going and coming. These are occasions when they have an opportunity to compare notes, opinions, attitudes, and philosophy; the supervisor can call to the attention of the student weaknesses which he has observed and plan with him those experiences in the student-teaching center or at Michigan State College likely to prove most useful. Evaluation becomes a daily activity, a vital part of teaching and learning.

In the total evaluation program several characteristics are worthy of emphasis. There is wide participation by student teachers and supervisors in the development and use of techniques and procedures. The evaluation is related to clearly defined goals and a rather comprehensive listing of types of activity through which they may be achieved. And the evaluation is, for the most part, inseparable from the work that is done in the continuous fulfillment of student-teaching responsibility. When evaluative activity is clearly a part of and contributes to the ongoing instructional program, the time devoted to it does not appear to be added on to regular duties.

EVALUATION IN A LABORATORY SCHOOL

At the College of William and Mary, students planning to become teachers enter the department of education in the junior year. The program the junior year, for prospective elementary teachers, includes two closely integrated courses in principles and methods plus observation in the Matthew Whaley School. The senior year's work includes practice teaching. Actually, however, practice teaching in the sense of doing responsible work with pupils and teacher in the laboratory school occurs throughout the two-year professional program. Several arrangements facilitate this relationship between college class and laboratory school. The two college classes in the junior year follow one another in the daily schedule and are taught by the same person. The teacher is also the director of student teaching and the elementary supervisor at the laboratory school. Moreover, the college classes are small (about fifteen students) and they meet in the Matthew Whaley School building. The opportunities which these arrangements give for students to have many contacts with pupils and to gain firsthand insights about the job of teaching are used to good advantage in the William and Mary program.

Evaluation of this program and of student progress in it is intimately bound to the daily teaching and learning activities and derives its evidence mainly from what the students do in fulfilling their regular responsibilities rather than from performance on specially prepared tests. While the evaluation activities vary from one class to the next, the ones we describe here are fairly typical.

Students usually begin their work in the junior year by observing children and classes in the Matthew Whaley School accompanied by their supervisor. The supervisor may direct the observation by asking questions or suggesting things to look for, or she may forego asking questions so as to discover in later discussions what they had seen and understood. After several weeks of group observation, individual students spend regular periods of time in one class with a single teacher. They begin to help the teacher in the preparation of class material, in administering and scoring tests, in recording anecdotes about different children, and in preparing reports. They may do some work with a particular pupil who is having difficulty, with a group of pupils who have a common problem, or with the whole class. In any case, these responsibilities are assumed gradually and are preceded by much planning between the student, the cooperating teacher, and the supervisor. Moreover, throughout the program there is much observing; the student teachers are observed by the cooperating teachers, the supervisor, and the other student teachers. And there are conferences which follow the observations.

As the program proceeds each student begins to develop four

different notebooks. In one notebook the student attempts to organize the ideas that she and the class reach concerning life in a modern elementary school. It contains forms for comparing and analyzing sets of criteria and scales by which to study certain activities of children. The second notebook is one which each student agrees to maintain for her classmates and for herself. In it she tries to make clear to the others the life in the particular classroom which she has been observing extensively. The third notebook consists of descriptions, plans, and materials for an imaginary classroom. Into the book about this imaginary room, the student puts her hopes and dreams along with commonplace plans. The fourth notebook serves to carry plans, techniques, conclusions, and other matters in relation to particular subject-matter fields. These four notebooks are started before the middle of the junior year and are added to throughout the professional program. The notebooks are a source of evidence that can be used in appraising the student's growth. They reveal ideas about education to which students are sensitive, values which students hold, their interpretations of pupil behavior, their use of test data and anecdotal records, their plans, and their selection of materials for teaching.

Within this general pattern—observing, discussing, and taking notes—the group often develops and uses more systematic evaluation techniques. For example, at one of the class meetings during the senior year, the supervisor without previous warning asked the members of the group to express what ideas or ways of doing things had become important to them as a consequence of their living with the children in the Matthew Whaley School. After a few topics had been suggested each student was given forty-five minutes to write what she wished in relation to the several topics. We have compiled here some of the statements which nine students wrote under the topics of planning and evaluation.

Planning

There is need for long-time planning, flexible and adjustable. Planning needs to be made for all types of personalities and for varied degrees of ability in children.

I need to plan in such manner that children will take on further responsibility.

Our planning should lead us to carry forward activities on a broad basis so as to include more phases of community life.

Planning should be based on detailed study of needs and abilities of each child.

Teacher should plan definite ways of working in skills to fit the particular needs of the individual pupils.

Planning should centralize on large lines of understanding for class.

Teacher should endeavor to stimulate the thoughts of the children, rather than pour out her own to them.

Planning should be very receptive to good ideas of children as teacher leads the class in considering possibilities.

Teacher should consider time element when planning.

. . . teacher should . . . delve into books in attempts to broaden the base for planning.

Variety of ways of planning for different kinds of job is important accomplishment.

A program of growth should be planned with each . . . child.

My planning should be such that I can fit in with the changing needs of the children.

In my own planning before meeting children I need to seek possible activities close to children's experience.

Teacher's planning with group should be such that children understand the large goals ahead.

Use cooperative planning in such manner that the child considers his own need for planning a well balanced program.

Evaluation

Encourage children to analyze themselves so as to see their own growth.

Teacher needs to analyze individual growth . . . of child from time to time.

Teacher should see needs and steps toward improvement.

Compare a child's ways of acting socially from time to time in order to see his growth.

Use varied ways and means to help oneself to find values.

Judge carefully the complexity of material a child can use.

Find by experimenting how much help a child can use.

Seek the thoughts back of words.

Teacher should find ways of evaluating her own planning.

Compare children's own evaluations of what ideas they have

gotten from work with the aims you previously listed for the children when planning.

Experiment with forms to help you in watching for growth in each child.

Compare children's criticisms and suggestions for further efforts with your own analyses.

Check on your own ability to work with the children.

Experiment with forms for recording development.

Analyze process rather than product[7]

In so far as this composite list contains ideas about professional education uppermost in each student's mind, it reveals some of the strengths and weaknesses of the over-all program. The students' responses to this assignment were discussed in class and the list of understandings finally derived was used to revise a rating scale that had been developed to cover these matters in a previous year. The rating scale was then used by cooperating teachers, supervisors, and the student teacher as one means of evaluating effectiveness in working with pupils. And the lists together with the rating scales became parts of the students' notebooks.

At the end of the senior year students write a summary of their two-year experience. The excerpts from the account below indicate further how direct experience (student teaching), courses, and evaluation move forward together. They are significant as an evaluation of one individual and as an appraisal of the program:

I vividly remember my first day in education. The more I heard and saw, the more surprised I was. It all seemed such a drastic change from the elementary school I had attended that I could not imagine for the life of me how it could work. . . . There were many questions in my mind to which I intended to find satisfying answers. After all, it is not so easy to discard something you have accepted all your life. . . .

As we became acquainted with the classes, we began to help the teachers and the children. The teacher of the room into which I settled helped me all she could to feel at home. I had many conferences with her in which she answered . . . questions, gave helpful suggestions and analyzed children and situations for my benefit.

[7] Final Report of the College of William and Mary to the Commission on Teacher Education, Appendices, pp. 84 ff.

Sometimes I helped the children with construction, sometimes with reading.

In the college classroom our professor encouraged us to ask questions, the answers to which she sometimes helped us to formulate and at other times left for us to find. Our classroom discussions were most significant. They were invaluable to me during my junior year and have helped me immensely during the proceedings with the children in the senior year. I had never felt too free before in any class to give my opinion. In most classes I have listened quietly and taken notes. In my education classes I didn't want to be quiet; I wanted to think, say what I thought, and hear what my classmates had to say. Our professor created, fostered, and stimulated this desire in all of us. . . .

We discussed education from all angles, learned the fundamentals together and filled in the details for ourselves. As we saw the same principles carried out again and again, they became natural to us. We understood the philosophy, for we saw it applied, and we were beginning to forget the situations in which we were educated. Teaching took on a new meaning for me; it was going to be so much more interesting than anything I had ever expected. . . .

Did we have notebooks? . . . we did, and nothing was left out of them. Although at the first of the year getting these notebooks together seemed to be more work than we could hope to do in a whole year, we always managed. What I . . . got . . . out of making those notebooks was certainly worth the time and work it took for they have helped me in planning and recording during my senior year and I know will help me when I go out to teach. Our own questions and answers about teaching in general and about the various subjects took up a great deal of the space in these notebooks. We learned how to analyze ourselves as well as the children. We learned practically to reproduce, on paper, life in the classroom by making charts of movement, writing plans, keeping a diary, writing the stories of the rooms, recording incidents and evaluations.

We had a review of all that we had learned in the first semester of the junior year when in the second semester we planned for a year's work in an imaginary room. I remember how slow I was in getting started in this. . . . Ideas never seem to come to me quickly. . . . But I got busy . . . and soon it kept increasing until I hardly knew where to stop.

In Matthew Whaley I had many experiences in different rooms until I thought I had covered the whole school program. Fortunately for me, the teacher whom I was with first gave me freely of her time. In the afternoons we would often sit and analyze situations and the children and talk over future plans. She was really marvelous at getting at the core of a situation or of a child. Every once in a while she would write me notes full of stimulating suggestions. . . . Those hours I spent talking with her in the afternoons just flew and it always seemed as if we could have talked forever. . . . We student teachers were all given a group of about seven children to analyze as thoroughly as possible and . . . we helped the teacher make out her own analysis sheets. Most of our regular Monday and Wednesday afternoon conferences for quite a while were spent in analyzing first the children and then ourselves.

. . . There were varied experiences . . . one day we received a note in the class in which I was then living, asking us to give a "happy story" [children's name for stories about life in their school] in the auditorium. We discussed the idea and the entire class was very much in favor of it. Then followed a week of eager story writing. . . . We wanted a play so we discussed the characteristics of a good play and . . . voted for the best. . . . We then began organizing the story. . . . Our main aim was that the audience be able to understand the point of the . . . story. The children decided on the scenery, made it, and put it in its place on the stage. . . . Characters were chosen and their parts decided on but no child had anything definite that he was to say—he had the main ideas and made up the words that came naturally to him. We dramatized first in the room and then in the auditorium. The play was darling, and I know their classmates were as proud of the participants as I was.

. . . You can see why I think so much of this experience. I saw many sides of the life in the room. I helped with reading, writing, and dramatics. Developing the . . . story into a play for the school made me feel as though I was accomplishing something. The teacher turned the class over to me and I felt the responsibility of guiding the children. I carried out my own plans; . . . I felt self-confident, responsible, and happy. This was my big experience. . . .

I think if I had had short experiences in more rooms under more teachers it would have prepared me better than the longer experiences did. But as it is, I have seen good and poor work. I have seen indifferent rooms with teachers or student teachers struggling in ways I hope to avoid. . . . I saw children adore the teacher. I also heard children call a teacher names. . . . A teacher must win her class if she is to succeed. I think a teacher can emphasize too much the good she wants in the children. I saw a teacher think and analyze genuinely in terms of the children and yet they resented her; maybe it was the age of the children but I think not. . . .

My last experience was in analyzing growth in myself and the children. I observed whatever hours I could and tried to see in the varied situations what growth there had been during the year. Experience in analyzing is valuable for us since it is so much a part of a teacher's life.[8]

In the program as a whole the main source of evidence for evaluation is in the student's teaching, how he works with boys and girls and his cooperating teacher and supervisor. Observation is the chief means of gathering this evidence. The notebooks provide a second source. Individual conferences and group discussions and reports sometimes lead to the development of familiar evaluative techniques—such as a rating scale or test. The dominant focus of the whole program upon the individual student and upon the importance of learning by doing helps to make evaluation, within the program, center on personal records and on activities that are in many ways indistinguishable from the regular learning activities of the courses. Thus, teaching, learning, evaluating—all drawing their material from direct experiences the students are having—are closely related throughout the professional program.

UNIQUE OPPORTUNITY FOR EVALUATION IN STUDENT TEACHING

The approaches to evaluation we have described, though different, have elements in common. At Ohio State University, we centered our attention on the development and use of an observational guide and record. Observation and rating were the chief techniques described at Furman University. At Michigan State College our chief interest was in the use of student diaries or logs and in an activities checklist based upon the program's objectives. At Teachers College the use of student reports of problems and needs met in their practice teaching was described. At William and Mary we described the use of discussions and notebooks for evaluation. With the possible exception of the activities checklist none of these techniques is what we would ordinarily think of as objective. They all involve a large element of subjective judgment. They may all be called descriptive records. In the guide to observation, the descriptive record and interpretation are usually written by some observer. In the diaries

[8] *Ibid.*, "Report," pp. 60-62.

or logs, and in the statements of problems and needs, the record is written by the one who is having the experience; it is a personal document.

Each of these methods is well suited to the unique possibilities of evaluation in student teaching. Their focus is on the overt behavior of the student in his daily work as a teacher. Their focus is on application, on evidence that the student is recognizing and taking advantage of opportunities, is putting his knowledge into practice in his relationships with people— pupils, peers, administrators, parents. Student teaching is what the student does when he works with his pupils face to face, when he plans with them, when he asks and answers questions, when he counsels with them, when he develops illustrations and expositions and discussions. It is what he does when he works with parents and supervisors and principals and other teachers. It is this emphasis upon the behavior that is *teaching* that makes the use of descriptive records well adapted to the unique possibilities of evaluation in this phase of teacher education. Paper-and-pencil tests to measure student ability to apply theory are one fairly long step removed from the real thing. The abilities they reveal are heavily loaded with linguistic and intellectual factors more or less isolated from the personalities, emotions, visual cues, and changing conditions that are always present in face-to-face teaching. Intelligence and the ability to interpret the abstract symbols of language are most certainly important in teaching. But the student teacher's ability to draw conclusions from observing Mary's behavior is not identical with the ability to interpret it from a written description. Of course, the two abilities are related, but their relation is not so high that we can use a measure of the one as a substitute for or index of the other. In the colleges whose programs we have described in part, the emphasis in evaluation has been on trying to observe and record as adequately as possible the dynamic behavior that is involved in student teaching. We believe that this focus is good and that it is the most appropriate one we now have for the evaluation of student teaching. But there is much to be learned about the use of observational records and personal documents.

IMPROVING OBSERVATION

What are some of the conditions requisite to good observation and recording? The quality of observation depends upon many things. It depends on the observer's ability to see what happened. This, in turn, depends on his background, on what he is "set" to see, on how well he understands the purposes of his observation, and on his sensitivity to behavior that is significant as evidence of the teacher's competence. Good recording likewise depends on all these as well as on a number of mechanical or technical matters—for example, on the observer's ability to express himself in writing, on the time elapsing between the observation and the recording, on the extent to which the record consists of facts separated from rather than interwoven with the interpretations and opinions of the observer, and on the extent to which the simple facts of what happened are supplemented by a brief account of the situation or circumstance in which they happened.

Beyond these considerations is the matter of interpreting the record. Here it is important that the interpreter be able to see the significance of an activity or item of behavior in relation to goals, to place appropriate value on the data. Schemes for classifying the observed behavior are of special importance in this connection. Classifications may be incorporated in the guide to observation, with illustrative types of behavior organized under headings describing the goals or competence to be looked for; or some system of classification may be imposed upon the anecdotes after they have been recorded. The former method is probably preferable. In either case the ability to interpret correctly depends upon one's knowledge and insight into human behavior and teaching and the basic sciences underlying them. It is also desirable to keep one's interpretations highly tentative until the results of several observations can be seen in some perspective. Moreover, because similar behavior can be exhibited in response to quite different purposes and motivations, the observer by himself is frequently not in a position to interpret a particular event fairly. It is therefore important to find out what the person who was observed was trying to do, to discover his purposes and intentions. That is one reason why, in the description of procedures at Ohio State University and Michigan State College, such stress was put upon conferences between the student teacher and the observer or supervisor. When the student knows that the observer will merely describe what happened and that the interpretation of what happened will be discussed cooperatively afterwards, he is quite willing to have the observer take extensive notes during the class period. Thus, the accuracy of final interpretation depends in part upon the techniques and procedures followed in the whole process of observing, recording, and judging. In this area of evaluation, as in so many others, genuine democratic regard for the integrity of all persons involved is an element that must not be overlooked. Cooperation contributes to both the accuracy and validity of the record.

Diaries, logs, and student reports of problems and difficulties met in practice teaching are first-person documents. The students' "planning paper," described in the orientation program at Ohio State University, was another example of a personal document used for evaluative purposes. Many of the cautions to be observed in using them are similar to those we have just discussed in relation to descriptive records.

SOME PROBLEMS AND SUGGESTIONS

In concluding this chapter several major problems in the evaluation of student teaching might be emphasized. There are at least a few suggestions which seem to be justified by various experiences within the cooperative study of teacher education.

First of all, the purposes in evaluating student teaching need to be clarified. One purpose focuses on the student teacher. What kind of teacher is he? What are his strengths and weaknesses? What does he need to do to improve? What progress does he make? What competence does he reveal? A second purpose focuses on the situation in which he does his teaching. Does it offer opportunity for a wide variety of experience? Does it give him an opportunity to plan with students, with other teachers, to study children on the playground and at home as well as in the classroom, to develop or collect new materials, to

see the program of his special area in relation to the total program of the school? A third purpose of evaluation focuses on
the general and professional education which precedes, and
which is presumably tested in, student teaching. What are the
strengths and weaknesses of the student's preparation? What is
the relative success of students with different subject-matter
backgrounds? Does the preparation of students in general and
professional education gear in to the needs of the pupils they
teach? All of these purposes are interrelated. One cannot judge
the success of the student fairly unless the program of student
teaching has given him an opportunity to reveal his talent. Nor
can one judge fairly the worth of the student's general and professional background without knowing much about the student
himself and about the opportunity he has had to demonstrate
his application of general knowledge and professional skill.

A second problem and suggestion for evaluation in student
teaching lies in the need for getting many people to share in
planning and carrying out the program. Students, cooperating
teachers, supervisors, and the faculty members responsible for
general and professional education, should all be concerned
about the performance of the student teacher; how well he does
reflects upon all of them. If one has a thorough evaluation of
the effectiveness of a student teacher in fulfilling his responsibilities, he has, from the same data, evidence of the effectiveness
of the student's general and other professional education. These
data need to be summarized, communicated to appropriate
faculty members, and used in the continuous improvement of
the educational program. Probably all staff members who have
contributed to a student's progress would profit from participation in the evaluation of student teaching, from observing the
student in action, examining the materials prepared, and appraising the situation in which he was receiving his experience.
Within the cooperative study there have been a few scattered
but notable examples of the value of such broad participation.
A science teacher in a college program of general education,
after studying a high school science program and observing student teachers in that situation, took the initiative in bringing

about badly needed changes in the science aspect of the institution's work in general education and its program for majors in the science area. A summary of technical skills unprovided for in the regular program of agricultural education but demanded of students in their practice teaching became the basis in another college for developing a skills laboratory.

A third problem relates to the need for a synthesizing framework in which the whole program of professional education including student teaching may be examined. One reason why the evaluation of student teaching has frequently been carried on apart from an evaluation of the rest of the students' program is that few institutions have developed, for themselves and with their students, any coordinated statement of goals toward which their total program is directed. This problem, of course, emphasizes again the importance of the fullest faculty participation in evaluation.

And finally, there is need for improving the methods of gathering and interpreting data relative to the effectiveness of student teaching. It is worth while here to repeat that student teaching can provide a rich opportunity for a person to express in action his ability to fulfill the responsibilities of a teacher. The problem is to observe and record accurately what the student does and to study its significance in relation to professional goals. It is the recording that is frequently omitted from the evaluation procedures. Often supervisors observe but enter only their judgments on a rating scale. Perhaps only a final grade is filed in the placement office. Judgments should be carefully supported by descriptive incidents, by concrete data that can be discussed with the student. There is need, also, to discover ways of making anecdotal records practical from the standpoint of content and the time consumed in keeping and interpreting them. We need to explore further the contribution a student teacher can himself make to the accumulation and interpretation of data concerning his own experience. We need to explore ways in which the student teacher and supervisor can gain from pupils evidence with respect to the student teacher's effectiveness. Since we have no automatic devices for measuring competence in student teaching, and perhaps never will have, we need to employ to the full the combined wisdom of all who may be in a position to help in arriving at valid judgments. Competence in observing and interpreting behavior is not a simple skill. Many hours and years of study and experience may be directed toward its improvement. And here, as in many other decisions, two heads are better than one.

VII

Follow-up Studies

THIS CHAPTER on the follow-up study as a focus for evaluative activities continues the sequence of problems or areas around which evaluations in the colleges and school systems associated in the cooperative study of teacher education have centered. The follow-up study represents both a culmination of evaluative activity at the pre-service level and a connecting link between pre-service and in-service activities. Its role as the climax of evaluative concern at the pre-service level is clear. Selection, orientation, general education, professional education, and student teaching have as their common objective the preparation of competent teachers. The ultimate test of their combined effect is how teachers behave on the job. The opportunity to apply this test comes when they first go to work. In a sense the evidence which one can obtain from follow-up studies constitutes the proof of the pudding—not only for the pre-service program as a whole but likewise for special aspects of that program. The function of follow-up studies as a connecting link between pre-service and in-service education is suggested by the fact that a follow-up study compels the college to look beyond its own boundaries, to appraise its program in the light of the performance of men and women under conditions which the college does not itself set up. This directs the college to look at the public schools and the larger community. Thus a need for cooperation and understanding between pre-service and in-service personnel is apparent.

The objectives or purposes that will guide the designing of a follow-up study may be as broad as the purposes of the program of pre-service education. Whatever objectives are held for the latter are pertinent leads for inquiries in the former. If an objective of the college is to develop student interest in community affairs such as participation in church programs, young people's clubs, civic organizations, local government, then a follow-up inquiry might appropriately discover the extent to which this hoped-for interest actually found expression in the lives of the graduates. The objectives for a follow-up study should, in other words, be the same as those which define the educational program of the college. Of course, the details and the manifestations of the objectives—that is, the evidence to be looked for— would not be identical in the two cases. If objectives for neither have been clarified the college can begin at whichever place it chooses—with institutional objectives, or with a description of the behavior which it believes should characterize its graduates.

Depending on its scope, the follow-up study can contribute to many phases of the college's program. From it suggestions can be drawn for the selection and guidance program, the general education program, the professional program. It can contribute to staff members' understanding of in-service needs. It can help students gain keener appreciation of what is likely to face them after they leave school. It can contribute substantially to the improvement of college instruction.

A FOLLOW-UP OF GENERAL EDUCATION

An example of an extensive follow-up study designed to con tribute to the evaluation and improvement of general education is the one made at the University of Minnesota.[1] In the belief that general education should focus its content in part on the problems and needs which students were likely to face in the adult world, the General College set out to collect a great many specific facts about the lives of former university students. To a sample of men and women who had been away from the campus from one to twelve years, some having graduated and some not, the General College mailed an elaborate, illustrated fifty-two-page questionnaire. The answers to this instrument provided the basis for an evaluation of college education and the springboard for generalizations regarding its possible improvement.

Although the questionnaire was exceptionally long it was re-

[1] C. Robert Pace, *They Went to College* (Minneapolis: University of Minnesota Press, 1941).

turned completely filled out by 70 percent of the former students
to whom it was sent. Several factors may account for this high
proportion of returns: the attractive design and format of the
questionnaire, the use of five follow-up notices and, perhaps
most important, the satisfaction of a comprehensive self-analysis
for those who filled it out.

CHECKLISTS OF ACTIVITIES

The content of the questionnaire was divided into four sections, dealing respectively with earning a living, home and family life, socio-civic affairs, and personal life. Within each section
there were checklists of pertinent facts or activities, needs for
more information, interests, and opinions. Most of the items
were submitted by General College staff members. Some were
taken from published tests. For all items the criteria for inclu-
sion were their probable value in judging and improving general
education, and the extent to which they would round out a significant picture of the lives of young adults.

The questionnaire as a whole sought to find out what young
men and women were doing, feeling, and thinking since they
left college. It did not ask directly their opinions about the
values of college experience. The staff believed that a summary
of the status and behavior of former students would give a
better index of the effectiveness of education. The staff could
make its own interpretations from the lives former students
were living. For example, a question such as "Of what value
was your university experience in developing interest, participation, and insight into current social, political, and economic problems?" was not asked. Rather, an attempt was made
to find out what activities these former students actually participated in, what attitudes toward social, political, and economic issues they held, what problems they were concerned
about, what current topics they most frequently talked about,
and what sources they actually used in keeping informed about
contemporary affairs. Checklists of activities and discussion topics, and a scale of social, political, economic attitudes were
among the specific techniques for gaining this information.

The following questions are selected from one of the check-lists in this area:[2]

SOCIO-CIVIC AFFAIRS

Your Activities

Please place an x before each activity in which you have engaged during the past year.

_____1. I voted.

_____2. I campaigned for one or more election candidates.

_____3. I signed one or more petitions to be presented to govern-ment officials.

_____4. I wrote a letter to a government official or a newspaper about a social, economic, or political problem.

_____5. I attended meetings of a political club.

_____6. I borrowed books from a public library.

_____7. I attended one or more public musical concerts.

_____8. I was a member of a church organization.

_____9. I gave aid to the Community Fund, Red Cross, or similar agency.

_____10. I deposited money in a bank.

_____11. I carried public liability automobile insurance.

_____12. I was involved in a legal dispute.

An analysis of the replies to some of the questions in the socio-civic area revealed that:

Their [the former students'] attitudes toward fundamentally re-lated social issues were markedly inconsistent. They exhibited con-cern about governmental policies, but except for voting they failed to make use of the political processes through which public opinion in a democracy is expressed. They were interested in national prob-lems but not in specific attempts being made to solve national problems. They expressed a desire for more reliable sources of in-formation about current affairs, but they read biased magazines. They failed to take an active interest in community affairs.[3]

THE PROBLEM OF INTERPRETATION

The breadth of specific information collected in each of the four areas made possible the type of analysis quoted above and provided the faculty not only with bases for generalizations re-

---

[2] *Ibid., passim.*
[3] *Ibid.,* pp. 121-22.

garding major modifications needed in the educational program but also with a vast store of facts and illustrative material to implement the new emphases that seemed to be called for. Moreover, the type of follow-up study that centers its attention on behavior rather than opinions is not vulnerable to the criticism that people cannot appraise the value of their own education fairly or reliably. The appraisal, in this case, is made by the faculty and research experts. There are, of course, limitations to the checklist technique and these will be discussed later.

Because the burden of interpretation falls upon the faculty and technical staff, a brief description of the way in which the study proceeded may be helpful to others. In the Minnesota study it was possible to assume that the faculty wished to receive and use the results of the follow-up study. Most of the items for the questionnaire had been prepared by the faculty. The study itself was part of a program of curriculum revision in which the faculty was closely involved. Changes in the content and organization of courses were being made and the study was designed to contribute to those changes. Moreover, the technical staff sought and got from the faculty many suggestions for analyzing the data in ways that would be most useful to them. As the data were tabulated they were fed back to the faculty. They were not presented in complicated statistical tables, but in relatively simple lists showing the percentages of replies to different items. And these lists were conveniently grouped to show what activities, problems, and attitudes characterized the majority of former students and what characterized only a very small proportion of them. Only the data from the published tests were given in statistical tables. The director of the study discussed the results with the faculty, both in individual interviews and in group meetings. Committees on the interpretation of results were set up, one for each major curriculum area of the college. The chairmen of these committees prepared reports setting forth the generalizations and interpretations they were willing to make in their areas, and the implications for better teaching in their areas. Differences in interpretation were discussed. Out of this process came a composite picture of the meaning and significance of the study to the college. Through participation in the process, interest in the product was maintained and developed.

A COMPREHENSIVE ANALYSIS OF OPINIONS

A follow-up study of graduates who had gone into teaching was made at Stanford University.[4] An all-university committee was set up to supervise the investigation, reflecting the belief that the teacher-training practices of the entire university should be considered, not just those of the School of Education. A director was responsible for carrying out the study. After preliminary conferences, readings, and inspection of many instruments, the director constructed three questionnaires, each to serve a different purpose. A description in some detail of these questionnaires and the groups to which they were sent will help to define the nature and scope of the project.

The first and longest questionnaire was designed for Stanford graduates engaged in educational activity. The group selected for the inquiry was as follows: all who received doctors' degrees between the years 1930 and 1940; all who received masters' degrees in 1930, and between the years 1935 and 1940; all who received credentials between the years 1935 and 1940. There were 2,372 graduates of the university during this period who received doctors' and masters' degrees or credentials, and 1,012 of them were found to be engaged in teaching—48 percent of the total group. The questionnaire was sent to this group of 1,012 former students, and replies were received from 61 percent. That 48 percent of the larger group were engaged in teaching was rather convincing proof that a major function of the graduate program, whether recognized or not, was the training of teachers. When the departments of law, business, and engineering were eliminated from this total group, it was found that 59 percent of the remaining graduates were engaged in teaching. It is possible that many colleges and universities would find similarly high percentages of their graduates engaged in teaching if they would assemble the necessary figures. Specific information of this sort

[4] Walter W. Isle, "The Stanford University Follow-Up Inquiry" (unpublished dissertation for the Ed.D. degree in the files of Stanford University, 1942).

might lead many colleges and universities to devote a larger share of attention to a task which they do not at present realize as being so important to so many students. Further facts about the 616 questionnaire respondents are the following: 24 percent had received credentials, 44 percent had received masters' degrees, and 32 percent had received doctors' degrees; 45 percent had graduated with majors in education, and 55 percent with majors in academic subjects; 43 percent were holding teaching jobs in high schools, 45 percent in colleges, and 12 percent in administration. Most members of the credentials and masters groups were employed in high schools, while most of the doctors were employed in colleges.

QUESTIONNAIRES TO ALUMNI AND EMPLOYERS

The questionnaire itself was designed to cover all aspects of Stanford's teacher-educating procedures—the general education program, the counseling and guidance, student teaching, extra-curricular activities, professional subjects, research for advanced degrees, and so forth—rather than centering attention on a few aspects of the total program. Almost all of the questions were of the kind which call for subjective judgments or ratings, rather than simple checklists of behavior or facts. The twelve-page questionnaire was concerned with nine major topics treated under the following headings:

General considerations
Courses, procedures, and services
Appraisal of attitudes and indirect influences
General education
Placement
Growth and promotion
Professional and academic background
Activities and responsibilities
How do Stanford-trained teachers keep alive and up to date?

The following excerpt illustrates the typical form of question used:[5]

[5] *The Stanford University Follow-Up Inquiry: A Study of Stanford's Teacher Preparation Services, Form A*, Stanford University, 1941, pp. 3-4.

II. Courses, Procedures, and Services

1. List what you consider the three most valuable courses in your Stanford program:

_____

2. List the three courses which, in your estimation, represent the most of wasted time and effort in your Stanford program:

_____

3. How much of value did you receive from the following:

	Much	Some	Little
a. Research for master's degree dissertation			
b. Research for doctor's degree dissertation			
c. Foreign languages to satisfy degree requirements			
d. Background courses required for degree program			
e. Work done by independent study plan			
f. Classroom procedures: lectures, discussion, etc.			
g. Conferences with other students			
h. Personal conferences with faculty members			
i. _____			

Explanations and suggestions:_____

4 Indicate your appraisal of the Stanford services listed below as to how adequately they met your needs as a prospective teacher:

	Adequately	Somewhat Adequately	Inade-quately
a. Personal guidance			
b. Vocational guidance			
c. Educational guidance			
d. Physical health facilities			
e. Library facilities and services			
f. Housing facilities			
g. Variety of courses available			
h. Facilities for recreation			
i. Cultural services, as Tuesday evening hour, artists series, etc.			
j. _____			

How might these services be better utilized for teacher preparation?

_____

5. How much of value did you realize from your practice teaching at Stanford?

	Much	Some	Little
a. Through the work of the general supervisors:			
1) In developing broad concepts of teaching			
2) In assistance with problems through private conferences			
3) _____			
b. Through the work of the supervising teacher:			
1) In providing sufficient actual teaching experiences			
2) In providing specific helpful suggestions			
3) _____			
c. Through the general weekly conferences:			
1) In outlining of problems and procedures			
2) In giving patterns of school organizations, programs, etc.			
3) In demonstrations of skills and procedures			
4) _____			

239

The second questionnaire was designed for the employers or supervisors of Stanford-trained teachers. Its purpose was to obtain judgments from them regarding the effectiveness of the individuals concerned. It was sent to the employers of the 1,012 Stanford graduates engaged in teaching. Altogether, there were 376 separate employers (so far as their names and addresses could be determined) to whom this form was sent, from one to thirty-three copies of the form going to each, depending upon the number of Stanford graduates he had under his jurisdiction. Sixty-nine percent of the questionnaires were returned. A quotation from the final report of the inquiry will serve to describe the scope of this questionnaire:

. . . Part I lists ten qualities or aspects of the individual's training for appraisal "in terms of your own standards as to what constitutes adequate training for the work being performed," this appraisal to be expressed as "superior," "average," or "inferior." Part II lists thirty descriptive qualities of "attitudes, knowledge, and other basic equipment which are currently proposed as desirable for a satisfactorily trained teacher." The respondent is requested to "indicate the extent to which you think the possession of these qualities is indicated by the work of this individual." The captions "to a great extent," "to some extent," and "to little or no extent" are provided for this appraisal.

Part III submits more general questions which do not tie the respondent to a checklist for his replies. He is asked simply to note any specific items of strength or weakness in the training of the teacher, as evidenced in the performance of the teacher in question. Part IV seeks to establish the relation, or lack of relation existing between the weaknesses cited and Stanford training.[6]

The third questionnaire was mailed along with the second one to 305 of the employers and supervisors of Stanford-trained teachers. Fifty-one percent of the questionnaires were returned. It was designed to obtain answers to the following basic questions: "What information concerning prospective teachers do employers desire? What do employers and supervisors consider important in the training of their teachers? What suggestions for the improvement of training practices do they have for an institution desiring 'to set up the best program of teacher edu-

[6] Isle, *op. cit.*, pp. 248-49.

cation that can be devised in the light of present knowledge and experience'?"[7] These matters were considered supplementary to, rather than a part of, the main purpose of the investigation— namely, an appraisal of the Stanford program. Both of the questionnaires to employers were much briefer than the single questionnaire to former students.

VALUES OF THE STUDY

The chief source of data in the Stanford study was the former students themselves, and their replies to the questionnaire were conscientious, thoughtful, and enthusiastic. They were, indeed, more discriminating about the Stanford program than were their employers. They used all possible choices on the checklists and ratings in expressing their judgments, and more than 90 percent of them wrote some comments or suggestions supplementing their answers to the questions asked in the study. In contrast, the employers tended to use superlatives so freely that "the interpretation of the results [was] seriously handicapped."[8]

The outstanding impression from the questionnaires was that "Stanford-trained teachers are well satisfied with their Stanford experience, and that employers and supervisors are well pleased with Stanford-trained teachers."[9] Within this over-all belief there were aspects of the program which received special praise and others which were mentioned as particularly in need of improvement. For example, one of the most valued features of the program was "the individual attention paid the student and the close relationship between the student and the instructor."[10] Thorough grounding in subject matter was regarded as another strong feature of the program. On the other hand, practice teaching was an experience which many of the former students criticized. They thought that practice teaching should be more realistic. The time devoted to it should be lengthened, it should come earlier in the training program, and the schools in which it is done should be more nearly like the ones in which most

[7] *Ibid.*, p. 271.
[8] *Ibid.*, p. 317.
[9] *Ibid.*, p. 319.
[10] *Ibid.*, p. 320.

Stanford-trained teachers will find employment. Another suggestion was to draw more extensively upon opportunities for participation in campus life and for participation in the community life of the San Francisco Bay region. Former students said that these resources were not drawn upon extensively in their own preparation for teaching and their jobs called for considerable participation in and supervision of the activities of their own students in relation to school and community affairs. Another recommendation called for improving the services in counseling and guidance. Former students said that while the university does a good job of teaching counseling and guidance in theory, it does not exemplify these procedures in its own program. Still another recommendation called for a more complete and continuous program of follow-up service. Such a service, the alumni said, would provide the college with a continual check on its teacher-training curriculum and instructional procedures and with a means of keeping them both in tune with the experience of teachers in the field.

These recommendations are typical of many others in the full report of the Stanford inquiry. The extent to which such recommendations will result in changed policies, practices, and procedures is a question which will be decided ultimately by the college faculty and administration. Few people, however, will fail to recognize the incentive to action and the basis for wise action provided through this systematic appraisal of the college by the consumer.

A BRIEF SURVEY

A similar type of follow-up study was conducted on a much smaller scale at Teachers College, Columbia in the spring of 1941. Approximately sixty students had graduated from the special fifth-year program at Teachers College the previous year, and a four-page questionnaire was sent to as many of these as could be located. Replies were received from thirty-seven, of whom twenty-eight were actually engaged in teaching. The questionnaire itself consisted of three types of item. First there were questions of fact, such as: What is your job? What are your duties? What is your salary? Will you be continued in the job next year? The second type called for general ratings, such as: How well do you like your job? How well do you like teaching as a profession? What is your estimate of the value of the special pre-service program as compared with the conventional program? The third type called for brief essay responses. The pre-service program had been divided into approximately three equal units: a central seminar, a divisional seminar, and practice teaching. With respect to each of these three units, two questions were asked: What experiences proved to be especially helpful to you in your job? What additions or modifications would you suggest in the light of your job experience? A final question requested suggestions for improving the pre-service program as a whole.

The significant results of the study may be summarized very briefly. Former students said that the chief values derived from the central seminar had been increased understanding of educational philosophy and a broad concept of the role of the teacher; from the divisional seminar the chief value had been the consideration of actual teaching problems; from practice teaching the chief values had been the general nature of the experience itself and the contacts with children. For the central seminar, they recommended more emphasis upon psychology and upon the practical illustrations and consequences of educational theory. For the divisional seminar, they recommended closer relationship to practice teaching experience so that the discussions and assignments would be more evidently applicable. For practice teaching, they recommended more of it and greater variety.

The results of this study, with their repeated emphasis on the importance of the practical aspects of the training program, suggests the importance of so teaching that the maximum transfer of ideas and information from college theory to classroom practice will be attained. In the opinion of these alumni, greater contact with children in school would help the program attain a greater amount of practical value. Former students of both Stanford and Teachers College expressed this judgment.

THE TECHNIQUES OF FOLLOW-UP STUDY

In the illustrations of follow-up studies we have given, one technique seems to be basic—the questionnaire. There are, of course, variations in the use of this technique, variations in the purposes for making follow-up studies, and variations in the types of person from whom information and views are sought. These variations are interrelated. Some discussion, therefore, of the relative values and limitations of different approaches and the possibilities of other techniques such as direct observation, interviews, and conferences may prove helpful.

Questionnaires have been of two major types. They have sought to find out the activities, behavior, or practices of the group being studied; or they have sought to find out directly the group's opinion regarding the values of previous educational experience. Within the first type there have been both checklists and items of a more general or essay type. Both have their advantages and disadvantages.

Suppose a teachers college wishes to find out the kinds of activity its graduates engage in on their jobs, or more specifically, suppose the college wishes to discover the extent to which its graduates are using desirable methods in their teaching. The faculty could prepare a checklist of activities which could be sent to the graduates. The graduates would then check those activities they had engaged in. The list may, of course, suggest to them a number of activities in which they did not engage but which they feel they should have undertaken. They may, consciously or unconsciously, check some things they have not really done. But clear, specific, and brief items plus good rapport between the college and its alumni should minimize whatever tendency there may be to check items falsely. On the other hand, the checklist of activities may be too short; it may not include some of the important practices a particular teacher has been following. One of the advantages of the checklist type of instrument is that a large number of specific factors can be sampled without demanding too much of the graduates' time in answering them. In general, this advantage should not be lost by limiting too drastically the number of items in the checklist.

A particular faculty may wish to use the essay type of question instead of a checklist. They might phrase the same question given above somewhat as follows: "The pre-service program of the college emphasized, among other things, the value of such educational practices as field trips, visual aids, community studies, case studies, and so forth. Have you had any opportunities during the past year to engage in some of these activities? If so, which ones, and what successes or difficulties did you meet?" Individual answers to such a question may be more revealing than responses to a checklist. On the other hand, because of the pressure of other work, or for a variety of reasons, the graduate may answer the question very briefly. A weakness of essay questions is the unevenness of response one invariably gets. Failure to mention an activity does not mean that the teacher has not engaged in it; it may simply mean that he forgot to mention it, although it is probably true that the ones he does mention are considered most important. The task of summarizing and interpreting essay responses is usually more difficult and time consuming than it is for responses to checklists. This is especially true when one has gathered the opinions of a large number of people. If checklists have been used the task of summarizing 500 replies is not much greater than it is for 50 replies. Thus, while essay responses may reveal more about individuals, checklists may give a better picture of the total group. In many follow-up questionnaires, both types are used. A checklist of interests or activities, for example, is followed by space for the graduates to add other items or by a request to explain and comment on those which they have checked. Thus the advantages of both methods may be gained.

A questionnaire, instead of seeking to survey the behavior of alumni may consist of direct questions designed to reveal their opinions concerning the value of their pre-service training. The items, for example, might be of this type: "How would you rate the value to you of your course in educational psychology?" Obviously, the success of any attempt to measure directly alumni opinion regarding the value of various phases of their school preparation depends on the alumni's ability to introspect reliably. Among graduates who have been out of school for many years the answer to the question, "Was college worth while?" tends definitely to be affirmative, perhaps largely because a halo is put upon education by society in general. This halo tends to make the judgment of "old grads" unreliable; memory of what they actually got in college is blurred. This is much less true of the opinions of recent graduates. Experiencing the demands of new tasks during their first few years out of school, they are in a much better position to reflect critically and reliably on the values and shortcomings of their preparation for discharging these responsibilities effectively. If their jobs have made demands on them which they felt ill prepared to meet they are likely to be vividly aware of it.

Although other techniques for follow-up studies were not illustrated, the possibilities of observation, interviews, and conferences may be noted briefly. All require personal relations of some sort, as contrasted with the questionnaire technique which demands no person-to-person contact. Some of the values and limitations of observation as an evaluation technique were discussed in the preceding chapter. Perhaps the fact that alumni are difficult to reach individually, together with the time-consuming nature of observation, accounts for the failure to use the technique oftener. The method does have, however, some special values. By getting members of the college faculty to visit their former students, to observe their classes, to discuss their problems with them, the college can succeed not only in collecting data for the appraisal of its program but also in sensitizing its staff to the needs and peculiarities of the area served by the college. Because such visitation cannot be made except through agreement and cooperation with school superintendents, principals, and supervisors, the process can help to develop better relationships between pre-service and in-service institutions. If the college places many of its graduates in nearby public schools where many of its current students also do practice teaching, a combination of services can be effected involving three functions—supervising student teachers, helping recent graduates, and gathering data for evaluation of the college program.

Observation is an eyewitness technique; in this respect it is similar to the type of questionnaire which is focused on activities rather than opinions. The interview technique is more like the opinion survey. One gets facts and judgments by talking with graduates rather than by observing their activity in some particular situation. Interviews can foster the same by-products of mutual understanding and service as the observational technique.

Conferences are a third variety of direct-contact technique. From conferences with alumni groups, or with employers, one can get an interplay of ideas, resulting either in a consensus or in the revelation of several trends in group opinion. Adequate records of conference discussions are a prerequisite to the use of this technique for evaluation. What one gets from a questionnaire is an expression of individual judgment, and the sum of these judgments reveals the trends of thinking in the group. In a conference the views of many individuals are submerged, or at least are not identifiable as readily as they are from questionnaires. For many purposes this may, however, be adequate.[11]

The most meaningful follow-up evaluation of a college's program will come from an analysis of the behavior and opinions of the direct consumers of that education. While the questionnaire has been the method most commonly used for this purpose, no single technique is adequate for the issues a really comprehensive follow-up study will encounter. We may hope that some day a college will dare to evaluate its program not only through extensive questionnaires, interviews, and observational probing into the activities and thinking of its former students, but will add to these techniques some well prepared tests designed to measure the understanding of important facts and principles and ideas.

[11] Fuller treatment of discussion as a technique of evaluation will be found in Chapter IX.

VIII

Growth in Service

THE TRANSITION from pre-service student to in-service teacher is not always smooth; evaluative practices could help make things a lot easier in many cases. Out of college, the recent graduate finds himself confronted with many new conditions and responsibilities. He is working among new people. No matter how excellent his preparation he finds much that is different from what he is used to or has anticipated. Frequently the principal or superintendent who hires him does not know very much about him. True, he has the new teacher's credentials: a record of his college grades, perhaps a list of his extracurricular activities, some census data (age, sex, and so on), and a brief paragraph by one or two professors commending his talents. The principal may also have interviewed him. But the total picture is usually sketchy. If typical placement credentials could be enriched by data from some of the evaluation practices we have described in the preceding chapters, they might be much more revealing and hence give a much better basis for the transition from college work to professional responsibilities.

During the whole of the pre-service program an educational history of each student is in the making. This may not be clear from the preceding chapters because we have described evaluation in aspects of programs from many different colleges. But it is apparent if we think of the activities as coordinated in a single institution. The chief authors of the history are the student, his adviser, his instructors, and the cooperating teacher with whom he does his student teaching. Sometimes they have collaborated in writing it and at other times each has written independently. The history begins with the potentialities and competence discovered in the student when he came to college (perhaps before that). It shows the emergence of various goals—individual, general, and professional—and what progress was made toward their attainment. It reveals achievements and failures, strengths and weaknesses. It contains personal documents, test data, ratings, records of observation, and much more. It has accumulated as the student progressed through the sequence of experience that constitutes his preparation for teaching. And it can continue throughout his professional career. Collaborators with him in the unfolding document will now be supervisors and principals instead of counselors and professors. One may hope that the potential value of such records will lead to more widespread demand for them.

The accumulation and use of comprehensive records of this sort, however, presupposes a pattern of attitudes and practices with respect to evaluation that does not always prevail in colleges and schools. It presupposes the practice of self-evaluation. It depends upon self-motivation, upon personal respect and security. It depends upon how the data are used. It depends, in short, upon many of the practices of cooperation and democracy which we suggested were important as we described evaluations in various colleges. At the in-service level, however, the basic importance of these attitudes and practices is revealed most clearly.

The significance of some of the ideas we have come to about evaluation is particularly well revealed by a consideration of evaluation as applied to teachers in service. From the beginning of the cooperative study it has been difficult to initiate studies of teacher effectiveness on the job. Evaluation was mistrusted. New attempts at appraisal were therefore resisted. Teachers were adults and they were privileged to resist what they disliked. But why was there resistance?

Teachers thought of evaluation in terms of the way it had been used on them. They recalled that supervisors and principals had rated them once or twice a year. Sometimes the ratings determined promotions or salary raises. Often the teachers remained relatively unfamiliar with the bases on which they were rated, and they got little professional help as a result of the ratings. Such procedures made frank discussion difficult. They put barriers between teachers and their employers. Teachers felt they must conceal their weaknesses to preserve their security.

Few had thought of evaluation as an activity calculated to improve their effectiveness.

Then too, and perhaps unconsciously, teachers did not want to submit to appraisal practices which might be similar to those which they exercised on pupils in their own classes. A teacher may have been willing to tell Mary, time after time, that she was at the 25th percentile in reading. But that teacher did not want to be told by the supervisor, time and again, that he was very poor at fulfilling some phase of his responsibility; he did not want to participate in an appraisal through which the supervisor might discover such a fact.

In the third place, many teachers were critical of evaluative procedures. They had seen so many tests given and ratings made which resulted in little use that they were impatient with attempts to appraise their own progress and accomplishment. Being adults and having adult responsibilities they regarded evaluation that was not aligned with their purposes as a waste of their time which they could not afford. In groups where teachers have been free to express their feelings this impatience has been quite evident. It has been noticeable, for example, in workshops where teachers' eagerness to make progress on their own problems has made them resist preparing special reports to determine what academic credit they should get, or filling out questionnaires to help someone evaluate the workshop. Evaluation which has not produced results which they could use has been disliked. This resistance to previous appraisals emphasizes the importance of trying to see the process of evaluation as inseparable from teaching and learning, and as characterized by genuine regard for individuality and personal security.

The appraisals of teacher growth which we describe in this chapter, and the evaluations of various programs and projects (chiefly workshops) which we shall discuss in Chapter IX, all illustrate these fundamental attitudes and concepts. The Ohio experiment will show some of the problems which arose when a project to observe teachers in service was carried out. The study of teacher-pupil relationships will demonstrate some of the precautions that were necessary in collecting significant professional data; it will also reveal the enthusiasm of teachers for knowledge which they regard as helpful and as contributing to their effectiveness. The account of evaluation in the Norris Schools will show what can happen to an apparently promising plan which does not prove to be in accord with the dominant interests of the teachers. The story of evaluation in the Moultrie High School will illustrate a close relationship between evaluation and both teaching and learning; it will indicate how evaluation may be a natural part of the teachers' regular work. Various implications about evaluative practices will be brought out in connection with each of the accounts.

AN EXPERIMENT IN DIRECTED OBSERVATION

When we described the development and use of the Ohio Teaching Record in the chapter on student teaching we indicated that it had been employed extensively with in-service teachers as well as student teachers and, in fact, that the ideas and experience of public school people had played a major role in its evolution. We can now give the details and at the same time emphasize several concepts about the evaluation of teacher growth in service. The story illustrates the importance of democratic procedure in evaluation projects which involve adults; it illustrates a useful technique of appraisal; and it illustrates a method of cooperation between college and public school personnel.

A workshop in teacher education held on the campus of Ohio State University in the summer of 1940 was one of a series of cooperative enterprises designed to bring the teacher-preparing agencies and the public schools of the state into more effective working relationship. One group at the workshop was particularly interested in evaluation. This group studied the "Observational Record," which had recently been drawn up at Ohio State University, and suggested many ways in which it could be made more usable with teachers. From these suggestions the Ohio Teaching Record, experimental edition, was devised. Moreover, tentative plans were made for an experiment aimed at the improvement of teaching in the school systems represented at the workshop, these improvements to be stimulated by observation and evaluation in which the Ohio Teaching Record would be used. At the close of the workshop administrators in each of the sixteen school systems represented agreed to discuss with their teachers the desirability of participating in such an experiment, and to meet in the fall for further planning.

Participation in the experiment was voluntary. Teachers in two of the school systems declined to take part. And nowhere was the decision to join made without much questioning. Some teachers were skeptical because the plan called for frequent observation of their work. Some were afraid that it was an entering wedge for a type of supervision the universities might want to exercise over the public schools. It was necessary to convince teachers that the experiment was motivated by a genuine desire to bring the resources of the universities and the schools to bear upon the one problem that is the concern of both, namely the improvement of education for the boys and girls of Ohio. The confidence between these two groups that had developed at the workshop did not transfer automatically to all teachers.

The fall planning meeting was attended by teachers, administrators, and members of the faculties of the several state-supported universities of Ohio. It was agreed that teachers would be observed once a week for ten weeks, that the anecdotal evidence from each observation would be discussed with the teachers, and that the copies of the Ohio Teaching Record on which the observations were recorded would be sent to Ohio State University for further study.

In all, there were nearly 600 teachers from 41 schools who took part in the project. Many details of the experiment were worked out by local groups—absolute uniformity not being required—and much was learned about observing, recording, and using the data as the study progressed. Also many problems arose. For example, it was necessary repeatedly to allay teachers' apprehensiveness about being observed: teachers and supervisors alike had difficulty grasping the full import of using the Record as a means for improving teaching rather than as a conventional rating scale. In some schools most of the observing was done by the local administrators; in other schools most of it was done by representatives from the universities. Nearly everyone failed to estimate adequately the amount of time the project would take. The time given to follow-up discussions with the teachers was sometimes cut short. In the concluding weeks of the experiment teachers were encouraged to visit each other.

At the end of the project a conference of representative participants was held to review and appraise the outcomes. Three questions were discussed: How can the Ohio Teaching Record be used effectively to improve teaching? What are the implications for teacher-preparing institutions? What major revisions need to be made in the Record and what supplementary data are needed? Much of the discussion led to changes that were incorporated in the revised edition of the Record and have already been described in Chapter VI. It was the consensus of the conference members that the following could be counted among the positive outcomes of the experiment:

1. The experiment has been a definite step in the direction of better relationships between the public schools and the universities.
2. The experiment has actually contributed to the improvement of teaching in many schools.
3. The experiment has resulted in improved observational practices.
4. Teachers understand more clearly the difficulties and problems associated with observation and supervision.
5. Increased sensitivity to some new concepts of good teaching has developed.
6. Teachers have become more sensitive to the procedures they employ; they see what they do moment by moment in relation to pupil outcomes; teaching has become more a *conscious process*.
7. Some new concepts concerning effective supervision have emerged.
8. The experiment has resulted in bringing down to the ground certain abstractions, or philosophic concepts about teaching.
9. New importance has been attached to the character and quality of pupil-teacher relations.
10. University people have had a refreshing direct contact with actual public school practice.
11. Teachers are more on their toes; frequent observations and conferences have stimulated them.
12. New concepts about the comprehensiveness of teaching have

developed; school people are no longer looking for short cuts or for simple answers to the problem of effective teaching.

13. Teachers have begun to understand each other's problems; teachers of different subjects see themselves as doing the same thing after all.[1]

Questionnaires circulated among the teachers and observers in the study and returned by three-fourths of them provided another means of evaluating the experiment. Forty-six percent of the teachers said they enjoyed being observed as much as once a week for ten weeks; 26 percent did not like it; the others had no definite opinion. Liking or disliking being observed was clearly related to rapport between observer and teacher: to such factors as note taking during the observation, and the nature of the follow-up conference. When both the observer and teacher were confident that the sole purpose of observation was the improvement of the educational program for boys and girls, the teachers welcomed frequent, extensive observations followed by individual conferences. One-third of the observers believed that more time should have been spent by the local school systems in planning for the project and studying the guide to observation to the point where it was more thoroughly understood. The most valuable part of the entire experiment, they thought, was the conference between observer and teacher. In general the reactions to the questionnaire again emphasized the use of the Ohio Teaching Record as a tool and a guide, rather than as an end in itself or as a rating device. Other responses to the questionnaire emphasized the values of the study that were expressed in the thirteen statements quoted above.

Perhaps one major weakness of the project grew out of its short-term nature. It had not been planned as an ongoing project; it was planned to run for ten weeks. In some schools it was introduced rather hurriedly. If it had been entered into gradually as a continuing part of local programs and expanded as local insights, needs, and interests developed there might not

[1] William John Jones, "Improving Teaching in Ohio through the Experimental Use of a Cooperatively Developed Anecdotal Observational Record" (unpublished dissertation for the Ph.D. degree in the files of Ohio State University, 1941), pp. 241-42.

have been a tendency, on the part of some schools, to add the activities of the experiment to already crowded schedules—with resultant disadvantages.

In spite of the care exercised in setting up the experiment there were still more than a few teachers who continued to regard evaluation as something done to them which might affect their security and status. If such an attitude had been widespread —as well it might have been if there had been no protests against it—it would clearly have prevented the experiment from yield- ing positive results. The experiment was designed to improve teaching. The teachers and observers, working together in this experiment, believed that they developed increased ability and desire to discuss common problems, greater awareness of educa- tional philosophy and values, and greater readiness to encourage pupil participation in their classroom activities.

A STUDY OF TEACHER-PUPIL RELATIONSHIPS

The Ohio experiment threw considerable light upon the sort of relationship between teachers and supervisors that could best promote evaluation as a means to the improvement of teaching. We turn now to an experiment which is concerned with a differ- ent sort of relationship as a focus for evaluation and a stimulus toward the improvement of teaching. Of the fact that the rela- tionship between a teacher and the pupils in his class powerfully affects both teaching and learning there can be no doubt. Yet this relationship between teacher and student, so important in the educative process, has seldom been analyzed directly and systematically. One such comprehensive analysis, however, has been made within the cooperative study of teacher education. And the stimulation to efforts at self-improvement which it provided among the teachers who participated—to say nothing of teachers' enthusiasm about its value—leads us to believe that an extensive description of some of the techniques and pro- cedures for analyzing pupil-teacher relationships would be use- ful to many readers.

In 1940-41, under the auspices of the Stanford Social Educa- tion Investigation, the relationships between nine social studies teachers and their pupils in a small private junior college were studied by Robert N. Bush.[2] The potentialities of the study were so promising that it seemed desirable to test the procedures further in public schools with more teachers, larger classes, different subject-matter fields, and more heterogeneous student groups. Teachers and administrators in the Denver and Spokane public school systems, participants in the Commission's cooperative study, had carried on a number of study groups and conferences through which teachers were sensitized to problems relating to their relationships with students. Consequently arrangements were made for Dr. Bush, acting assistant professor of education at Stanford, to visit administrators and teachers in some of the schools of these two systems and describe the nature and outcomes of his previous investigation. As a result, he was invited to organize similar studies in the two cities, and the administrations of those two school systems made careful and generous provision for carrying out the work. In both Denver and Spokane the relationships between nine high school teachers and their students were studied during the winter of 1942. In all, since the beginning of the investigation, the pupil-teacher relations in twenty-seven classrooms have been analyzed.

For the project as a whole there were several purposes. One purpose was simply to describe as accurately as possible the relationships that exist between a number of teachers and the students in their classes. A related purpose was to develop appropriate techniques for studying these relationships. As a result of consequent analyses it was hoped that some hypotheses concerning the characteristics of effective teacher-pupil relationships might be suggested. From the outset of the study, the objective of furthering the growth of teachers in service was clearly in mind.

The particular teacher-pupil relationships which were considered are indicated in the following questions:

[2] This preliminary study has been summarized by Bush in "A Study of Student-Teacher Relationships," *Journal of Educational Research*, XXXV (May 1942), 645-56, and described in more detail in his "A Study of Student-Teacher Relationships" (unpublished dissertation for the Ed.D. degree in the files of Stanford University, 1941).

1. What does the teacher know about his pupils aside from their achievement in class?

2. How do the teacher's interests in various academic fields and leisure-time pursuits compare with his pupils' interests?

3. How do the teacher's purposes in teaching a particular course compare with the purposes of the pupils who are taking the course?

4. What are the similarities and differences in social beliefs between the teacher and his pupils?

5. How does the teacher's knowledge of his subject matter compare with that of his pupils?

6. How is the teacher's personal appearance, personality, ability to work with students, effectiveness with instructional procedures, and knowledge of subject matter rated by his pupils, his supervisors, and himself?

7. How does the teacher appraise the motivation, quality of academic learning, emotional and social adjustment, and the probable future success of his pupils?

All these particular relationships were aspects of the general question of personal rapport and its relation to effective teaching.

Various rating scales, questionnaires, tests, and other devices were used to get answers to these questions. Some of the techniques are illustrated below in connection with the description of a sample case. To get forthright answers it was necessary to establish a confidential relationship between the investigator and all those from whom data were to be gathered. Many teachers would not wish to have their pupils or supervisors know the facts with respect to some of the questions raised above. And equally, students and supervisors would hesitate to express certain judgments about a teacher if they thought the teacher could later identify those judgments with them. Therefore, the procedure adopted in the study was to assure all teachers, pupils, and supervisors that the information which they provided would be held strictly confidential, or at least would not be described to anyone in a way that might reveal its source. Under this arrangement the investigator was free to seek the information he wanted. After getting the information the investigator discussed the findings with the teacher; together they analyzed and interpreted the strengths and weaknesses in the teacher's relationships with his pupils, and planned various steps that might be taken toward their improvement.

The techniques and procedures of the study can be illustrated best, perhaps, by giving a rather complete case study of the relationships between one teacher and the pupils in his class. The case of Mr. Brown is typical so far as procedures employed are concerned, but is of course unique as to the personalities involved. Brown himself, for example, would not be classifiable as "average." He is young, has many outstanding qualities, and promises to develop more. Yet despite his superiority, everything considered, he has weaknesses that provide opportunities for improvement. The following case study concerns Brown and the twenty-eight youngsters in one of his classes.

THE CASE OF MR. BROWN AND HIS PUPILS

Brown teaches in a large high school. The socio-economic status of the school community is neither as high nor as low as in other sections of the city. No one industry, family, or group dominates community life. There is a mixture of racial, religious, and national elements. The principal of the school considers it very important to maintain academic standards. For example, he keeps a follow-up record of the students who go to college, but none of those who do not do so. The school itself is neither markedly traditional nor progressive.

Brown has two major fields in which he is qualified to teach. All of his teaching, however, is in the field of his second choice. He has altogether more than 100 students—fewer than have most teachers in his school. He has no special counseling duties; he is a member of one committee; he teaches in night school and does some tutoring; he belongs to a few professional fraternities and to the teacher organizations suggested by the school system; he teaches a Sunday school class, but otherwise is not active in community and civic organizations. All of this activity, he says, "certainly keeps me busy all the time." Before entering the teaching profession, he had some business experience.

Knowledge about pupils

Brown was asked the following ten questions about each of the twenty-eight pupils in one of his classes, which he had to answer without looking up the pupils' records:

1. What school did he attend just prior to (this school)?
2. What academic success did he have there?
3. What is and was his home situation (i.e., lives with father and mother, broken home, with guardian, and so on)?
4. Approximately what is his IQ?
5. What are his interests, special abilities, hobbies, and school activities?
6. What is his health status (i.e., any problem presenting difficulties, and the like)?
7. What are his educational plans for the future after leaving (this school)?
8. What are his vocational plans for the future?
9. Do these conflict with his parents' or guardian's ideas on the subject?
10. Any other facts about the pupil that seem important in giving a brief picture of him?

An analysis of Brown's answers to these questions revealed that, by and large, he knew relatively little about the boys and girls in his class. On the average he answered correctly only 1.8 questions. He failed completely in the case of seven pupils, and his best score was six correct answers in the case of a single individual. This record may be compared with an average of 4.7 accurate answers for all nine of the teachers including Brown, who were studied in the same school system. Only two of the nine knew less about their pupils than Brown. Brown knew something about the academic or family background of two pupils; he knew the vocational plans for the future of two of the boys; and he knew something about the interests of seven pupils. His knowledge of IQ's was correct for about a third of the class; he estimated eleven correctly within five points, overestimated six by more than five points, underestimated eight by more than five points, and hazarded no guess about the remaining three.

Another line of evidence about Brown's knowledge of his pupils was obtained by asking him to divide the pupils in his class into three groups: those who were most ignored by the others; those who were most sought after; and those who had a few, but mutual friendships. Then each pupil was asked to write down the name of his best friend in the class and the name of the one to whom he would go, if he had been absent from a class, to find out what had been missed. From the answers to these questions it was possible to construct a sociogram depicting the pupil relationships in the class. When the friendship patterns revealed in the sociogram were compared with the teacher's estimates of pupils' popularity it was found that the teacher had judged nearly three-fourths of his pupils incorrectly. Again it seemed clear that Mr. Brown was relatively unacquainted with his pupils.

Interests

The Progressive Education Association Interest Index, form 8.2a,[3] was used to measure the likes and dislikes of Mr. Brown and his pupils. Figure II shows the proportion of activities liked and disliked in each of a number of interest areas: by the class generally, by Brown, by George, a pupil whose interests are most like his teacher's, and by Henry, whose interests are most divergent from the teacher's. In the areas of biology, physical science, business, and sports, the interests of Brown and the class run in the same direction, but Brown's interests are greater. On the other hand, the teacher has much less interest in foreign language, home economics, and fine arts than most of his pupils. The likes of Mr. Brown and George are practically identical, except in the areas of social studies, industrial arts, and music. The relation between Brown and Henry is very different. Whereas Brown likes a great many activities in biology, physical science, mathematics, and business, Henry actually dislikes a great many activities in those fields. In the fields of foreign language and music, where Henry has special interests, Brown is

---

[3] For a discussion of the way this instrument was used in the study for which it was developed, see Eugene R. Smith and Ralph W. Tyler, *Appraising and Recording Student Progress* (New York: Harper and Brothers, 1942), pp. 338-48

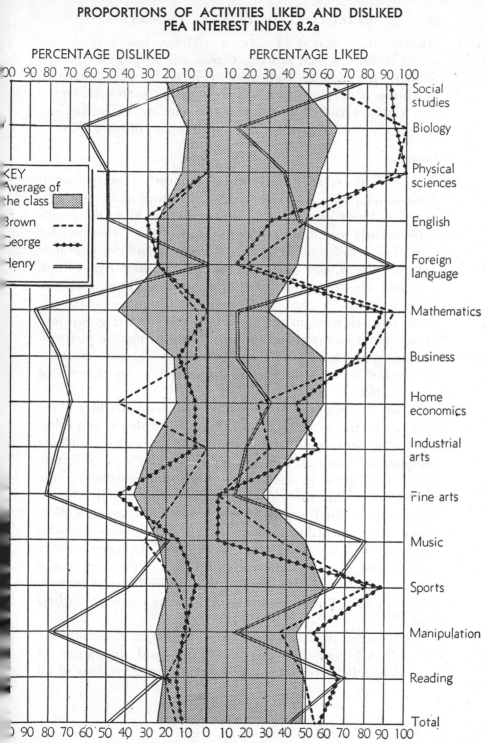

Figure II

PROPORTIONS OF ACTIVITIES LIKED AND DISLIKED
PEA INTEREST INDEX 8.2a

PERCENTAGE DISLIKED   PERCENTAGE LIKED

00 90 80 70 60 50 40 30 20 10 0 10 20 30 40 50 60 70 80 90 100

KEY
Average of
the class
Brown — — —
George •—•—•
Henry ——————

Social studies
Biology
Physical sciences
English
Foreign language
Mathematics
Business
Home economics
Industrial arts
Fine arts
Music
Sports
Manipulation
Reading
Total

0 90 80 70 60 50 40 30 20 10 0 10 20 30 40 50 60 70 80 90 100

generally uninterested. In contrast to Henry, however, who has strong dislikes as well as likes, Brown has no pronounced dislikes. Even in foreign languages where he likes few activities, he dislikes none. One other point is worth mention here. Of the nine teachers studied in the school system, Brown ranked second in the similarity of his interests to those of his pupils.

Purposes

To study the relationships between the teacher's purposes and those of his pupils a special "Purposes Rating Scale" was constructed. There are ten sections to the scale. First, the pupils indicate their reasons for taking the course. Then, they give for each of nine different classroom activities an indication of how well they like it, how often they do it, how valuable they think it is, and what their purposes are in doing it. These activities are as follows: examinations and tests; oral reports; written reports; research work in the laboratory and library; group projects, committee work, and the like; lectures; motion pictures; excursions and trips; and class discussions. The directions for the test and the items under one sample section are reproduced on page 263.

So that Brown's purposes could be compared with those of his students, he was asked to answer the rating scale as "you think an ideal student would" or "as you would like to have students complete it." Because the responses to the "Purposes Rating Scale" were given in confidence, it was not possible for the consultant to show the teacher how his purposes differed from those of individual pupils; it was possible, however, to show him to what extent his purposes differed from pupils' purposes generally. This was done by averaging the differences between the responses of pupils and teacher for each of the ten items of the scale. The procedure revealed that in similarity of purpose with his pupils Brown ranked second among the nine teachers studied.

Pupil ratings of class activities with respect to frequency, liking, and valuing were also summarized, and the ratings of Brown's pupils were compared with the average ratings of all

PURPOSE RATING SCALE[a]

Name_____ Class_____ Date_____

The following pages contain statements which students have given as their reasons for or purposes in taking this class and engaging in its activities. With these suggestions before you, would you please encircle the appropriate number as follows:

1. If this is the most or a *very* important reason for, or purpose in, taking the course or engaging in the activity
2. If this reason or purpose is of only secondary importance
3. If this reason or purpose is of little or no importance

There is a space provided under each major heading for you to check if you do not engage in the activity and there are also three rating scales to indicate (*a*) how well you like the activity, (*b*) how frequently you engage in the activity, and (*c*) how valuable you think the activity is.

Please answer these items frankly; try to indicate clearly how *you* actually feel. There are no "right" or "wrong" answers, and *all material will remain confidential.* Be sure to check this blank in terms of *yourself* in relation to *this class.* Be sure to encircle either 1, 2, or 3 for each of the listed reasons or purposes.

V. GROUP PROJECTS, COMMITTEE WORK, AND THE LIKE

_____ We do not have them in this class.

Check on the scale the point most nearly indicating your feeling:

1	2	3	4	5
I have a strong dislike or them	I like them less than most things in the course	I like them about as well as most things in the course	I like them more than most things in the course	I like them extremely well

Check on the scale the point indicating how often *you* usually have group projects, committee work, and the like in *this* class:

1	2	3	4	5
About once a semester	About once every six weeks	About once every month	About once a week	Constantly Several times weekly

Check on the scale the point most nearly indicating your feeling:

1	2	3	4	5
This kind of activity is a complete waste of time	This kind of activity may be valuable to me sometime, but I doubt it	I think this kind of activity is about average in usefulness and value to me	I think this kind of activity is above average in usefulness and value to me	I think this kind of activity is extremely valuable and useful to me

My purpose for engaging in group projects and committee work is (*encircle the appropriate number*):

1 2 3 a. To obtain the opinions, ideas, and points of view of others on the subject under consideration
1 2 3 b. Because they are required
1 2 3 c. To learn to work with other people (cooperation)
1 2 3 d. To obtain the necessary grades and credits
1 2 3 e. To prepare myself better for college and / or future life work
1 2 3 f. To increase my information, knowledge, and understanding of the subject
1 2 3 g. To satisfy my interest
1 2 3 h. Because I can get some other member of the group to do the work and I usually don't have as much to do myself
1 2 3 i. To enable me to cover more material than I would be able to otherwise
1 2 3 j. To give me an opportunity to develop some leadership
1 2 3 k. To help me to become better able to solve problems
1 2 3 l. To give me an opportunity to compare myself with others
1 2 3 m. (List others)_____
1 2 3 n. _____

[a] Prepared by Robert N. Bush, Stanford University.

the pupils studied. In those activities in which Brown's pupils participated most frequently (examinations, oral and written reports, lectures, and discussions) they like and value them to a greater extent than do the pupils in other classes. Tests, however, are among the least liked activities in all classes. Brown's class almost never has group projects or excursions; yet group projects are fairly common in other teachers' classes, well liked, and valued. These data are shown in Figure III.

Social beliefs

Both Brown and his students responded to the Progressive Education Association test on Beliefs on Social Issues (forms 4.21 and 4.31 of the Scales of Beliefs).[4] This test was designed to measure attitudes of liberalism, conservatism, and uncertainty with regard to democracy, economic relations, labor and unemployment, race, nationalism, and militarism. Compared with his class, Brown was markedly more liberal with respect to race, nationalism, and militarism, and markedly more conservative with respect to economic relations, and labor and unemployment. Brown was also more frequently uncertain than his pupils on the topics of democracy, economic relations, and labor and unemployment. An over-all summary showed him to be somewhat more liberal and uncertain than his pupils. There was one pupil whose beliefs were almost identical with Brown's, and there was another whose attitudes differed sharply from Brown's on most issues.

Knowledge of subject matter

To make this comparison Brown and his pupils took one of the achievement tests published by the Cooperative Test Service. The teacher's scaled score was almost three standard deviations above the average of his class and one standard deviation above the score of his best pupil. Brown is clearly outstanding in his knowledge of his field, so far as that knowledge is measured by the test.

4 *Ibid.,* pp. 215-29.

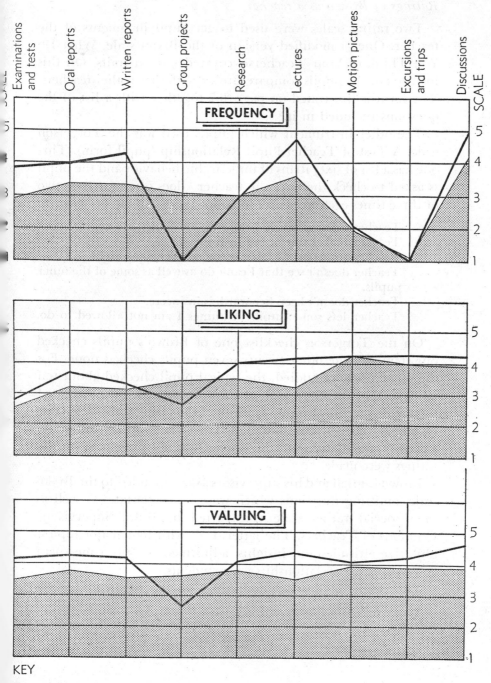

Figure III
STUDENT RATINGS OF FREQUENCY, LIKING, AND VALUE OF CLASS ACTIVITIES

FREQUENCY

LIKING

VALUING

KEY

Average for Brown's class

Average for nine classes

Ratings of Brown as a teacher

Two rating scales were used to get pupil judgments of the teacher. One—a modified version of the Bryan scale, What Do You Think of Your Teachers?—covered sixteen traits. On this instrument the pupils compare Brown with three other teachers. The form is illustrated on page 267 together with a list of the questions included in it.[5]

The other instrument which pupils used was the Torgerson scale, A Test of Teacher-Pupil Relationship (pupil form). This one has a list of sixty items of undesirable behavior and the pupil is asked to check the ones the teacher "does often (at least two or three times each week)." The following six items[6] are typical:

____Teacher talks so much I can't do anything.
____Teacher makes fun of me in front of class.
____Teacher threatens to fail me for not behaving right.
____Teacher doesn't see that I can't do as well as some of the other pupils.
____Teacher doesn't keep her word, is insincere.
____Teacher lets some pupils do things I am not allowed to do.

On the Torgerson checklist one of Brown's pupils checked one item and the other twenty-seven pupils checked none. For the other teachers studied, the typical pupil checked about ten items in the Torgerson scale. Brown, in other words, was rated remarkably well by his pupils. Both of the rating scales filled out by pupils were collected and mailed directly to the consultant by a class representative and the teacher was not present when the ratings were made.

Brown himself and his supervisors also responded to the Bryan scale, omitting questions which were inappropriate, as well as to a special rating scale constructed by Bush, Supervisors' Opinions of Teachers. The latter dealt with four major topics: objective attitudes and insights, adjustment to job, time spent counseling, and relationship with students.

The results of the various ratings on the Bryan and Bush

---

[5] Quoted from Ewing Beatty, *A Study on Student-Teacher Relations* (Denver: Denver Public Schools, Department of Education, 1942), pp. 30-45 (mimeographed).
[6] Quoted from Beatty, *op. cit.*, pp. 50-52.

1. What is your opinion concerning the amount of knowledge each teacher has of the subject taught?

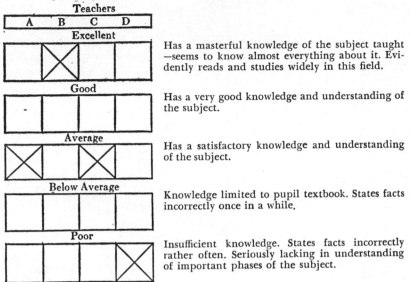

Teachers

A	B	C	D

Excellent

Has a masterful knowledge of the subject taught —seems to know almost everything about it. Evidently reads and studies widely in this field.

Good

Has a very good knowledge and understanding of the subject.

Average

Has a satisfactory knowledge and understanding of the subject.

Below Average

Knowledge limited to pupil textbook. States facts incorrectly once in a while.

Poor

Insufficient knowledge. States facts incorrectly rather often. Seriously lacking in understanding of important phases of the subject.

2. What is your opinion concerning each teacher's fairness in grading?

3. How well do you like each of your teachers personally?

4. How much are you learning from each of your teachers?

5. What is your opinion concerning each teacher's ability to maintain discipline?

6. At present, how well do you like the subject taught by each of your teachers?

7. What is your opinion concerning the sympathy shown by this teacher?

8. What is your opinion concerning the fairness of this teacher's decisions regarding the students?

9. What is your opinion concerning the value that the study of the topics and problems of this class has for you?

10. What is your opinion concerning the ability of this teacher to assist students in planning and organizing classroom work?

11. What is your opinion concerning the ability of this teacher to explain things clearly?

12. What is your opinion concerning the general (all-round) teaching ability of this teacher?

13. What is your opinion concerning the pride this teacher takes in his personal appearance?

14. To what extent do students in this class share decisions with the teacher?

15. To what extent do you have individual working freedom in this class?

16. What is your opinion of the extent to which this teacher has a genuine understanding of and concern for you and your problems?

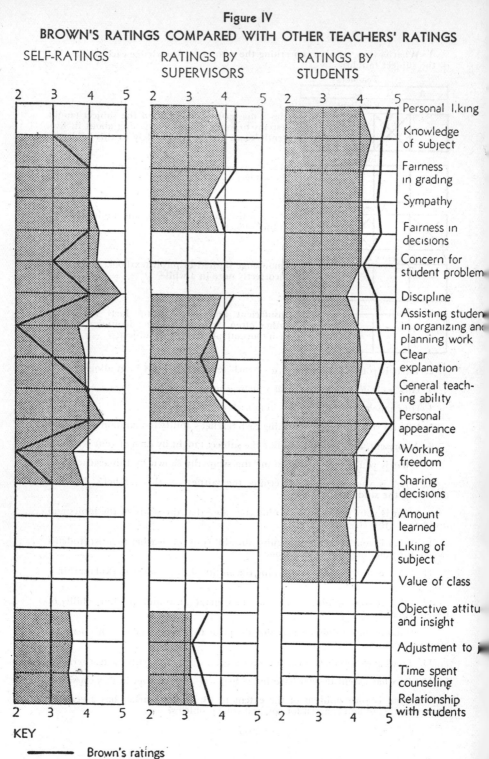

Figure IV
BROWN'S RATINGS COMPARED WITH OTHER TEACHERS' RATINGS

SELF-RATINGS   RATINGS BY SUPERVISORS   RATINGS BY STUDENTS

Personal liking
Knowledge of subject
Fairness in grading
Sympathy
Fairness in decisions
Concern for student problem
Discipline
Assisting student in organizing and planning work
Clear explanation
General teaching ability
Personal appearance
Working freedom
Sharing decisions
Amount learned
Liking of subject
Value of class
Objective attitu and insight
Adjustment to j
Time spent counseling
Relationship with students

KEY

——— Brown's ratings

▓▓▓ Average of other teachers' ratings

scales are shown in Figure IV. It is apparent that Brown's pupils rate him higher on all sixteen traits of the Bryan scale than pupils generally have rated the nine teachers studied. Brown is, however, rated relatively low on the value of his class, his concern for pupils' problems, and on sharing decisions. Supervisors also rated Brown highly on the Bryan scale. Why the supervisors ranked him relatively low on clarity of explanations when his pupils considered that one of his strongest points is not evident from the data. Brown does not regard himself as highly as do his students and supervisors. He does, however, recognize as his strong points those on which supervisors and pupils also rate him as strongest, namely fairness, sympathy, discipline, general teaching ability, and personal appearance. On assisting students in organizing and planning their work and on working freedom for students Brown feels he has real weakness. His judgment is supported in part by student ratings of him on these same traits and, more forcefully, by their liking for and the value they sensed in group projects as revealed in Figure III. All in all, the various comparisons and ratings should give Brown confidence in himself and free him to work on the few problems that seem to be only relative weaknesses.

Brown's appraisal of his pupils

In a comprehensive appraisal of a teacher's relationship with his pupils it is important to know what he thinks of them as well as what they think of him. Brown rated each of his students, in the class studied, on a Teacher Rating of Student form adapted by Bush. Two sample items from the scale are reproduced on page 270.

Other questions included in the rating scale are (1) What are his work habits and study skills? (a) effort, (b) methods; (2) Conduct in class; (3) His outlook for the future; (4) How well do you like this student personally? (5) Does he need prodding? (6) Has he a program with definite purposes in terms of which he distributes his time and energy? (7) How well is he accepted by others? (a) adults, (b) peers; (8) What is your judgment as to the quality of his thinking? Brown's ratings of his students follow closely the average ratings which other teachers make of their students except for "quality of thinking," which he rates high, and "definiteness of purpose," "need for prodding," and "probable success in college," which he rates low. Brown, like the other teachers, rates his pupils highest on "conduct in class" and "emotional balance."

TEACHER RATING OF STUDENT

What is your estimate of _____? We are in-
(Name of student)

terested in obtaining your opinion as to his present and future success and adjustment. Will you please check the items as directed.

1. At present he is planning to attend _____ college after leaving _____ (school). Which of the following indicates your opinion as to his probable success?

_____a. He should not attend (this) college:

_____ He is incapable of college work.

_____ He might get by in a college with low(er) standards.

(If you place a check in the blank before "a," indicate which of the above two statements applies.)

_____b. As I see him at present, he would do a very poor quality of work.

_____c. Would probably do mediocre work.

_____d. Would probably complete his work and do an above-average job.

_____e. He should go on to college as he will do a very superior job.

. . . .

9. How well balanced emotionally does he appear to be?

_____a. Very easily and often moved to fits of depression and anger or becomes very unresponsive and apathetic.
_____b. Frequently shows instability, although not always.

_____c. Sometimes shows balance and at other times a lack of it.

_____d. Usually has good balance; only occasionally does he show emotional difficulties.
_____e. Unusually good balance of responsiveness and control.

Another basis for examining Brown's relationships with his pupils was provided by asking him to list the names of the one-fourth of the pupils with whom he thought he had the most effective relationships and the one-fourth with whom his relationships were least effective. Although no statistical analysis of the differences between the two groups identified in this way is available, it is possible to point out some of the differences which appear to be the greatest. Achievement test scores and honor points in Brown's class are quite a bit higher in the group with which Brown considers he has the most effective relations. There is also evidence that he knows more about the pupils in this group, likes them better, and gives them better general ratings. On the other hand, there was no appreciable difference between the average IQ's of the two groups or between their ratings of Brown.

One other important aspect of Brown's appraisal of his students can be stated briefly. As compared with students of other teachers, Brown's students are rewarded with slightly higher grades. The ratio of Brown's "A" and "B" grades to lower grades is approximately three to two, whereas the ratio is about equal in the other classes.

Brown and one of his pupils

Before summarizing the study of Mr. Brown, we can learn more about him from an analysis of his relationship with Henry, one of his pupils. Despite the fact—which the reader may recall—that he differed more in interests from his teacher than any other member of the class, Henry was included among those with whom Brown felt he had most effective relationships. Actually, however, Brown had some very mistaken judgments about the boy and was unaware of many problems that the boy was facing. For example, he gave him a B in the course; yet Henry's score on the achievement test which was given as part of this investigation was the lowest in the class. Brown overestimated his IQ by twenty points: it was only 92 on a short form of the Otis test. Before the social structure of the class had been analyzed Brown characterized Henry as very popular; yet the analysis showed him to be sought by no one. In his attitudes toward economic relations and labor and unemployment he was markedly more liberal than Brown. On the Teacher Rating of Student scale Brown judged him average or better on all the characteristics listed. Henry rated Brown superior on all characteristics but one included in the Bryan scale—the value of the course was rated very low, and Henry added the comment that the course was "quite useless."

All of the data regarding this pupil (with the boy's permission) were laid before the teacher by the consultant; Brown was quite astonished to discover such striking differences between him and Henry. Brown and the consultant decided to learn more about him. Brown began to observe him more closely and to gather data from Henry's cumulative record and other sources. He noticed that in and out of class the boy was always very pleasant around other students, but was generally ignored by boys and girls alike. He discovered that the boy was an only child, that his mother was employed full time in one of the professions, and that his father was a semiskilled laborer. The boy's interests were more like his mother's than his father's. From these and other data Brown and the consultant tentatively guessed that, if the results of the intelligence and achievement tests were valid, Henry was being pushed academically, probably by his mother, beyond his normal ability. They discovered that Henry was spending a great deal of time studying, and they suspected that this might be keeping him from developing normal social relations with other boys and girls. They agreed that Henry was facing important problems of social adjustment and of intelligent educational planning in the light of his ability, interests, and background. And it was clear that such problems were new to Brown. Brown had not been much aware of them and felt quite incompetent to help.

SOME RECOMMENDATIONS OF BROWN AND THE CONSULTANT

The method by which the consultant acquainted the teachers with information about their effectiveness had to be adapted to the readiness of each teacher to accept such data objectively. With Brown the procedure could be quite direct. On the whole, the results of the inquiry were favorable to Brown and furthermore he was eager for help. He and the consultant, therefore, studied the strong and weak points in his record, compared the appraisals with averages for other teachers, and in some instances made comparisons with the individual records of other teachers—where identity was not of course revealed.

The over-all picture of Brown can be summarized briefly. He has many interests in different academic fields, and no marked dislikes. His attitudes toward some social issues are rather liberal, toward others conservative, and where he is most conservative he tends to be uncertain. His purposes in teaching his course center largely on disseminating knowledge of the subject matter, and developing skill in observing, thinking, and expression. His pupils' purposes are more like his than is true of most other teachers and their students. Aside from their achievement in his class, he knows little about his pupils, is not greatly concerned with their individual problems, and lacks ability to help them or work with them in the planning of group projects. Like other teachers studied in the same system, he makes little use of excursions and motion pictures. His pupils think he is particularly good at explaining the subject matter clearly. Students and supervisors generally like him and rate him higher than other teachers in most respects. An examination of specific relationships between Brown and individual students, however, shows that he is not equally effective with everyone—and that there are a few students with whom he is quite ineffective. In general, his pupils like him, like the subject matter, and like the way he explains it. On the other hand, they do not think he has much concern for their personal problems and they do not think his course is very valuable. In the light of Brown's lack of knowledge about his pupils it would seem that he makes the most of what may be termed the value that adolescents generally can see in academic subject matter, but that he fails to arouse the interests among students that can grow out of a feeling that their needs are being individually met. Moreover, it is unlikely that such interest can be captured until Brown knows his students better, understands their needs and problems, and provides for necessary flexibility to meet them.

As the consultant and the teacher reviewed these data they developed many suggestions and planned several next steps by which Brown might increase his effectiveness. For example, they agreed that he should study several pupils intensively. Accordingly, they selected the boy whose social acceptance Brown had grossly misjudged and whose case we have already described; a girl whose general adjustment and relationship with Brown were judged very effective; and a girl whose relationship with Brown was considered poor. Later, as time permitted, he should study and discuss with their other teachers the cases of four pupils whom he disliked personally. Then, to increase his general knowledge about boys and girls he should undertake to read some books on adolescent psychology and to join one of the teachers' child study groups in the city or a class or seminar in adolescent psychology in a nearby college. Also, within his own course he should begin to study ways in which he could modify his teaching to meet individual differences in ability, interest, and background; expand the course purposes to include individual planning and group work; find out what further school and community resources were available to enrich his teaching; and consider the possibilities, with other staff members, of using motion pictures to better advantage in the school. In carrying out these plans Brown should, of course, seek help from his school principal and supervisors and draw upon other resources which the school system made available.

SIGNIFICANCE OF THE STUDY

The pattern of testing, analyzing, comparing, discussing, and planning which we have illustrated in the case of Mr. Brown has been followed in the studies of all the teachers made up to the present time. Although the number studied so far is not large it is possible to make a few rather obvious generalizations about teacher-pupil relationships from the data that have been analyzed. Every teacher is highly effective with some pupils, and every teacher is quite ineffective with some pupils. However, there are some teachers who have effective relationships with a large proportion of their pupils while others are effective with relatively few. In general, the teachers who know most about their pupils and are aware of and sympathize with their individual needs and interests have effective relationships with a larger number than do the teachers whose concern is pretty exclusively with knowledge of subject matter. Teachers of the latter sort usually develop very effective relations with students who have marked academic talent and interest; but students generally tended to experience more success and satisfaction in work with teachers sensitive to broader needs and interests. Brown was an exception to this tendency.

The value of this comprehensive study of teacher-pupil relationships has been acclaimed enthusiastically by the teachers who participated in it. Both the Denver and Spokane teachers said that the study was the most valuable service they had ever received. One main reason they gave for this opinion was that the data were applied to their particular problems. All but one of the teachers further agreed that the experience had resulted in definite changes in their teaching procedures, and they attributed the changes to a greater awareness of their shortcomings and strengths. They believed that the study gave them a picture of their strengths and weaknesses that was most revealing, and that was sufficiently specific and clear to enable them to plan a program of professional improvement. They learned new things about the boys and girls whom they faced daily in the classroom, and they believed the knowledge helped them to establish better relationships with more of their pupils. Subsequent tests, observations, and interviews will reveal what justification there is for these beliefs. At the present time teachers are nearly unanimous in their conviction of the study's helpfulness to them.

The procedures and techniques of the study are, perhaps, too complex for general application. In both Denver and Spokane it took about ten hours of each teacher's time, six hours of each student's time, and three hours of the administrator's time to gather the necessary data. The consultant spent a month in each city. This may represent more of an investment of time and money than the average school system can readily afford; although it is interesting to note that there was general agreement among the teachers themselves that the amount of time taken from the classroom and the amount of their own time required was not unreasonable and impractical. However, there are a number of ways in which the extension of such work could be made more feasible. For instance, it should be possible eventually to reduce the number of tests, rating scales, questionnaires, and other instruments, or reduce their length, or both, without sacrificing coverage or reliability seriously. Doubtless some of the tests will be found to contribute relatively little to the analysis while others will be considered indispensable. Moreover, the need for some of the precautions in collecting and using the data so as to maintain confidence may decrease. As teachers come to see that the data are being used to help them and as they gain security through that aid they may be increasingly willing to share information. Thus it should be possible to put more responsibility upon teachers and pupils and regular sources of supervisory assistance, thereby reducing the work of the outside consultant. Whether a special consultant from outside the local school system is required if forthright personal data are to be collected is, perhaps, a moot question. (The Denver and Spokane teachers believed that the consultant services should be clearly divorced from the local school administration.) That a good sense of professional ethics is required on the part of all who use the data is unquestionable.

So far as evaluative procedures are concerned the study of teacher-pupil relationship emphasizes again the importance of a thoroughly democratic approach. Teachers were, at first, apprehensive; they became enthusiastic when they saw that the information and opinions they were giving out were redounding to their personal benefit. As a means of promoting teacher growth in service the main value of the study probably comes from its concrete, personal, and clinical nature. It begins by focusing upon, and ends by offering insight into, the fundamental domain of the individual teacher—namely, the teaching-learning relationship with boys and girls.

CHANGES IN TEACHERS' CONCEPTS ABOUT EVALUATION

During 1940-41 the staff of the Norris School in Tennessee began, with the help of a full-time consultant, a project to evaluate the school's program.[7] Their plans were directed toward two purposes: to clarify the objectives of the whole school (nursery through high school), and to develop instruments and procedures for determining how well the objectives were being achieved. It was not intended that all this should be accomplished and the program fully appraised during one year. By the end of a year, however, the staff did hope to be well on the way toward the development of an evaluation program that would keep the school responsive to student needs and provide dependable evidence of the extent to which those needs were being met.

Plans for getting the project under way called for two steps. First, the teachers were to conduct discussions for the purpose of defining the general objectives of the school. These objectives were to be further clarified and illustrated by committees and served as guides to the development of evaluation techniques. Second, committees of teachers were to construct tests and other similar instruments suitable for appraising progress toward each of six major objectives that had been tentatively identified. Provision was made for staff meetings where the work of each committee would be explained and discussed. To coordinate these activities they organized a staff steering committee specifically to plan agenda for staff meetings, receive and analyze reports from the various committees, and recommend changes in emphases and working procedures as they saw various problems emerge.

The first two steps in the project were logical enough. A series of tasks was to be carried out in order, beginning with the definition of general school objectives. The organization of a staff steering committee (with rotating membership) was something relatively new. In reality it was an evaluation committee, but this was not clear when it was first formed. As it reviewed records of group action and sensed increasing or waning interests the committee saw that in order to give intelligent direction to the work of any particular group it had to evaluate the group's

[7] A report presented by Donald J. McNassor at the second evaluation conference in teacher education at Columbus, Ohio, March 1942, was the major source of material for this account.

progress and help the group to evaluate itself. When the steering committee did this it led to modifications in the work of the other committees. In fact, the plans for the evaluation project were considerably changed as the staff worked together during the year. A description of what these changes were and why they came about reveals several modifications in the teachers' conceptions of evaluation.

As the plans for staff work were carried out during the first couple of months of the school year, the steering committee became sensitive to considerable dissatisfaction with them. Teachers did not feel that they could spare the time to meet regularly as members of several committees. Although committee membership was voluntary, some teachers became impatient with group meetings to discuss general objectives; they were more concerned about immediate problems of some of their boys and girls and about some of the group work in their classes that was not going well. The staff developed a tendency to regard evaluation as something apart from learning, something tacked on. They began to question seriously the advisability of continuing discussions about objectives as a basis for the development of a program of evaluation.

During late October and early November, as the significance of these attitudes became clearer, the staff altered their plans of evaluation. A formal and logically planned study gave way to informal and pragmatic processes that took their cue from conditions in the school that challenged the attention of the teachers. Teachers felt that they did not understand the needs of many of the children; they saw evidence of their lack of understanding every day in the behavior of individuals and groups. Why does John head for the library at every possible opportunity? Why does Bill contrive in every possible way to avoid the library? Why is Mary so uninterested in planning her work, so haphazard in getting things done? Why do certain boys loaf so much in the halls and washroom? These were the problems on which they wanted to work. They decided to take them as they came. Some called for individual attention, others for group study and action. As teachers turned their attention gradually to these problems they did not, however, really turn away from problems of evaluation. Rather, their conception of what evaluation was and of how to go about it changed. Moreover, their concern with these questions about pupils brought them face to face with questions of what to do about the school's program, for it was clear that pupil problems were not unrelated to the school's program. Thus evaluation became closely tied to child study and through that, in turn, to program revision.

During the year a careful record was kept of discussions at committee and faculty meetings, and the consultant kept an account of his observations. Toward the close of the year members of the Norris staff held a three-day weekend conference during which they reviewed critically the year's activities. At that meeting they decided that the consultant should analyze the records of the past year and the conclusions of the special weekend discussion, and prepare a report for the Norris staff and the Commission showing changes that had occurred during the year. The consultant prepared the report and submitted it to five members of the Norris staff for their approval. This document[8] gives an analysis of staff thinking and action in relation to the whole program of the school. While our particular concern is with changes in concepts about evaluation, we have listed here several other major changes that were identified:

Approaches to the improvement of the school's program
 1. From areas of specialization to correlated efforts on broad fronts
 2. From generalized school objectives to individualized objectives
 3. From committees on philosophy and theory to committees on the solution of immediate school problems
 4. From pupil grouping according to subjects and large units of study to pupil grouping according to needs of individual pupils
Approaches to the evaluation of the school's program
 1. From committees on school objectives to informal groupings of teachers on the basis of mutual concern about a learning activity
 2. From formal testing and measuring to study of pupils in life situations

[8] Donald J. McNassor, "Teachers in Transition," a report to the Commission on Teacher Education and a study of the Southern Association of Colleges and Secondary Schools, August 1941 (mimeographed).

3. From evaluation of the curriculum to evaluation as inseparable from the curriculum
4. From appraisal by teachers to appraisal by pupils and teachers together

These statements should be regarded as illustrating changes in emphasis among the staff, or changes in their way of looking at problems; they should not be regarded as definitions of any scale or continuum with poles which represent opposing beliefs. It is quite possible, for example, to think about objectives for individuals and solutions of their immediate problems and, at the same time, consider their relation to general objectives and matters of philosophy and theory. Moreover, the report indicates clearly that these changes were not made by all teachers. Our concern here is not with the extent of changes but with the nature of the changes and how they came about.

Analysis of appraisal procedures used by teachers at the beginning of the study and ideas expressed in the early meetings of the committees on objectives showed that teachers believed that certain types of specified behavior should be achieved by all pupils, that such behavior should be appraised with test instruments that could be easily administered to large groups of pupils, that progress of pupils should be judged on the basis of standard behavior (test norms), and that evidence of progress toward all of the schoolwide goals should be collected for each pupil. The following factors are believed to have contributed to the modification of these views:

The teachers concluded that their earlier approach to evaluation was impracticable. Whereas, at the rate they were going, it would be at the earliest the following winter or spring before measuring instruments of any significant degree of validity or reliability could be completed for use, they desired to secure evidence of changed pupil behavior during the fall months. Many of them concluded that the most practical way of doing this was to observe boys' and girls' actions in the classroom, in the halls, on the playground. . . . This approach, the teachers agreed, could be used with varying degrees of intelligence and validity by most teachers, and it would not require additional time on their part in their already crowded school day. . . .

A second relevant factor in the transition involved the teachers' experience in trying to define their objectives. As the teachers got well into this job, they found themselves confronted with doing something which contradicted previously held values. In specifying behavior which was to exemplify attainment of a school objective, they were, in effect, saying that it was a good thing for all boys and girls in the school to acquire these specific behavior characteristics. . . . Several teachers had to reject this procedure because they believed that to try to have all pupils exhibit *certain specific* behavior characteristics . . . ignored individual configurations of behavior and individual needs, and . . . assumed that a certain kind of behavior was an end in itself, irrespective of its significance in the life of an individual child.

Another factor that influenced the decision of several teachers to lessen emphasis on pencil and paper and other indirect means of measurement was their intense interest in pupils as individuals. Rarely did such teachers discuss "what my class is doing" or "what my pupils need." Their references . . . were to individual cases. . . . This interest . . . seemed to make the teachers more sensitive to the individuality of pupils and the necessity to deal with . . . individual drives and motivations. . . .

A fourth factor was the growing . . . belief of some teachers . . . that evaluation should be as much a pupil concern as it was a teacher concern. In a classroom where evaluation deals primarily with teacher concerns . . . the problem [of evaluation] is simple: the teacher wants to know how her pupils are getting along with respect to some objective, and she wants to know now. . . . The problem is solved by giving the class a test. Some teachers began to ask such questions as: What is happening to the pupils? Do they consider the behavior measured by the test important in their lives? Are they anxious to take the test and to study the results in relation to their life goals and drives? (Not to be determined simply by asking all those who want to take a test to raise their hands.) What would happen if taking the test was to be made optional? To what extent are *their* criteria of achievement compatible with those of the teacher? (Not that incompatibility is to be considered undesirable. When it exists, however, it has implications concerning *how* the teacher secures evaluative evidence.)

The teachers who began to ask such questions as these have been trying to insure a maximum of pupil participation in evaluation. . . . When the classes of these teachers have a discussion to appraise some project, or decide to write up something as a class paper, or respond to a questionnaire, or . . . take a test, the decision usually is one which most members of the class have arrived at themselves without pressure . . . from the teacher.

The next . . . factor . . . was the desire of teachers to . . . know what aspects of the child's experience account for his changes in behavior. Some teachers were not concerned with . . . changes . . . apart from those elements in the . . . environment that account for them. . . .

They considered knowledge of the processes through which an insecure child develops greater security to be as important . . . as the fact that a change in the child's security status did occur. . . . Many testing instruments (interest indices, etc.) would reveal only . . . likes or dislikes and would not relate them to classroom procedures which produced . . . them.

A sixth factor which helps to account for the shift from indirect to direct methods of getting evaluative evidence is that some of the teachers indicated a growing dislike for picturing the growth of pupils in terms of statistical numbers and percentages. Such a procedure "loses the flavor," as one teacher stated, which comes from studying boys and girls in flesh and blood as they participate in school activities. . . .[9]

These experiences and shifts in viewpoint have an important implication for the way evaluation at the in-service level is carried out. One cannot avoid the implication by suggesting that the Norris teachers may have had some questionable notions about evaluation to begin with. The belief that evaluation is a formal process, or a logical sequence of steps, or something that can be defined in terms of objective tests, standard scores, and statistics is widespread. What is significant is that when the teachers tried to practice evaluation in a way which they thought was consistent with this belief they failed to get enough satisfaction to continue. A program of appraisal in which mature and busy teachers are to take part needs to make some clear contribution to tasks which seem significant to them.

There should not be a conflict between observing and testing as methods of gathering data about the behavior of children. The two methods should reinforce each other. Some teachers are shrewd observers, others are quite unperceptive. Some teachers do not understand or get much meaning from tests, others are greatly helped by them. Impressions about a child gained from

[9] From Donald J. McNassor's report to the second evaluation conference in teacher education, March 1942.

a few observations can be checked against performance on tests which sample a wider range of reactions, and test interpretations can gain color and significance when seen in the light of a few dramatic incidents. Many of the Norris teachers were deeply concerned about the problems of individual boys and girls and, tentatively at least, they believed they could satisfy this interest better by drawing upon observations than by using tests as a chief source of evidence for their evaluation. The choice they made and the pattern of attitudes revealed in their report emphasize again the need to keep evaluation practices closely in line with teachers' major concerns.

EVALUATION IN AN ONGOING PROGRAM

Evaluation of the growth of teachers in service takes on added meaning when the changes occurring in individuals can be viewed in relation to changes in the staff generally, in the students, in the curriculum, and in the community. The report from Colquitt County, Georgia and from Moultrie, its county seat, illustrates this point; it is an evaluation of an ongoing program of teacher education as well as of individual teacher growth.

For several years before the cooperative study of teacher education began the Moultrie High School had been a participant in a study sponsored by the Southern Association of Colleges and Secondary Schools. Teachers had been clarifying their objectives and modifying their program with the help of consultants, workshops, and other resources. Curriculum revision had been undertaken in the elementary school systems. A series of reports by committees representing the entire state of Georgia had thrown the spotlight on economic conditions. And the schools accepted them as a challenge. Teachers in the school systems of Colquitt County were thus already engaged in many activities aimed at the improvement of their educational program when the cooperative study of teacher education began.

During their association with the Commission the teachers from the Moultrie High School, Moultrie elementary and junior high schools, and from the county elementary schools have continued to study a great many problems together. Committees and study groups have formulated objectives; children have been studied; school and community surveys made; new curricula and programs of action developed; and results appraised. The account which follows is concerned chiefly with some of the activities of high school teachers. It illustrates how data were gathered, outcomes appraised, and results used.

SOME GOALS OF THE SCHOOL

During 1936-37, a statement setting forth a point of view for education in the Moultrie Public Schools had been worked out. In 1939, when the teacher education study focused attention on the competence required of teachers in the fulfillment of their responsibilities, this statement was re-examined in order to see what directions for teacher growth it implied. These implications are reproduced below[10] in italics, following quotations from the statement of point of view:

The program of a school should be based primarily on a comprehensive study of the community served by the school, its background and its specific and peculiar needs. It should be by no means static, but a dynamic changing program, paralleling as closely as possible the changing needs of society. . . . Therefore the primary function of education is to help youth to develop an understanding of the social and economic structure of the community and the consciousness that the worth of an individual in a society is directly proportionate to his contribution to the welfare and progress of society. . . .

Teachers should grow in social understanding

. . . The interest of society . . . can best be served when the program of the school affords the means of discovering the individual pupil's peculiar talents, abilities, tastes, and gives opportunities for their fullest development.

Teachers should grow in understanding of child growth and development

. . . The school through its entire program should direct its efforts toward making its organization democratic. . . . Democratic living

[10] Final Report of the Moultrie and Colquitt County Schools to the Commission on Teacher Education, pp. 7-8.

in the school is the best preparation for the understanding of and participation in democratic living outside the school.

Teachers should grow in the ability to work democratically with others

. . . In providing for the interests and needs of pupils the instructional program [should] not be limited to the traditional subject matter, but [should] include activities and worthwhile experiences in meaningful situations that serve to identify the problems of the pupils with those of the school and community. This implies extensive use of environmental materials. The activities must have a close relationship to the out-of-school life and the children must see this relationship. As children are constantly bringing into school for school use experiences, information, objects gathered out of school, and carrying out into the out-of-school life that which they experience in school, they are being educated.

Teachers should grow in the ability to utilize community resources

To these purposes, derived from the statement of point of view, the teachers added three others: (1) teachers should increase their understanding of the total school program, (2) teachers should improve in physical, mental, and emotional health, and (3) teachers should grow in ability to promote learning on the part of boys and girls. These were the needs they sensed as they examined their responsibilities.

ACTIVITIES CARRIED OUT

The high school teachers did not proceed to organize a program to meet these needs directly; instead they attacked the job of improving education for the boys and girls in their school and community. That is to say, they did not organize study groups for the general purpose of increasing their understanding of children and the community. Their efforts were not oriented toward their own needs, rather they were oriented toward the needs of children. They knew, for example, that there were serious health problems in the school and the community; they proceeded to work on those problems. As they tackled such tasks, however, they grew in their understanding of children, the community, and the school's program. They also discovered needs for more resources and help. Consultant services, local workshops, attendance at special workshops in other institutions, and reorganizations in their own manner of working together, constituted some of these aids.

Local and countywide surveys of health and recreational needs were among the major projects carried out. Teachers throughout the county, working in cooperation with social agencies, doctors, dentists, and nurses, organized programs for immunizing children against certain contagious diseases and examining them for hookworm, dental defects, and social disease. Programs for treatment were developed. Clinics were organized. Parents and children needed to be educated to accept and support these activities. Follow-up study showed that treatment was not the whole solution to the problem of hookworm infection: for example, there needed to be an educational program to improve diet and sanitary conditions. An analysis of foods served in the school cafeteria, and observation of children's choices of foods, showed that some of the dietary standards were not met in the school itself. Through the combined planning of the cafeteria manager, a committee of teachers, and the NYA, it was found possible to offer two vegetables, meat, and a drink for ten cents. Other inexpensive combinations also became available. Reading materials on food content and balanced diet were prepared for use with the children. Subsequent observation by the cafeteria manager, the principal, and several interested teachers convinced them that the boys and girls had improved in their choice of food. Children who were unable to buy their noonday lunch at the cafeteria were given luncheon ticket books privately by their teachers.

There were other community projects. The high school teachers made an economic survey of the community, interviewing 123 business and professional men. Beyond gathering data on economic conditions, the teachers made new acquaintances, and got a clearer picture of parents' and employers' attitudes toward education. School, community, and home beautification programs were developed. Still other projects were directed toward getting people to screen their windows and doors, improve their methods of laundering, develop better habits of personal cleanliness. The agriculture, home economics, art, and biology teachers carried the initiative in some of these projects but there was also schoolwide interest and participation.

Another type of project in the Moultrie High School grew out of one teacher's attempt to deal with a perennial school problem. Many boys in the school were taking little interest in their classroom work, and teachers were finding it difficult to provide meaningful experience for them. One teacher undertook to plan a program with about thirty-five of these boys. As they discussed personal, school, and community problems, they discovered, among other things, that most of the boys had jobs during out-of-school hours and knew from experience that unsanitary conditions existed in meat markets, dairies, drug stores, and restaurants. This led the class to decide to visit such establishments. After having done so they discussed their observations. They also consulted the local health office about its effort to promote sanitary practices, the character of sanitation laws, and the obstacles in the way of their enforcement. Interest developed concerning other laws and ordinances and a study of local government services resulted.

Thus it was that teacher participation in a broad survey and various community projects led to modifications and extensions in the educational program of the high school. Their activities also brought changes in the sort of records and reports they kept, and in the ways in which they worked together. For example, they had often come together according to grade levels or by subject-matter areas. Community problems, however, required the formation of diversified working groups. In addition, routine faculty meetings held every other Tuesday evening gave way to committee and smaller group meetings on problems of special interest. Daily after-school teas became popular as an opportunity for relaxation and an occasion for small groups to discuss new problems and report progress on various activities.

The staff discovered that the new flexibility of this program increased the need for careful planning. Accordingly, a pre-school conference to block out general activities for the year was held in September 1940. Progress and problems of the past year were reviewed and groups were organized to continue work on those problems. Various committees were set up—a committee on the induction of new teachers, on health, recreation, distribution and care of instructional materials, care of buildings and grounds, beautification of community and homes, cafeteria, and several others. Teachers could choose the ones on which they wished to serve.

While the brief description given above is by no means complete, it is hoped that it does give a fair picture of the sort of school and community enterprise which was tackled, and a useful background for the evaluative reports which follow.

EVIDENCE OF CHANGE

It will be recalled that when the teachers examined their responsibilities in the Moultrie schools, they acknowledged several needs: for increased understanding of children, of the community, and of the total program of the school; for increased ability to promote learning among boys and girls, to work democratically with others, and to utilize community and academic resources; and for the improvement of their physical, mental, and emotional health. To judge the extent to which growth has been made in these directions evidence from several sources is available. Teachers have written appraisals of their own progress, of changes in the school's program, and of changes observed in children. Principals and supervisors have recorded observations of the teachers under various conditions. Records of student progress have been examined; participation in community projects summarized; incidental observations of group and individual behavior recorded in the notes of teachers' meetings; and data examined from teachers' personal files relative to units taught during the year, judgments of children's physical condition, social attitudes, and other factors. Some of this evidence is presented below.

From teachers' statements

Teachers were asked to write critically about their individual progress, their efforts to improve the educational program in the high school, the help they may have received from various sources, and the progress of the school and faculty generally. While these accounts were written as part of the report to the Commission they also served a very useful purpose locally in helping the staff summarize its own experience and identify some of the conditions that promote teacher growth. The following appraisal reveals some of the changes that came about in the teacher who wrote it and illustrates as well some of the potentialities of personal accounts as a technique of evaluation.

As I survey with a critical eye the growth of Moultrie High School over a period covering the last eight years, it seems to me that two developments stand out above all others. . . . These two philosophies appear to have guided its other phases of growth. They are:
1. The realization of the great social significance of educating for citizenship in the democratic way of life
2. The realization that every individual's growth as a well rounded personality better fits him for that democratic citizenship
As a member of the faculty of this school, I believe that my own growth has been largely determined by those principles. I believe I always thought that education for citizenship was important and even uttered words to this effect, but I'm afraid they were often just words. Always I was working toward some achievement of the future rather than realizing that every individual student is a citizen in a democracy now. I think the philosophy of this particular school and its principal has led me to realize this truth far more than words. It is learning to work together for the good of the whole group; learning to plan and make decisions that affect that group; learning many more principles of democratic living.

I think my workshop experience and the national crisis have . . . given stimulus to my actual classroom emphasis upon this phase. I am sure I have done more this year than ever before to help students to a realization of their benefits from, responsibilities to, and individual importance in, a country devoted to the democratic way.

As we study and work with boys and girls our knowledge of them inevitably grows. As we watch hopeless "hoodlums" miraculously grow into fine young men and steady heads of households, and silly, giggling girls mature into purposeful homemakers and mothers, we naturally gain perspective. I believe, however, that some very definite experiences have contributed to my growth in the understanding of human nature.

Although I had studied child and adolescent psychology and have continued to read about and study at first hand boys and girls in and out of the class, I believe I have begun only recently to appreciate fully the significant influence of environment in shaping the emotional life of students. I think this insight has come about through my own marriage, homemaking, and motherhood experiences. These experiences have also given me a contact with mothers from the home's and mother's final viewpoint as well as the school's. This has been of inestimable value in understanding and reaching individual children. My husband, through his knowledge of the physical and emotional reactions of adolescent boys, has helped me more than all the books I've ever read to a broader understanding of growing boys.

The appreciation of the great part that the school may play in offering a variety of opportunities for growth of a well rounded personality has been a part of my growth as a teacher in this school. I have always tried to achieve an informal give-and-take atmosphere of comradeship between pupil and teacher. I have believed that pupils should have a part in plans because it was the fair thing, but I have only gradually realized the significance of pupil participation in planning as an educational experience. With this realization there also grew a belief that it is not so important what a student chooses to study but that in determining goals, making and carrying out a plan of work, and evaluating his progress he is developing his personality. This development teaches such traits as ability to think for himself, to exercise initiative, to become a leader or an intelligent follower, and to measure his own growth.

These theories grew and developed gradually in my own thinking. My teaching for carrying out my theories did not grow so rapidly, however. I was working with a freshman group . . . to determine the following things:

1. Suitable problems for study based upon needs and interests
2. Goals or things we would want to get out of such a study
3. Materials we would need
4. How we were going to study
5. Activities which would be involved
6. Work plans and schedules
7. Evaluation of finished product and growth during study by group and individuals

As the work got under way my first reaction was discouragement and I'm afraid there was confusion. The children were somewhat baffled and hesitant because they lacked initiative and faith in their ability to judge and decide for themselves. I couldn't be in enough places at the same time to approve each individual's every movement and each student was afraid to go on unless the teacher said so and how. After analyzing the situation I realized that I needed to make the transition more gradually. The difference was immediately evident in the purposefulness of the students and their growth in developing independence.

My next problem was to learn to evaluate the full growth of the student rather than the finished product of the work done. When I finally got through my head the fact that progress is the focal point for measurement it was like a form shaping itself out of a maze of shadows.

I believe the next phase involved a theory that a great deal of the personal growth of the student hinged upon his ability to take inventory of himself and of his class and diagnose his own weaknesses. I believe this self-evaluation gives greater impetus to his purpose than any other one thing. More recently I have been trying to determine better techniques of helping the student evaluate his own progress with a frank and critical eye.

In my own classroom I tried to remember that most individuals need encouragement by a word of praise here and there. I am not happy in my work unless I feel I have the support of the administration, the community, my fellow teachers, and the students. I am one of those people who must have approbation and a word of praise occasionally. I will work unceasingly and happily for those who I feel appreciate my efforts.

Although our emotional state always affects our work, I think my actual physical well-being influences my classroom work more than any other one factor. If I begin to get too discouraged about the results of my work, I know that I have overtaxed my energy and that I am at the point of exhaustion. A little rest is all the medicine I need.

To have some sympathetic person whose opinions I respect and whose interest I enlist, with whom to talk things over, means everything to me. Just to think out loud with such a person clears the cobwebs from my mind.

It is a different thing for me to analyze my classroom work and determine my greatest work weaknesses and strengths. One so far outweighs the other and the scales leave me wanting. In certain times I am inclined to expect too much academically from a student and to use an adult yardstick for measuring progress. According to my own theory, I believe I sometimes do too much for the student that might be excellent training if he were to do for himself. On the other hand, when I examine the classroom procedures of some of my fellow workers, I find I don't do so much as many of them do. I have not yet determined a suitable criterion for my own use. Occasionally I have been inclined to get lost in a mass of details and become sidetracked from my big underlying purpose.

I consider that my greatest strength in the classroom is learning to know my students personally—their interests, home background, etc. It is gratifying to know that many of them come to me with intimate details of problems, triumphs, etc. Many come even after I no longer teach them.

What is revealed in this account? This teacher has made a number of shifts in her thinking about the role of education: from democracy as something to prepare for, to democracy as a way of life in the school; from planning as a fair thing to do, to planning as an educational experience; from product to progress as the focal point in measurement; from evaluating students, to helping students evaluate themselves. These concepts of education have led her to increased study of children in and out of school, to new insights about motivation in learning and evaluating, and to seeing that new ways of working with children call for much learning on the part of both teacher and pupil. She has, moreover, come to understand better her own limitations —to know symptoms of fatigue, and to identify the relations with students and colleagues which make for mutual helpfulness.

One must recognize of course that what this teacher has reported may not check entirely with the observations of other teachers or the principal. Its general tone, however, is in harmony with evidence collected from other sources. From such data it is quite apparent that teachers in the Moultrie High School were free to admit weaknesses, were accustomed to open discussions with their administrators, and were therefore not inhibited by any fear of the consequences in writing these reports. At least, the tendency toward artificiality which often goes with assigned reports was reduced to a minimum by the conditions surrounding the preparation of these documents.

From observation of teachers

Independent observations of teachers at work lend support to personal opinions and descriptions. The following is a report of one classroom observation and follow-up conference:

Another class labeled as mathematics, visited without warning the first period of a Monday morning, revealed some interesting activities. As soon as the opening bell rang, several students, with no apparent reminder from the teacher, moved around the room attending to a variety of responsibilities. One student checked the daily budgets of money obtained and spent. These budgets were checked once a week and a discussion held as to the problems arising in connection with obtaining, earning, and spending money. Other children attended to definite responsibilities connected with cleaning and straightening the classroom. Another child checked on the defense stamps bought and brought the chart of the class total up to date. Another checked on the number who had brushed their teeth regularly. As the class was studying percentage, the teacher used the figures concerning the stamps bought and teeth brushed to begin the work on percentage. The teacher appeared cheerful and vigorous in speech and manner. She asked the students to make a list of things to be done during the period. As the group carried on the various activities listed they had freedom to discuss their difficulties and to ask questions. A considerable portion of the period was taken up by the students checking their own individual folders. In these folders each child kept a list of words encountered which he didn't understand, assignment sheets, a chart showing the number of times he had brushed his teeth, an expense account, a notebook of class notes, a list of Bible verses and quotations, sheets of problem exercises in mathematics, a calendar, and a list of defense stamps bought. At the close of the period the class stopped long enough to evaluate its work for the period. They discussed the value of each thing done, the way the time had been used, ways of using the time better, and set up tentative plans for the next day.

A conference was held with this teacher after the observation. When asked how she developed the practice of giving students a share in the planning, giving them definite responsibilities, and getting them to evaluate themselves, she replied, "I think workshop experiences helped me see the value of students' assuming responsibility and evaluating themselves. There is no comparison in the interest of students now and when I did all the planning myself and handed it out. Oh yes, in the home economics room I saw a chart of household duties that gave me the idea of delegating routine responsibility." She also stated that she attempts to utilize experiences of interest to students as leads (motivation) to achievement of mathematical skills. She listed as the most helpful resources contributing to her growth a former principal, her present principal, two or three fellow teachers, certain textbooks, and the *Mathematics Journal*.

In speaking of her relationships with students this teacher said,

"It has taken me years to develop friendly, easy relationships with my students. I tend to work under tension and 'blow up' easily when I have minor interruptions and things of that nature. Two things have been of real help to me in developing friendly relations: visiting the children in their homes and helping them with projects to get spending money, such as selling eggs, etc."

Although the observational report does not give evidence concerning student achievement in mathematics, it leaves little doubt that students are participating in activities of service to the group, learning to plan, evaluating the use of their time, and capitalizing on problems growing out of their interests and activities to learn mathematical skills.

Another observational report reveals something about relationships among teachers:

One Friday after school, when no regular meetings were scheduled and when conceivably the teachers would be anxious to get away from the school after a hard week, one teacher decided to go around and see the things teachers were doing. His findings were significant. One hour after school was closed he found many small groups of teachers in the home economics rooms where they had stayed after being served tea. It was evident that most had struck some common interest with other teachers and had stayed to talk. Three teachers working at the same grade level were in one corner of the room discussing various students they taught. They were informally pooling their information about, attitudes toward, and plans for helping each student. The discussions were emotionally charged because the teachers had a sincere desire to help the students being discussed. These teachers remained in this discussion for over an hour. In another corner of the room two apprentice teachers were describing some of their experiences to each other and discussing their problems. They continued in the discussion for over an hour. Two other teachers were in the kitchen discussing plans for putting on the junior play about three weeks from that date. About six freshmen and sophomore teachers were sitting around a table discussing the best way to do immunization work in the classes. This was not a scheduled meeting; it formed spontaneously. A home economics teacher was busy getting materials for some adult evening classes. A chemistry teacher was in her room working with some students giving the laboratory a thorough cleaning. Two other teachers were in a classroom discussing ways and means of improving writing skills. Thus on a Friday afternoon with no meetings planned, seventeen teachers [more than half the total group] voluntarily stayed after school for well over an hour to work on things which they hoped would improve the job they were trying to do.

Few would question the validity of using the observations reported above as evidence that these teachers are genuinely interested in their professional responsibilities and that they are working together on common and related problems. Few could doubt that growth in professional competence must be taking place.

From student progress

So far the evidences of change we have reported have been concerned with such matters as more pupil participation in planning, more democratic relationships with and among teachers, more attention to student and community needs, and so on. It is presumed that these matters are not unrelated to the ultimate goal of teacher education—namely, to improve the learning of boys and girls. The next two reports give evidence relative to student achievement and to tasks accomplished. The first describes some changes in the program for teaching English and shows student progress in adequacy of written expression.

Since 1938, the English and social studies classes in all but the senior year have been combined. The senior teachers plan and work together as closely as possible. English has become a supplementary skill subject used in connection with other subjects and has ceased to be a separate body of subject matter. . . .

Every effort has been made to make English a part of the work in every class in the school by close collaboration between English teachers and others. In teacher-teacher conferences efforts have been made to show teachers of science, home economics, and other fields how they can be teachers of English. One of these is the system of checking papers by a chart prepared by all the English and social studies teachers. . . . The plan called for a checking system using numbers to denote [common] errors. A copy of the list of errors and their corresponding numbers was given to every student. . . . In some cases the teachers send written work to the English teachers for correction. . . . In the senior year students do much individual study on interests discovered in other classes. The teachers stress reading as an important part of English and feel that such reading should, wherever practical, grow out of the special interests of the students. . . .

Widespread student self-evaluation and checking of oral and written work place responsibility for good work on the students. English courses have become more functional through the above and through the use of a uniform system of grading papers. Grammar is taught when the need appears, but in most cases the teachers attempt to make the learning have transfer values into actual writing and speaking. In 1940-41, the seniors' written work showed the following decrease in errors:

TABLE IV

TOTAL NUMBER OF STUDENT ERRORS IN SUCCESSIVE GROUPS OF EIGHT PAPERS EACH

Type of Error	Groups of Papers					
	1–8	9–16	17–24	25–32	33–40	41–48
Spelling	1,875	1,958	810	762	659	503
Agreement of subject and predicate	579	403	352	267	238	146
Agreement pronoun and antecedent	324	193	106	92	70	53
Run together sentence	258	174	157	102	71	46
Incomplete sentence	360	182	127	94	78	59
Misuse of tense	319	180	75	56	48	39
Misuse of case	378	209	171	106	87	60
Misuse or omission of comma	630	451	382	327	240	218
Other punctuation	1,248	752	451	406	385	206
Mechanics: capitals, abbreviations, syllabification, etc.	816	690	572	520	371	243
Sentence unity	237	164	150	123	91	75
Double negative	67	51	45	33	30	24
Clearness	631	409	357	296	223	167
Diction	1,008	890	768	710	249	452
Subjunctive mood	41	49	57	52	50	23
Paragraphing	104	87	72	67	56	24
Misuse of adjective or adverb	125	105	78	70	56	29
Total errors	9,000	6,047	4,730	4,083	3,402	2,367

The second report gives an impressive picture of tasks done in the school and community beautification programs:

Prior to the year 1939-40, the school had made no organized effort to encourage beautification. The home economics and vocational agriculture teachers had included beautification as a part of their courses, however, and served as leaders for the remainder of the school.

The campaign since 1939-40 was organized about two main activities: (1) home beautification and (2) community beautification.

While certain classes undertook an intensive study of beautification, the greater part of the program was carried out through the advisory groups. Each student was urged to plant at least one tree on his home grounds and to take part in planting trees on the campus, hospital grounds, and on vacant lots. . . . The trees were secured by the agriculture students and sold to the students for a small amount. Some of the trees were bought from a nursery while others were brought from the woods. A number of fruit trees were planted on the farms by the students. Some of the types of tree planted were: dogwood, oak, willow, youpon, mimosa, red bud, crabapple, and pine.

Certain classes undertook a more comprehensive study of beautification and engaged in projects such as the following: landscaping home grounds, building rock gardens, building flower stands, making curtains, reupholstering furniture, and planting flower gardens. The agriculture students landscaped the grounds around the [school] building, around the Happiness Cottage, around an orphanage in the city, planted trees on the hospital grounds, and built a school nursery.

One group, the Future Farmers of America, summarized their accomplishments as follows:

1. 2500 pine trees were set out at hospital
2. 5000 pine trees were set out in community
3. 20 homes have been landscaped
4. Approximately 30 homes have been screened
5. 6000 shrubbery cuttings were set out
6. County clean-up campaign sponsored
7. 14 bookshelves and 17 flower boxes were made for homes
8. Boys sponsored tree-planting campaign in community
9. 14,145 pine trees were set out on eroded land

From incidental sources

During the first year or two of the Moultrie High School's association with the cooperative study little attempt was made to record incidental observations of student behavior and of various school attitudes. Later however, a feeling that much valuable evidence of change was thus being lost led to the keeping of memoranda and notes. Some of the observations were discussed in teachers' meetings and were put into the records of those meetings. Teachers came to feel that many evidences of change in themselves and their students were brought out in these discussions. In the next chapter we shall discuss the use of secretarial records in evaluation. Here, we shall simply present a few excerpts from such records made during 1941-42 in Moultrie to illustrate some of the changes teachers believed were taking place.

Changes in teachers' attitudes toward meetings:

... It is the opinion of some who work in the program that teachers are inclined more and more to make statements before the group which they formerly made only in private to their best friends after the meetings. Statements made in private such as, "Half these meetings are unnecessary; we get in there and waste our time talking about things that are unimportant," changed to statements made to the group such as, "I think we ought to get clearly in mind just what it is that we are going to try to do in this meeting. We've got to distinguish between what's important and what's not." And again, "Our meetings drag out until we don't have time for anything else in the afternoon," made in private has changed to "I believe the morale of the group would be better if we began and closed our meetings on time," made before the entire group.

Changes in children growing out of improved pupil-teacher relationships:

... A few years ago students would stiffen up and say "sh-h-h" when they saw certain members of the staff approach. The students had a tendency to look upon these persons as policemen. Today when students see most of these same persons they are quick to speak in a warm, friendly manner.

In general there seems to be less nervous tension on the part of the students in the school. This can be noted in the classroom and on the campus. In many spots there is much less fighting and rough playing on the campus and much more organized, orderly playing. In some cases it is reported that recesses and play periods run more smoothly now with student recreation leaders than formerly when play was unorganized and not guided, but when the teachers stood around on the campus to see to it that fighting and disorder did not break out. Several teachers at the lunch table recently remarked that fewer instances of boys and girls breaking out in open rebellion or doing things purposefully to annoy the teachers in the classroom have occurred in the last few years.

Incidental observations such as these are sometimes very revealing in themselves; more often, however, they are a useful stimulant to systematic observation and survey.

WORKING TOGETHER FOR FURTHER IMPROVEMENT

The testimonial, observational, survey and other evidence presented in the preceding pages is, we believe, representative of the larger body of data in the report of the Moultrie High School. Equally extensive accounts could be given of the elementary programs in the city and county school systems. Looking back over the events of the past few years the teachers of all three systems have tried to summarize the evidence of progress. There is no clear description of their status at an early stage against which an outsider can compare their status later, but within the data they report there is evidence of change, and it would be difficult to discount the validity of their conclusions. In their opinion the following generalizations are warranted:

1. More teachers have a sincere desire to grow and improve.

2. The relationships that exist between the human beings connected with the program are freer, more democratic, and more friendly. This applies to the relationships that exist between the school board, the administrators, the teachers, the parents, and the children.

3. There are more sincere efforts made to work together on common problems and toward common goals on the part of the schools in the unit, the administrators, the teachers, the parents, the children, and community agencies.

4. More teachers have a better understanding of the children with whom they work and of the nature of child growth and development.

5. More teachers believe that school experiences should be centered around the problems, interests, and needs of the individual.

6. More teachers believe that the function of the school is to serve the community in which it is located.

7. Teachers understand better and are more sensitive to certain social problems which now exist in our community.

8. More teachers use community and academic resources effectively.

9. More teachers have a broader understanding of the total school program.

10. More teachers are willing to use an experimental approach as they function in the school program.

11. More teachers have a greater respect for themselves and the work they are trying to do.

A comparison of these conclusions with the seven goals or needs for teacher growth identified earlier shows not only considerable accomplishment in the direction they wanted to go but also the discovery of some additional achievements—for example, an increased desire to improve and an increased willingness to experiment. The teachers in the Colquitt County and Moultrie schools took an important step beyond drawing conclusions about their progress. They asked themselves: What are some of the conditions conducive to teacher growth? As they looked back over their experience with this question in mind they came to the following conclusions:

1. Teachers grow when they have a feeling of achievement and when they have the respect of others.
2. Teachers grow when they set up clear and worthwhile purposes within their reach.
3. [The] clarity of [the teachers'] purpose increased as they saw definite results in the lives of students. . . . On the other hand, as teachers try many types of things and see results, they come to have an increasing clarity of purpose that will act as a guide for future action.
4. Teachers grow when they have many varied, free, and open avenues of communication with others.
5. A feeling of belonging to the group is necessary for teacher growth.
6. Teachers must have freedom to experiment with their own hypotheses and plans, and must not be limited too much by established procedures.
7. Teachers grow when school activities are centered around environmental problems.
8. Cooperative efforts among teachers in which they feel themselves a part of the group, find common purposes, and work together to break down barriers make for teacher growth.
9. Teachers grow as they participate in experiences leading to an understanding of the total school program.
10. Teachers grow as they have responsibilities they are capable of fulfilling.
11. When personal matters are satisfactorily adjusted teachers tend to grow.
12. Teachers grow when they are working in jobs they are trained

to handle and for which they are emotionally and physically adapted.

13. Teachers grow as they are able to develop gradually and when they do not have to take on duties and responsibilities they are not ready to assume.

14. Free and easy relationships with children promote teacher growth.

15. Teachers grow when they find economic security and have sufficient money to live the "good life," to buy the small things necessary to mental ease, and when they do not have to make teaching a continual battle against penury.

The term "growth" as they have used it here is in many ways synonymous with "learn." One could perhaps also substitute for "growth" the expression "increase in effectiveness." That conditions conducive to growth or learning or increased effectiveness are, in the opinion of these teachers, so heavily weighted with considerations of human relationships, personal security, social acceptance, respect, and so on is a fact of very great importance. It is important for education generally and it has some special applications in evaluation.

Three facts about the Moultrie evaluation deserve further comment for they have, in our opinion, significant implications for in-service education and appraisal. First, the teachers succeeded in developing a spirit of good will that was conducive to forthright self-evaluation. Second, the evaluation found its place within the continuous teaching and learning of the school. And third, the motivation for teacher growth came from doing jobs and meeting needs which teachers believed to be important.

That personal and job security free the teacher to admit weakness, as well as strength, there can be no doubt. Forthrightness and objectivity in teachers' self-evaluations and their appraisals of the educational program are not likely to be found unless there is this basic freedom. At Moultrie there was extensive opportunity for teachers to check their own appraisals against the judgment of others in group discussions, and this tended to make for greater objectivity in their evaluation. Furthermore, there was an absence of perfectionist standards in the administration and among the teachers. No individual or group of individuals was making punitive judgments with a set of criteria, pronouncing certain practices as good or bad, and identifying teachers as strong or weak. Instead, teachers and administrators recognized the magnitude of certain educational problems and understood that no universal solution had been discovered for them. They saw, too, that as changes occurred in the school and in the social and economic order new problems arose. And they realized that there was much to be learned about democratic methods of work. All of these conditions served to set the teachers free to examine themselves and their program and to proceed within the limits of their understanding, time, and energy to work out solutions to their problems.

In many schools appraisal activities are something added to the primary business of teaching and learning. The group at Moultrie tried to capture evaluative evidence in the ongoing activities of students and teachers. In all the plans and reports students made, teachers sought evidence of students' adequacy in expressing themselves in writing; in student behavior in the lunchroom, on the playground, and in individual conferences, teachers looked for evidence of their own effectiveness and of their students' progress; in the records of staff meetings, in the classroom observations, and elsewhere they found further data of evaluative significance. The only evaluation activity that was "added on" was the written self-appraisal report from individual teachers. These accounts were written in order that a more complete record of progress could be made to the Commission. But the Moultrie teachers were ready for that "assignment." Indeed, they used it themselves as a step leading to a formulation of their convictions about factors that make for teacher growth— an action voluntary on their part.

Evaluation activities in the Moultrie High School originated at the source of need and were developed by those who sensed the need and could use the results. There are implications in this fact relevant to group organization and the role of a central administration. The Moultrie High School is not small: it enrolls over 800 students; it serves both rural and urban areas;

most of its departments have three or more teachers. In large cities where there are many schools and where there is a large central administrative and supervisory staff, there is a tendency for the central staff to originate policy, identify needs, prescribe programs, and impose evaluation procedures. It is well to re-call some of the experiences at Moultrie which made teachers self-propelling, which stimulated action and appraisal: students were seen to be fidgety and aimless in class and unruly on the playground; individual conferences and visits to homes sharp-ened teachers' sensitivity to student needs; community needs were revealed through surveys; stimulation and support were coming continually from the principal and from the other teachers. These and other experiences led the teachers to seek help in meeting their problems—to find better ways of adjusting the program to individual needs, better methods of helping students evaluate their progress, better ways of communicating between those who were directly responsible for a program and those whose passive if not active support was needed, better ways of inducting new teachers, better ways of planning with children. The role of a central staff in a large school system, like the role of leadership in the individual school, is best con-ceived as one of service. Its role is not to give answers, for who knows the answers to these questions? Its role is to help teachers work experimentally toward solutions, to free teachers to tackle their problems vigorously and objectively.

No one would be quicker than the teachers and administra-tors in Colquitt County to deny any notion that they had per-fectly evaluated their program or the growth of teachers and students. They have used tests, observations, questionnaires, descriptions, records. Some of their evidence is convincing; some of it is not much better than a guess; much of it is subjective. Of this they are thoroughly aware. Yet all of their data fit to-gether to give a general impression of growth and progress. And their methods of work give promise that they will improve their bases for evaluation as rapidly as time and resources per-mit.

SUMMARY

The descriptions included in this chapter have been related in varying degrees to the central topic of evaluating the growth of teachers in service. The Ohio experiment sought to promote and evaluate teacher growth by the observation of teachers in their classrooms followed by discussions with them in the light of a carefully prepared outline which had served as a guide to the observation. Most of the teachers and supervisors thought that they were benefited by the procedure; they became more keenly aware of a philosophy of education; and they felt that they had modified some of their methods of teaching and working together as a result of it. The studies in Denver and Spokane sought to promote and evaluate teacher growth by analyzing comprehensively and in detail the teacher's relationships with the pupils in his class. The teachers were enthusiastic about the help which they got from that service; they liked it especially because it was specific and pertinent and personal; and they also said that they had modified teaching procedures as a result. Both the Ohio and the Denver-Spokane studies were dependent in part upon special consultants from outside the local school systems, and both focused their attention more or less directly upon individual teachers in their classroom situations. The Norris and Moultrie descriptions, on the other hand, were of teachers working together on local projects in which they were commonly interested. The evidence of teacher growth and increased effectiveness, particularly striking in the case of Moultrie, was found in changed attitudes, revised curricula, more functional ways of working together, and as well in pupil attitudes and accomplishments.

Within this variety of experiment and procedure relative to the evaluation of teachers in service one can find two common threads and two corresponding implications for evaluation practices: In each description the importance of genuinely democratic procedures was evident—evaluative procedures in which the security and individuality and status of the teacher were respected. Evaluation was an activity teachers did with others;

not something others did to teachers. When such cooperative relationships obtained, teachers were free to face weaknesses and to experiment. And second, in each description the importance of beginning with problems and needs locally felt was evident. Evaluation was most helpful in stimulating teacher growth when it focused on problems about which the teachers were personally concerned—their effectiveness in class, their relationships with pupils, their own programs, their part in the life of the school and community. Teachers grew in effectiveness as they participated fully and freely in attacks on such problems.

IX

Special In-Service Activities

IN A VERY IMPORTANT sense the present chapter is a continuation of the previous one. Growth in service is influenced
by conditions within teachers and within their environment.
And the effectiveness of an environment, in turn, is judged by
the growth of individual teachers in it. Thus, the topics "Growth
in Service" and "Special In-Service Activities" are but aspects
of one broad problem. The point of departure for the present
chapter, however, is in-service activity rather than the individual
teacher.

There are, of course, a great many types of in-service teacher
education. Summer schools and extension courses, for example,
have long been familiar and widely used services to teachers.
Evaluation in them has been concerned primarily with individual teachers' progress. The common techniques of examinations and term papers are employed, and grades are given sig-
nifying mastery of the course content. Appraisal of their value
for those who take them—as a group, and in individual cases—
has however been rare. In such an appraisal, teachers and their
administrators in the local school system would have to participate, and the criterion would be improved teaching rather than
mastery of course content.

Other types of in-service activity include travel, independent
study, summer work experience, field trips. All these may be
thought of as individual activities as may summer schools and
extension courses. And for all of them the ultimate test of value
must be sought in improved teaching. This test is hard to apply,
not only because improved teaching is a difficult criterion to
define but also because applying it satisfactorily seems to require the cooperation of a great many people—the teachers
themselves, their administrators and supervisors, and their pupils.

It is perhaps unfortunate that more attempts at appraisal of this sort with regard to these common in-service activities have not been made. In the cooperative study of teacher education only one of them—field trips—was evaluated systematically. Special evaluators accompanied teachers and an instructor on several field trips sponsored by The Open Road, in the summer of 1940. And during the winter an extensive follow-up study was made to judge the changes in teachers and teaching that had taken place as a result of the experience. Certain aspects of these evaluations have been described elsewhere.[1]

Our discussion in this chapter will be limited to a selection of activities with which participating institutions did the most experimenting. Among such activities were study groups, the use of consultant services, the sending of local staff members to visit other institutions, participation in local planning committees, participation in conferences of both a local and national character, and workshops. The experience of colleges and school systems with most of these enterprises is described more fully in two other of the Commission's publications.[2] Our selection here is limited to three of them—study groups, consultant services, and workshops. The first two may be considered as activities teachers participate in or make use of on the job—that is, during the regular school term, while workshops are comprehensive special activities usually scheduled during the summer months.

APPRAISAL OF STUDY GROUPS

Study groups (and committees) are such familiar devices that no explanation of them is needed. Like any other human enterprise, they accomplish their purposes with varying degrees of success. Sometimes procedures are studied, decisions made, accepted, and implemented by such groups to the satisfaction of

---

[1] Gordon W. Blackwell, "Studying the South Firsthand," *The Educational Record*, XXIII (April 1942), 271-82. Joseph J. Romoda, "Field Trips for Teachers," *Phi Delta Kappan*, XXIV (September 1941), 13-16.

[2] See the forthcoming volume in this series on in-service education by Charles E. Prall and C. Leslie Cushman, and the volume on pre-service education by W. Earl Armstrong and Ernest V. Hollis.

all concerned. Sometimes they move too fast; they come to superficial conclusions in their study of a problem, or they move so far beyond the thinking of the larger group for whom they are working that they propose solutions which others are not ready to accept. For lack of leadership, inadequate resources, personality clashes, or various reasons, some groups make little or no progress.

Evaluation in such situations means, primarily, thinking about the effectiveness of group activity with a view to discarding or modifying what fails to contribute to the accomplishment of group purposes and to retaining and improving what works well. Viewed broadly, it is not only the members of a study group who are concerned with its progress, and hence its evaluation; there is also concern on the part of the administration and the nonparticipating teachers. In a comprehensive evaluation, there would be at least three lines of evidence that would need to be considered. First, there would be the progress of the study group itself: the extent to which it achieved the group purposes it had set for itself, and the effect on individuals of participation in the group's activity. Second, there would be the point of view of the administration: this would be concerned with the relation of the particular study group to other in-service activity and its impact upon the total program of the school system or college. And third, there would be the influence of the group on the nonparticipating teachers, particularly those teachers who were facing problems similar to the ones being faced by the study group. Our special interest is in the sort of evaluation that is an integral and indispensable part of the work of teachers and administrators as they participate together in study groups and committees of various sorts.

USE OF SECRETARIAL RECORDS

In the cooperative study secretarial records of group activity have proved useful many times in identifying weaknesses and strengths of group work, and in furthering progress. The usefulness of the record, however, depends upon anticipation of the demands that are to be made on it. Often these demands have not been anticipated by the group in delegating secretarial responsibility or by the secretary who assumes the responsibility. The chore of recording may have been given to whoever is willing to take it or perhaps to someone who has had stenographic training. What often results is a bare record of motions approved and recommendations made, or a nearly verbatim account which few people will ever read. There are, of course, records varying in length and quality that stand between these extremes. The value of any record depends on the extent to which it serves the purposes of a particular group; and the members of the group might profitably discuss these purposes during one of their early meetings. Do we need a record of our activity? What purposes should the record serve? What should go into the record in order to fulfill those purposes? Whom should we appoint as secretary? How often and to whom should reports be made? Obviously, complete answers to these questions cannot be given at the beginning of the group's work, but an early discussion of these questions can help to clarify responsibilities and give clues to the kind of record needed.

In a number of the institutions in the cooperative study secretaries and chairmen of committees and study groups have held meetings to discuss the purposes and content of secretarial records. Under the two headings, suggested purposes and suggested content, we have given a composite of their deliberations. And their responses indicate a number of ways in which records can contribute to the effectiveness of group work.

Suggested purposes

A first purpose of records is that they should be such as to facilitate periodic self-appraisal. When studied individually and in sequence they should reveal accomplishments and failures, along with suggestions for subsequent meetings, when progress is slowing down, when discussion is going in circles, when new resources (such as consultants) should be brought in, when professional literature should be explored, when work between meetings should be delegated. Also, they should reveal as clearly as possible the original and emerging goals of the group. In revealing such information as this the records can contribute to the group's effectiveness.

Certain aspects of group work perhaps need special mention. Work on any important educational problem should result in learning which, in addition to solving that problem, may have important by-products. The record should show what some of these by-products are: new ways of discussing issues without being stymied by personality clashes; newly discovered resources within the group; improvements in leadership ability; new and constructive ways of achieving goals when the solution tends to affect the security of some staff members; better ways of communicating to others outside the group.

The second major purpose which records should have is that of providing a basis for communicating to others what the group has done, and why it has done certain things and reached certain conclusions. Such communication may be important contemporaneously. Frequently a group discovers that the original purposes for which it was organized cannot be achieved until some other problems are solved. Communication of this fact to some coordinating agency or administrator may reveal that others are already at work on that problem. Thus, communication at the proper time may bring about coordination of effort and avoid duplication or conflicting solutions. An unexpected direction in the work of the committee may call for communication to other groups or individuals whose status may be affected by the outcomes. Such changes may call for temporary or permanent additions to the group personnel. Eventually, the records should provide a basis for the kind of report that will show not only derived recommendations or programs, but the reasons for making them. In preparing such a report one cannot assume that those who receive it will have fewer obstacles to understanding than the members of the group had in arriving at their solutions. In fact, effective implementation is one criterion that can be applied in judging the success of a group's activity.

Communication may also be important historically. Committees appointed for similar and related purposes in subsequent years can profit by access to records of previous study. Such groups or persons should be able to find from previous records how the committee worked, what sources they turned to for help, how helpful the sources were, what obstacles they encountered, why they derived a particular solution or made a certain recommendation rather than another, how the attitude and point of view of the group changed as they studied the problem. In other words, they should be able to profit from the prior experience of others. Incidentally, they should be able to identify members of the former committee—they may want to talk with them. Actually, adequate historical records of faculty committees and study groups are rare. The following condition is more typical: in one of the colleges in the cooperative study a large faculty committee was set up to reorganize the general education program. This same task had been delegated to committees twice within the eight years immediately preceding. Both times the committee had studied the problem, made recommendations which were approved, and had been dismissed. The records were the only source of information about their work and these revealed only the bare recommendations—none of the considerations that led to them.

Suggested content

Much of the necessary content of records is clearly indicated in the foregoing statement of purposes. Other content is implied. For emphasis we have listed here some of the items that can contribute to these purposes and the usefulness of records.

1. The record should give the usual factual information about time, place, duration of meeting, and the names of those in attendance. These may seem to be unimportant mechanics, but in many discussions among secretaries and group chairmen there was repeated emphasis on the importance of knowing who came to certain conclusions, and when.

2. The record should show group objectives whenever agreed upon, with reasons for their acceptance, rejection, or modification. Original purposes should be fully given in the minutes of the first meetings.

3. The record should show the methods of work used by the group: discussions, field studies, case studies, experiments, delegated responsibilities, book reviews, special consultants, changes

in group leadership. Moreover, it should show individual and group appraisals of the usefulness of the various methods tried.

4. The record should reveal obstacles and issues that impeded or blocked progress of the group and any useful ways the group discovered for resolving issues and overcoming obstacles. Such data may contribute materially to the preparation of a final report. Moreover, procedures that contribute to the effectiveness of cooperative endeavor may be worth passing on to others, for there is still much to be learned about making democracy work.

5. The record should include preliminary and revised drafts of recommendations, proposals, syllabi, or other products of the group's activity, whether ultimately accepted or not, and should set forth reasons for acceptance, modification, or rejection. These data can reveal something of the evolution of the group's thinking. Final group action should of course be shown. When agreement has been difficult and the minority remains strongly opposed, it is especially important to give reasons for both positions.

6. The record should include plans and suggestions for implementing the recommendations of the group, and proposals for follow-up evaluation of them. This is very important though not usually done.

The chairmen and secretaries who have suggested these purposes and items of content for secretarial records recommend particularly that each new committee and study group first discuss the nature of its responsibility, determine whether or not it needs a secretary and, if it does, consider with him the purposes of his records and what he should try to write into them. Groups already established could hold similar discussions in an effort to improve the records of their work. Such discussions not only inform the secretaries but sensitize the members of the group to important matters so that they, in turn, become more helpful to the secretary in the keeping of records.

A SAMPLE RECORD

The experience of one study group associated with the Commission's program illustrates very clearly many of the considerations and values suggested in the outline given above. The supervisory group of the Pasadena City Schools has kept unusually revealing records of its activity; and its secretary prepared a report about it which was given at the Commission's second conference on evaluation. The following excerpts are from that report:[3]

First of all I considered it important to organize these records so that they would function as a learning device for the group. To accomplish this we made individual copies of all notes for every member of the group. This, it seemed, would help to provide a continuity of experience which is important if one wants to develop cooperation and unity within any given group. Instead of recording verbatim the activities and discussions, I chose to use a descriptive and interpretative technique. This was accomplished by recording key words of individual conversations and by concentrating upon thought content. . . .

In reporting our meetings I have always tried to use the individual's key words in my statements so that upon receiving the notes the person will feel a sense of ownership. This, I believe, helps the individual more closely to identify himself with the activities of the group.

To increase further the functional aspect of the records they were organized according to the following outline:
1. Those present
2. Place of meeting
3. Time
4. Purpose of meeting
5. List of problems
6. Motions
7. Discussions
8. Decisions
9. Summary

As we progressed in our study, we found new uses for our records. They proved to be an excellent device for keeping . . . our local administration . . . informed regarding our problems and activities. We also found them helpful in establishing better relationships between the principals and the supervisors by providing a means of communication between our two groups.

[3] Youldon Howell, "On the Record: A Brief Story of How the Supervisory Group of the Pasadena City Schools Has Organized Itself for the Study of Child Growth and Development," 1942 (mimeographed).

An actual record of one of the group's meetings will illustrate their organization and the nature of their content. The supervisors began working together as a study group in February 1941, when they set for themselves the problem of improving their understanding of human growth and its implications for the school program; the meeting reported here is therefore nearly one year later, and the group had been meeting semimonthly during the school year.

REPORT OF SUPERVISORY GROUP MEETING
January 20, 1942

1. Those present were: [Twenty names were listed.]
2. Meeting was held in the Board Room.
3. Time: 8 A.M. to 10:30 A.M.
4. The *purpose* of the meeting was to have a report of observations of children made by Miss A and Miss B. Dr. C was asked to lead the discussions which followed these reports.

   The following procedures adopted by the group: The principal, Mr. D, and the teacher, Miss E, were invited to sit with us while the reports were given by Miss A and Miss B. In this way they could contribute much to our understanding of the child under consideration. We are indeed grateful to [the superintendent] for making it possible for Miss E to attend our meeting as she made an important contribution to our study. We were also appreciative of the information regarding the child's home which Mr. D contributed to our discussion.
5. List of Problems

   Dr. C summarized a few of our problems for this meeting as follows:
      a. What have we gained from observations?
      b. What information was not evident in the observation that might lead to better observations?
      c. What other information do we need to understand better what we observe?
      d. How can we help the child to grow?
      e. How can we improve our own observations?
6. Motions: none
7. Discussion

   Dr. G, our study chairman, turned the meeting over to Dr. C, Miss A, and Miss B.

   Miss A started by giving us a description of a child named Donald.
      a. Not quite seven years old
      b. Thin

    c. Dark circles under eyes

    d. Clothes clean and neat

The observation was made on a fair, sunny day during a rest period. The child was lying on a table and there was soft background music.

Miss A then proceeded to describe in detail the various bodily movements during this rest period. She observed that Donald had difficulty in relaxing.

Miss B reported some of the observations that she had made. Then Miss E was asked to contribute some background material for our discussion. She gave the following:[4]

    a. IQ of 96

    b. Health

        (1) Normal vision

        (2) General appearance frail

        (3) Was 16 percent [underweight] when he was in kinder-garten

        (4) Eight percent when he was in first grade

    c. Listless, restless, and needs help in social appearance

    d. Difficulty in sharing

    e. Enjoys books

    f. Takes good care of materials

    g. Very careful of clothing and his personal appearance

    h. Great evidence of afternoon fatigue—does not do much in afternoon

Mr. D mentioned the home as being clean and tidy.[5] Miss H inquired if he liked to play. Miss G said yes—but the problem was again one of sharing; pinches ears in a teasing manner, etc. Dr. C asked what he does best. Miss G replied that Donald liked books very much. He also can concentrate indefinitely upon matching games.

Miss H wanted to know if he avoided children of his own age level. Miss E told how Donald would stand at the fence during play periods and watch the smaller children on the other side. Dr. G wondered if Donald's pretense of hitting other students was a sign that he really wanted to be more aggressive. Miss E said he definitely avoided fighting—in fact, all strenuous activity. Mrs. J wanted to know to what extent Donald was adequate in the class activities. Miss E pointed out that Donald was low in comparison to total group within the room but high within his

---

    [4] In the original record a list of twenty-five facts about Donald is given. We have reproduced a few typical ones.

    [5] The next two pages of the secretary's original record give further information about Donald—much of it in response to questions from members of the supervisory group. We have reproduced about half of these items.

small subgroup which is the lowest in the class. Mr. D questioned if he might not be bored with those of the slow group. Miss E said no, that when he was in the larger group he made very little response.

At this point Dr. C listed the problems recorded under 5. Miss A brought up the problem of what to do for Donald. Miss K suggested that perhaps the real problem was one of doing something about the mother.

Dr. L expressed the opinion that reports such as we have had in this meeting today do much to increase our sensitivity to the growth needs of children. Mr. M expressed the belief that much could be gained by continuing the study of Donald. Miss B felt that it would be valuable to hear other teams give reports on the children they are observing.

Miss E thought visits to the home would help the team which is observing Donald. Dr. G reminded us that we had a policy for our group of not establishing this kind of relationship, that we were relying [instead] upon visitations by teachers and principals.

8. Decisions

The group decided to postpone the study of Donald for one month, thus giving time for teacher, principal, and consultants to acquire additional information.

9. Summary

The important elements of these notes can be summarized as follows:

    a. Miss A and Miss B did a splendid job of reporting their observations of a child named Donald.

    b. Donald's teacher, Miss E, and his principal, Mr. D, contributed greatly to our understanding of Donald by giving us a background of health, home, and previous school experiences.

    c. It increasingly became apparent that to understand Donald we would have to have more information.

    d. There was a desire to do something for the child.

    e. The group expressed satisfaction with the meeting and felt they were becoming more aware of the needs of children.

Reviewing the year's records, the secretary notes the following evidence of progress:[6]

1. As the study has advanced, we have succeeded in increasing our cooperation between teachers, principal, and supervisor.

On March 31, 1941, the group brought up the question: "To

[6] Howell, *op. cit.*

what extent should we include principals, teachers, and parents?"

On April 15, 1941, Dr. C made the following motion: "Recognizing that it is impossible to include principals and parents in all of our activities, and recognizing that we need the help and guidance of these people, I move that as a matter of general policy we should invite into our group the principal of the child whose observational records are up for discussion."

By January 20, 1942, we find Mr. D, the principal, Miss E, the teacher, and one of our observational teams, Miss A, and Miss B discussing the case of Donald. Donald is an elementary school boy who was chosen by this team for observation. Thus we can see by the record that the group is progressing in terms of cooperation upon mutual problems.

2. Another goal was to increase our sensitivity to child behavior. For evidence of growth we turn to the notes of November 4, 1941. We find Mrs. J, a music supervisor, presenting a very practical problem to our group which indicated that our study was becoming functional. She wanted to know if in shifting the study of Mexico into the third grade from the fourth the students would encounter physical handicap due to their lack in muscular and bone development. The question was whether or not the younger child could use the same musical instruments. This was an illustration of how the records provide evidence of increased sensitivity [to child growth] on the part of our members.

3. In looking over the records I do not find enough evidence to indicate the extent of our growth in observation skills. There is, however, some indication that along with increased sensitivity our members are becoming concerned with the problem of using data of this kind in improving the learning experiences for children. In the notes for January 20, 1942, when the group was discussing the case of Donald, the members expressed a desire to do something for the child.

4. One goal we have not discussed has to do with our desire to operate within the framework of the democratic process. I believe we have evidence in the record to support the conclusion that we are making progress in this endeavor. We find that, for one thing, we have developed wide participation upon the part of our members. A sampling of nine meetings indicates that we have over 60 percent participation and that participation has tended to increase as we progress. Another indication is that everything we have done has been by the consent of the majority of the members.

We have still another aspect of this democratic process which could well be mentioned. I believe that whenever you have a group working together upon common purposes and goals and when individuals within that group begin to accept these goals and purposes as their own you have greatly increased the quality of the democratic relationships. This has been taking place within our supervisory group.

The secretary then offers evidence as to the usefulness of the year's records to various persons and for various purposes.

Let us now turn to the problem of evaluation as a part of the growth process of our group . . . one of our objectives was to develop a "simple program of evaluation designed to guide our continued growth." We have not in any sense of the word developed what might be called a "program." However, we have not been lacking in awareness of this problem. . . .

1. First let us consider the value of good notes in terms of evaluation of large programs or activities which involved more than one group. Last year our director of guidance was requested to submit a report of the various activities which were going on in Pasadena in relation to the teacher education study. She has reported that her problem of making this report was greatly simplified because the supervisory notes were comprehensive and functional. She found that these notes gave an accurate picture of the organization and the activities of our study group. . . .

2. . . . [The records have also been valuable] in establishing fine relationships with our elementary principals. . . . Mr. X who is the chairman of the Pasadena Elementary Principals' Association [has said]: "(a) The notes have served to give me a progress report upon the thinking of the study group. (b) My teachers have used these reports in order that they might understand what the supervisors are doing, and as a result have been able to cooperate with understanding. (c) The notes have aided me in becoming convinced of the value of the study and thus resulting in my being able to present a picture of the study to the Elementary Principals' Association. . . ."

3. Another valuable asset of adequate record keeping has become apparent to our planning group. We have found that by being able to refer to our notes we could more successfully plan for next steps. . . . In the fall Dr. C and her planning committee thought that we should reach some definite agreement upon matters of policy. After carefully rereading notes the committee evolved two checklists. One was "Do We Agree That." This list was composed of questions about which the notes seemed to indicate a general agreement. The second list, "Can We Reach an Agreement On," was composed of questions which seemed to represent some elements of disagreement

as revealed by the records. This serves to illustrate the value of good records for future planning in any given group.

4. There was still another use for these notes. [Two persons] used them in the [Commission's] collaboration center at Chicago for the purpose of relating their work and study to the growth needs of our group.

5. . . . I have asked various members of our group to write down their personal reactions to the notes. This was done for the purpose of preparing an agenda for an evaluation meeting which we, on the planning committee, hope to use in the near future. The results from this request bring out some interesting points. . . .

   a. "As requested by you last Tuesday, I have been looking over your notes reporting the activities of the supervisory group, and I find that I have no very specific suggestion for improvement to make. . . . it requires considerable amount of time to study them through. However, I think it better to have the reports complete rather than not enough. It also indicates that I have not participated much in the discussions. . . ."

   b. "The supervisors of special departments in the Pasadena City Schools have been an organized group for a number of years, meeting irregularly. . . . During the last year we have been meeting regularly and the meetings have taken on new significance. It [the record] has helped us to keep an important account of all educational ideas that have been presented to and by the group and when necessary to review the notes to see if we have moved ahead on plans laid out for ourselves.

   "The notes of our meetings have perhaps been as constructive an element in our study as any other activity participated in by the group. . . ."

   c. "I find the notes a very helpful reference and one that I should use more often. I hadn't gone back to the beginning for some time and I was impressed by our first planning when I looked it over. Notes such as ours can help keep us on even keel—we can use them to reaffirm our purposes or as evidence of growth for changing our purpose or at least our path to our goal.

   "One of our first problems [in] March 1941 was the felt need of knowing more about child growth. Our notes are a record of our strivings to meet this need. The monthly records of our working together show our interest continued in attempting to meet this need. However, the second problem of March 1941—"How can we work with teachers and guide them to an understanding of this important problem?"—has been more inadequately met. Our notes show our verbal concern about having teachers in on it, but they do not show any active participation of teachers in our study nor discussion of ways of arranging situations so that teacher initiative and interest may take an active part. We must consider this together to determine whether we have let it slip or have agreed that purpose number (2) is fundamentally one that must wait on purpose number (1)'s accomplishment.

"Our notes give a picture of the group structure. I think they also show the development of a more democratic way of working together. They show group growth and individual growth. More are participating and this participation is in wider fields. ... Reference to our notes can save us much time—too often we are prone to hash and rehash the same problem, adding no new insights to its solution. We have a ready reference in our *motions* and *decisions* and the discussions preceding the motions hint at our backlog of experience which prompts our decisions.

"Our motions and decisions also show our non-follow-up of certain matters. Some of these follow-ups have been made by the persons delegated to do them and since group action was not possible the matter was dropped without reporting the incident back to the group. . . . Rereading the entire notes at one time has pointed this up. . . . I think the notes are very fair—they represent the spirit and structure of the group—they show our weaknesses and our strength and from more careful analysis of them we can learn much—both . . . what not to do and what has worked and why."

These replies demonstrate the importance of records in terms of planning for evaluation activities which will be directed toward the improvement of our study group. In conclusion may we state the belief that there are unexplored values in records and record keeping which if found and used would make a significant contribution to education.

One of the main implications for evaluation in the foregoing discussion and illustration of secretarial records is the notion that within the regular activity of a group it is possible to find data from which to make a significant appraisal of the group's work. In fact it is not merely possible, it is highly desirable. Records of the sort we have described not only provide a basis for evaluation. They contribute materially to the effectiveness of group work. They give direction to activity. And they serve as a basis for communication to all interested in or affected by the outcomes of that activity—both contemporaneously and historically. By way of summary, the kinds of data that need to be included in records if they are to serve these purposes are listed briefly below:

1. Group personnel, present and absent; date, time, and place of meeting.

2. Minutes of the first meetings should certainly contain a statement of the purpose for which the committee or group was set up.

3. Extension or modification of purposes and reasons for such extension or modification as group work progresses.

4. Types of activity through which problems were attacked—group work, delegated activity, field study, others; resources used.

5. Evaluative comments on effectiveness of activity and resources.

6. Obstacles, issues, and problems arising out of activity toward the achievement of goals; important discussion of these obstacles.

7. Manner in which problems, obstacles, and issues were solved and reasons for the solutions finally derived.

8. Preliminary and revised drafts of recommendations, programs outlined or constructed, and so forth.

9. Record of formal action, consensus of opinion and divided opinion.

10. Periodic summary of progress—perhaps made by some member of the committee other than the secretary but from the secretary's records.

11. Plans and suggestions for implementation of recommendations.

12. Proposed provisions for and results of evaluative follow-up study.

CONSULTANT SERVICES

The use of consultant services by study groups, committees, and other working units in the institutions associated in the cooperative study was widespread. In general, the function of a special consultant was to work with a local group on its particular problems. His job was not primarily to make a quick survey and a subsequent list of recommendations; rather, it was to enter into the discussions of the local group so that together he and the local group could analyze difficulties and achievements and plan next steps. The analyses and plans would be joint products. Thus in many study groups and similar organizations, both in colleges and public school systems, the ques-

tion of how best to plan for, use, and evaluate consultant services has arisen.

While ideally the records of study groups should include such
matters as the reasons for calling in a consultant, the plans
worked out for using his service, his activity with the group,
and the results of his work, there are several reasons for discussing these questions as a rather special topic. For one thing, group
records did not commonly include such data. For another, drawing upon consultant services was one of the commonest methods
of working used in the cooperative study. And finally, consultants were sometimes used for purposes of stimulation and the
clarification of issues in advance of the organization of study
groups.

There was, of course, a wide range in the effectiveness with
which consultants were used. Some consultants were most helpful; others were unsatisfactory to the local groups and in their
own estimation as well. One outstanding consultant was brought
to a college under plans that were hurriedly and superficially
made. He had been chosen because he had played a prominent
part in the reorganization of the teacher education program in
his own institution; consequently he spent most of his time describing how that program operated. The provision of information about what is being done at other places and how it is
working is often a valuable function for a consultant to perform,
but in this particular case the staff members at the college were
disappointed because their resources and their students were
sufficiently different from those in the institution represented
by the consultant that they had not received much help; the
consultant left disappointed because what he had tried to do
had not been enthusiastically received. The same consultant
spent three days in another college to the genuine satisfaction of
everyone concerned. In this instance, the various staff members
who were seeking his help prepared a statement of their purposes, a description of their program, and a list of questions they
would like to discuss with him. These were sent to him in advance. The chief difference between success and failure in these
two institutions was in the planning.

Another consultant, with a rather clear understanding of the purposes he was to serve, arrived on one campus at eight o'clock in the morning. The local staff member who had planned his schedule was in conference at the time. A secretary handed the consultant his schedule. It called for eight half-hour conferences with as many staff members in as many different offices on a large campus by one o'clock in the afternoon. Beginning at 2:00 there were three short committee meetings in succession, and at 7:30 there was an unannounced meeting with department heads. In the short conferences there was not enough time for helpful discussion. The last meeting was the only one in which there was sufficient time for deliberation on problems, but the purposes of that meeting never became quite clear to the consultant. In this case the arrangements for using the consultant's time were poorly suited to the purposes he was supposed to fulfill.

In contrast to this situation is the experience of the same consultant in visiting another institution. His first conference was with the person who had arranged the visit. They spent a half-hour discussing certain questions regarding the plans for using his service and for bringing him up to date on some recent developments. They discussed the schedule for the two days he was to be on the campus. The local coordinator had provided for a half-hour at the beginning of each half day for the consultant to examine materials and committee reports; no less than an hour and a half had been provided for each group conference; most of the individual conferences were scheduled for the lunch and dinner hour; and time was provided at the end of the second day for the coordinator to draw appropriate people together to discuss with the consultant some of the over-all implications of his visit. Throughout the visit it was perfectly clear that staff members' schedules had been freed so that they could give their full attention to the problems that were being discussed. The local staff member responsible for the visit was present at most of the meetings and, with the consultant, budgeted the time so that there would be ample opportunity not only to explore problems and suggest procedures but also to plan the steps that would be taken between this and the consultant's next visit.

The importance of good planning is evident in these anecdotes. Planning requires thoughtful attention to a good many
questions. A group needs to decide, first of all, that a consultant
is needed and to identify rather clearly what he is needed for.
Then the right man needs to be picked and to be fully prepared
for his job—by being informed about the general situation at
the place he is to work and about the particular things he is
expected to do. Two further questions then arise—arranging to
have him long enough (at any particular time or for enough
times), and arranging wisely for the use of his time with the
right people in the right ways. Finally, what decisions or other
outcomes may reasonably be hoped for before he leaves need
to be anticipated, and what is to be expected of him after he
leaves—a report, response to written requests for further advice,
periodical return, and so forth—should be taken into consideration.

No matter what plans are worked out by the local group and
the consultant, their use calls for some flexibility. The consultant
may wisely want to do some things the local planners had not
thought of, and he may want to resist doing other things. For
example, there is a temptation, once the consultant is on the
job, to draw him into a consideration of problems concerning
which he has little background. The hazards of this are obvious.
The consultant in personnel turns out not to be helpful in general education; the general education staff, therefore, tend to
discount his ideas in personnel. The avoidance of this temptation is a responsibility of both the consultant and the local administrator, although it is not always easy for the consultant to
refuse invitations. Another temptation that sometimes arises is
the rather hurried calling of a general faculty meeting so that
the consultant can speak to the entire group. Some, and often
many, staff members are disgruntled when they come to such a
meeting because they have had to make last-minute changes in
their plans and because neither the staff nor the visiting consultant see clearcut purposes for it. Consequently, it is important that the consultant and the local staff member who is
chiefly responsible for working with him have some leeway in
following the general plans that have been set up.

The sort of planning and activity we have described here may be characterized as informal commonsense evaluation. It is a joint responsibility of the consultant and the local group. Moreover, we have been concerned with a particular kind of consultantship—a kind in which planning and working together are matters of special importance.

Out of various experiences in the cooperative study, members of the Commission's staff and representatives of participating institutions have tried to identify some of the factors that contributed to the effectiveness of consultant services. In any list of such factors, of course, there would be different degrees of importance attached to various items in accordance with different local conditions. Nevertheless, the items presented below may have some general significance. They are given in the form of questions which might profitably be considered by local groups and by consultants in planning for, using, and evaluating consultant services. They might also be used, depending on local conditions and purposes, for *post facto* evaluation.

1. Planning for consultant services
    a. Was the primary function of the consultant clearly defined? Was it that of stimulation, clarification of issues, or to serve as a resource person on already clearly defined problems?
    b. Were reading materials (for instance, statement of problems, committee reports, outlines, syllabi, statements of institutional objectives, etc.) complete enough and sent to the consultant sufficiently in advance of his visit that he could become useful without unnecessary waste of time?
    c. Were special interests and concerns of those people with whom the consultant was going to work sufficiently described to him so that he could make his contributions in a way most likely to be accepted by the group?
2. Activities during the consultant's visit
    a. Was time allowed the consultant before starting his conferences to discuss details of procedure, such as who will lead the discussion? will there be a secretary? who will be responsible for the budgeting of time? etc.

b. Was the length of time allowed for each conference sufficient? Did conferences begin with a statement of purpose? Was time apportioned for the issues to be discussed? Was time allowed for summary and planning of next steps, delegation of work, and setting of due dates?

c. Had time for local staff members been sufficiently freed that they could participate without interruption from local responsibilities?

d. Was the sequence of conferences such as to keep the work moving forward, or was it necessary with some groups to undo what had been done in others?

e. What specific help was received (increased sensitivity to what problems, what issues clarified, what possible solutions or avenues of work outlined)?

f. Were the consultant and those with whom he worked sensitive to the relationship of the problem under consideration to larger aspects of the institution's program?

g. Was the participation of the group broadly enough distributed to insure full support of conclusions and plans?

h. Was the consultant sensitive to the implications and contributions made by local staff members?

i. Did the consultant tend to force his ideas upon the group or to dictate the direction the institutional program should take?

j. Did the group tend to expect the consultant to give the answers, that is, tell them what to do, or did they expect him to help them arrive at a solution in terms of their own needs and desires?

k. Was the consultant suited to the task that was laid before him? Was his background of experience adequate and were his methods of work well adapted to the group?

l. Was the person who was to give leadership and sustained direction to the activities of the group in charge of group conferences while the consultant was present?

m. Were the room and the equipment (table, blackboard, freedom from distracting noises) satisfactory?

3. Follow-up relationships and outcomes of consultant services

a. Did the consultant and the institution prepare a written summary and statement of recommendations? Was the report helpful?

b. Did the groups which met with the consultant follow his visit promptly with a meeting at which the results were distilled and next steps initiated?

c. Did the group keep in touch with the consultant as prob lems arose in the carrying out of plans?

d. Do records of progress show need for continued consultant services, and if so, do they provide a basis for planning the consultant's next visit?

e. Were definite dates set for the fulfillment of responsibili ties?

f. Have plans been made and are they being fulfilled for an evaluative statement of progress at the end of six months or a year?

Evaluation of, in the sense of thinking about, each experience with the use of consultant service ought to lead to conclusions as to ways of maximizing success. This, after all, is the main purpose of evaluation. Having in mind the questions raised above, or a similar list better suited to the purposes and expectations of a local group, should enable interested persons to make the kind of commonsense evaluation that is often so necessary to the continued effectiveness of group work.

EVALUATION IN WORKSHOPS

Within the past few years workshops have become an increasingly important means for the continued education of teachers in service. The current use of the term "workshop" as applied to summer study originated with the Progressive Education Association in 1936. Since that date the number of workshops has multiplied rapidly. In the summer of both 1941 and 1942 there were well over 100 held in various parts of the country.

With the multiplication of workshops has come an increased interest in the role of evaluation in them. This interest is shared by several groups. There are first of all the workshop participants. Most of them come to study a problem which is of particular concern to them in their local school and they are, quite naturally, concerned about the progress they make in that study. Then, there are the teachers and administrators of the local school from which the workshop participant has come. Because the problems which participants bring to workshops are generally practical ones arising out of their jobs, what they do with respect to those problems has implications for their administrators and fellow teachers. Often too, participants are sent to workshops by their local school to study problems which have been delegated to them and which embrace considerations of school-wide importance. In the third place, the members of the workshop staff are interested in evaluation. They are interested in appraising their own effectiveness as advisers, the success of the workshop as a whole, and the progress of individual participants. Finally, there is the interest of the credit-controlling authorities —the graduate schools of colleges and universities. Theirs is the problem of deciding whether credit toward an advanced degree should be given to those who apply, and if so, what amount of credit and on the basis of what accomplishments.

Because the nature of workshops has determined to a large extent the sort of evaluation activity that has been carried on in them and the way in which the interests of the several groups that have a stake in evaluation have been expressed, it is important at this point to clarify further some of the characteristics of workshops. The following outline of "what seemed to former workshop participants to be the essential characteristics of a workshop" comes from a leaflet prepared by the Commission's workshop advisory service:

1. The participant brings a specific interest or problem which has arisen out of his experience as a teacher and is afforded an opportunity to make an intensive study of the interest or problem at a place where superior library, advisory, and other resources are available to aid him in the achievement of his goal.

2. The participant shares in the planning of a program of individual and group activities designed to meet his needs and those of his fellow students.

3. The participant is provided with easy access to the services of various staff members representing a variety of kinds of assistance

related to the student's problem, and he has ready contact with other members of the workshop group who have met problems akin to his own.

4. Formal and informal association with other workshop members of varied backgrounds contributes to the participant's thinking on his specific problem, broadens his general professional orientation, and provides opportunity for experiences in cooperative activities.

5. An effort is made, through the study of basic fields related to a participant's problem, to interest him in the whole child, the whole school, and the whole community.

6. The participant's total experience as he studies a specific interest or problem tends to prepare him for the solution of other professional problems in the future.

7. Since the workshops have been concerned not only with the professional problems of the teacher but with his life as an individual, efforts have been made to afford opportunities for balanced living.[7]

Implied in these characteristics is another that needs to be mentioned: participants have come to regard workshops as a significant experience in democratic living and good fellowship.

Because of the character of workshop programs formal examinations have not been usable. The participants have worked on individual problems, and while they have met in groups to discuss related problems, they have not done so to master a prescribed body of subject matter. Consequently, common examinations have not been called for. Rather, the evidence of an individual's progress has had to be sought in what he does toward the achievement of his goals. Thus the search for good methods of judging individual progress has been a major problem and a significant focus of evaluation in workshops.

Another major focus of evaluation has been upon the appraisal of the workshop as a whole. In a broad sense, the sum of the progress of individuals constitutes an evaluation of the workshop as a whole. But there are elements in this total appraisal that need to be specially identified. Such elements include the availability and usefulness of various resources—library materials, staff advisers, special consultants, group meetings, and similar items; they include, in short, an appraisal of

[7] "Workshops in Education," 1941, pp. 4-5.

the effectiveness of particular methods and leaders. Taken jointly, the appraisals of individual progress, group progress, and workshop methods and resources constitute a general evaluation of the workshop as a whole. And often special questionnaires, rating scales, and other techniques are employed in this over-all evaluation of the workshop's effectiveness.

INDIVIDUAL PROGRESS

From the time of the first workshop there has been a continuous effort to develop comprehensive means for appraising the progress of individual participants. There has also been a persistent attempt to keep evaluation procedures consistent with the purposes of individuals and the nature of workshops. Our discussion here is not a blueprint for the evaluation of an individual's progress; rather it is a review of several procedures that have been found useful.

Initial status

In order to obtain a basis for appraising individual progress and for providing help that will facilitate that progress it is essential to know where the individual stands when he comes to the workshop and where he proposes to go. What does he think his problem is? How does he plan to work on it? What does he hope to accomplish? It has therefore been customary for workshop directors to ask applicants for a statement of their problems and plans—along with certain background information such as education, experience, and so forth—in advance of enrollment. Often, of course, some revision of purpose occurs after a few days of workshop experience—of discussion with advisers, consultants, and other participants, and of a clear knowledge of available resources. Conseqently, it has also been usual to seek a restatement of problems, purposes, and plans by the end of the workshop's first week.

Various procedures have been tried to help participants clarify their purposes and give definiteness to their plans in advance of workshop enrollment. The purposes and plans of those who attended the first workshop in 1936 grew out of problems that had been rather clearly identified as a result of several years of participation in the Progressive Education Association's eight-year study. The Moultrie recreation institute for teachers in the summer of 1940 was organized as a result of a countywide survey made the previous year by a committee representing teachers from all school systems in the county. A report of the survey had been distributed to the teachers and discussed in staff meetings. Those who attended the institute did so with the needs revealed by the survey in mind, and many of them came feeling some responsibility for giving leadership to the school in extending its program of recreation and health when they returned.

In some instances, workshop participants have had responsibility delegated to them by their local school. This has helped to clarify the participant's purpose and to enhance his usefulness when he returned. The latter is an important point. A staff that has delegated responsibility to some individual or group has usually already become sensitive to some of the local implications of a problem and should, consequently, be prepared to receive and implement the report which the workshop participants will make.

One should not infer, however, that teachers without clearly defined problems are refused admission. Some of the teachers who have been most enthusiastic about their workshop experience have come with very vague problems. Their main purpose was to shop around for ideas or to enjoy the fellowship. According to their testimony the workshop served this limited purpose admirably. At the same time, if there were not many others in attendance with definiteness of purpose it is doubtful whether shopping for ideas would be so profitable.

Recognizing the inadequacy of early statements of problems by many participants, most workshop faculties have tried several methods during the first days to gain a clearer picture of the participant's needs. At Ohio State University in the summer of 1940, participants were asked to answer the following questions after the first conference with their adviser:

1. Revised statement of your problem, following the interview:

(Indicate what changes you have made, if any, and your reasons for making any changes. Include a discussion of any new relationships, broader implications, or different modes of attack which you think significant for your problem.)

2. What books, magazines, etc., do you plan to read?

3. What interviews or conferences do you plan to have?

4. What other steps are you planning?

5. What are the major difficulties, uncertainties, worries, or questions which occur to you as you think of going forward on your problem?

6. I believe (even if only tentatively) that I should join the _____ group.

At a workshop at Northwestern University in 1941, each participant interviewed at least two or three staff members during the first two days. These interviews helped both participants and staff to clarify individual problems and to facilitate the best selection of advisers. At the Commission's own workshop in Chicago, in 1940, participants were asked to write about their problems and purposes (following a prepared list of questions) during the first week. Thus, prior to enrollment or during the first days of the workshops, and usually at both times, efforts are made to get a reasonably clear statement of participants' problems, objectives, and plans.

Evidence of achievement

Among the commonest means of judging individual progress in workshops are observations, discussions, interviews, records, and reports. One of the characteristics of workshops is the close association between staff and participants which enables staff members to get to know individuals unusually well. Each staff member is an adviser to a relatively small number of participants. Interviews are frequent. Moreover, most participants and advisers have further contacts with each other in discussion and study groups. And finally, a good deal of informal association is promoted by social activities, field trips, and other events on the workshop calendar.

Notes on conferences and interviews are usually kept by the adviser to provide a record of what has been planned, tried, and accomplished. At the Northwestern workshop in 1941, for example, a special interview record was used. The record simply had space on one sheet of paper for noting "ideas," "persons to be interviewed," "references," and "next steps." In some cases it was filled out by the advisers, in others by the participants, and in still others by both of them.

In several workshops the participants have written weekly reviews of their work and progress, usually following an outline that was developed by an evaluation committee. A diary or log of activities and ideas has also been found very useful. Both the weekly reviews and the diaries help to facilitate self-evaluation as well as provide data for the staff in estimating individual progress. Because people vary greatly in their attitudes toward keeping diaries, this practice has not been followed systematically in any workshop. In connection with several field courses sponsored by The Open Road in the summer of 1940, however, all the participants kept daily logs in relation to the following points:

"An idea today that threw new light on my problem was. . . ."
"My thinking was challenged today by. . . ."
"What I am doing was called into question by. . . ."
"Ideas I would like to discuss further with ____ were. . . ."
"New materials I discovered today were. . . ."

The logs were regarded by some people as among the most useful of a number of evaluative techniques employed in a comprehensive appraisal of those field courses; they showed the emergence of new interests, challenges to philosophy, changes in social attitudes, and new ideas about the opportunities and responsibilities of education.

Formal and informal discussion among staff members of individual progress is likewise a part of the evaluation process. In some workshops special staff meetings have been held in which the cases of all participants have been reviewed. Questions such as the following may be raised: Who is his adviser and with what other staff members is he working? What is he like and what progress is he making? What are his needs that are not being met and how could he receive more help? Is he in a position to be of special help to other participants who are working on similar problems? Meetings centered around questions such as these help to acquaint the entire staff with the progress and special problems of all participants.

Most workshoppers prepare special reports relative to the problem they are studying. Sometimes they give such reports orally before a group for discussion. Sometimes they write them for ultimate distribution among colleagues in their local school. These reports, which are in some respects similar to term papers, are available to the staff and provide a major basis for judging achievement.

Generally the adviser or the participant or both keep a file which includes much of the above data about the individual's work: initial and revised statements of the problem studied, plans made and carried out, books read, persons interviewed, notes on interviews with the adviser and other staff members, and copies of outlines, reports, or other materials produced. The total of this material provides the basis for judging progress and achievement. Moreover, it is a common practice for the adviser and the participant to reserve their last conference for a review of the participant's work and a discussion of some of the problems of implementation which may be encountered. If the workshopper has registered for graduate credit the question of a fair grade for his work is sometimes raised and discussed.

OVER-ALL APPRAISAL

In addition to an evaluation of individual progress a good deal of the appraisal activity in workshops is concerned with the effectiveness of the workshop itself in accomplishing its purposes for the entire group. This includes not only an over-all appraisal of the program but likewise an evaluation of various aspects of it such as group meetings, equipment and resources, field trips, the art studio if there is one, individual guidance, the staff leadership, and so forth. Some of this evaluation occurs during the workshop period as a step toward improvement while in operation.

Since the basic purpose of a workshop is to meet individual

needs and since these needs are likely to vary widely and not be fully evident to the staff before the workshop begins, it is important to have a wide variety of resources available and to check on their adequacy as the program gets under way. Efforts can thus be made to improve the services for the benefit of those currently in attendance. A number of techniques have been used to keep the workshop staff informed regarding the adequacy of organization and resources. Special questionnaires, "ballot boxes" in which participants can anonymously drop "suggestions," representation on planning committees, and group discussions have all been tried and found helpful.

During the second week of the Northwestern workshop, for example, a brief questionnaire was circulated covering the following questions:

1. Are the library facilities adequate and convenient?
2. Are the arrangements for conferences proving satisfactory?
3. Have general meetings been helpful?
4. Have meetings of your interest groups been helpful?

Each question was followed by space in which to write "suggestions for improvement," and a final general question was asked calling for any other suggestions for improving the effectiveness of the workshop. The answers to these questions enabled the staff to make several changes in the workshop schedule and resources in ample time for the participants to benefit from them during the last three weeks of the program. The most notable change was an improvement in the workshop library: quite a few books and pamphlets were transferred from staff members' desks to the general reading room and the room itself was made more attractive.

Periodic evaluation by such means as this and others is generally considered important for several reasons. First, workshops are relatively new; the details of their organization have not become set. The participants themselves usually share in planning much of the program. Then special arrangements need to be made with the sponsoring university or school system for the use of various materials, and special resources need to be assembled for the particular use of the workshop. Both staff members and participants often come from widely separated parts of the country and they need to discover suitable means for working together. Thus, in new ventures of this sort, interest in appraising many details seems natural and necessary. One might add that more established organizations could also profit occasionally from a canvass of consumer opinion regarding their usefulness.

A major aspect of workshops is the program of interest or study groups. This is usually appraised from one or more of three types of data: materials which the group has produced cooperatively, evaluative discussions within the group, and secretarial records of the group's work. The use of secretarial records in evaluation has already been described and is applicable to workshop study groups. The use of evaluative discussions has been mentioned in Chapter VIII in connection with the Ohio experiment and the work of the Norris teachers. In workshop groups the setting aside of a little time to review progress is fairly common. Midway in the workshop period, for example, a group often spends an hour considering such questions as: What have we done so far? Are we clear about the direction we wish to go in? Are we spending our time to good advantage? What further things ought we to do? Sometimes a special effort is made to take notes on such a discussion—not only because it contributes to the group's planning but also because, when similar notes are taken in several groups, it gives the workshop staff and director a useful overview of what is being done. Finally, many study groups produce some sort of document at the end of the workshop. It may be a series of conclusions which the group has come to regarding the topic that has been discussed—for example, evaluation, or supervisory practice, or general education for teachers. Or, it may be a statement of point of view, or a bibliography. The participants often want to take back with them such a record of one phase of their work. Consequently, they prepare it with that purpose in mind. And the document, of course, provides further evidence for appraising the group's achievement.

At the close of most workshops some attempt has usually been

made—by questionnaires, interviews, or group discussions—to
gain a general appraisal of the workshop as a whole. Many of
these attempts have value for individual self-appraisal, for staff
appraisal of individual growth, as well as for the appraisal of
the effectiveness of the workshop itself. We shall describe a few
of them here because they illustrate these values and because
the responses to them give some indication of the success of
workshops in accomplishing their major purposes.

At the Commission's workshop in 1940

The responses to the evaluation questionnaires at the Commission's workshop in Chicago, gave primarily a picture of
individual progress and therefore had special value for self-
appraisal. But taken together those responses also furnished a
significant evaluation of the workshop as a whole. Each participant answered a questionnaire at the beginning of the workshop; he answered the same questionnaire at the end of the
workshop; he then compared his answers to the two and expressed his interpretation of the observable differences. The
questions asked were as follows:

1. Why are you attending the workshop?
2. What is your problem in relation to teacher education?
3. What are the conditions out of which your problem arises?
4 What plans have been made by you and your school for work
on your problem?
5. What is the relationship of your interest or problem to the
total program of the school?
6. What are the most essential activities or resources to be utili-
ized in the solution of your problem?
7. What do you hope to accomplish in your school program next
year as a result of your workshop experience?
8. a. What kind of help will you want from others in your local
   situation?
   b. What help will you be able to give others?
9. What do you anticipate will be the chief obstacles?
10. What additional knowledge, understanding, and experience
do you need?

These questions called for an analysis of the participant's problem, his plans for working on it, and his ideas regarding its im-

EVALUATION IN TEACHER EDUCATION

plementation in his school. The comparison between the first and second analyses revealed the direction of change in the participant's thinking. One such comparison was made by the participants and another was made by an independent judge who did not attend the workshop.

The general conclusion reached by the independent judge was that the most persistently occurring differences between the first and second analyses centered around increased appreciation for democratic and cooperative methods of work, greater awareness of interrelationships, and clearer and more definite conceptions of plans. More specifically, answers to question 5 at the end of the workshop were often expanded and amplified with illustrations, whereas on the first analysis a good many participants wrote vague generalities such as "guidance has implications for the whole program." The number of activities listed in response to question 7 was much larger at the end of the workshop than at the beginning. Moreover, a greater number of very specific activities was mentioned. There was also greater emphasis on helping others through group methods—committees and discussion groups, for example. Answers to question 9 indicated that a greater number of obstacles was foreseen at the close of the workshop than had been anticipated in the beginning. Quite specific obstacles were mentioned such as lack of clerical help and lack of space as well as the more general obstacles of complacency, tradition, rivalry, and conflicting philosophies.

The changes most frequently mentioned by the participants in their own comparison of first and second statements were exactly the same as those identified by the independent judge. That is to say, they believed that they had come to see their problems more clearly and definitely, that they had gained a broader perspective on their problems, and that they had come to have a greater appreciation for democratic methods of work.

When the participants attempted to give reasons for the changes they had observed they most frequently mentioned the name of some staff member. A great many of them also mentioned group meetings and general contacts with other participants. They mentioned, in short, the resources which a workshop is characteristically organized to give—helpful, friendly, stimulating associations in a democratic atmosphere.

At the Northwestern workshop in 1941

The Northwestern evaluation was focused primarily on the workshop and its several aspects; it was not a provocative self-appraisal device of the sort used in Chicago. An evaluation committee developed a rating scale which was circulated among the participants at the close of the workshop. The form of the instrument permitted both general ratings and free response; the fifteen topics included on it are indicative of what one group regarded as important aspects of the workshop. These are illustrated below:

Directions:
Cross out the appropriate number following each question to indicate your attitude.

    5—very well satisfied, or very much, or to a great extent
    4—well satisfied, or much, or to a considerable extent
    3—fairly well satisfied, or some, or to some extent
    2—somewhat dissatisfied, or little, or to a small extent
    1—frankly dissatisfied, or very little, or to a very small extent

1. How well satisfied are you with the progress on your individual problem? 1   2   3   4   5
    I feel this way because:
        [Space for remarks]
    I have these suggestions:
        [Space for remarks]
2. How well satisfied are you with the help you got from your adviser?
3. How well satisfied are you with the morning interest group of which you are a member?
4. How well satisfied are you with the afternoon interest group of which you are a member?
5. How well satisfied are you with your contacts with staff members besides your major adviser?
6. To what extent have you become profitably acquainted with other workshoppers?
7. How well satisfied are you with the amount and helpfulness of your readings?

8. Of how much value has your work in a committee been to you?
9. To what extent have the general meetings been helpful?
10. To what extent has the workshop contributed to your understanding of democratic procedures?
11. To what extent do you believe that workshop procedures have been democratic?
12. To what extent has the planned social activity of the workshop been satisfactory?
13. To what extent have the unplanned social activities of the workshop been satisfactory?
14. How well satisfied are you with the length of time allotted to the workshop?
15. How well satisfied are you with the fact that you came to this workshop rather than to some other type of summer school?

The highest median rating, 4.5, was given to question 15. The help received from advisers was rated 4.3; the help received from other staff members was rated 4.2. Next in order of value was the major interest group in which the participant worked. And following that were the help gained from other participants and the satisfaction derived from the many unplanned social activities—both of which were rated 3.9. The lowest rating for any item was given to the value of work on committees; even so, the rating of 3.3 which that item received was not unfavorable. Again, as in the Chicago workshop, the things which teachers prized most highly and from which they got the most satisfaction and benefit were their associations with staff members, with each other, with their study group, with the opportunity for friendly social contacts.

At the Philadelphia workshop in 1941

In contrast to the Chicago and Northwestern workshops, which were national in their representation, the Philadelphia workshop was a local affair for teachers and administrators in the Philadelphia school system. Two methods were used in evaluating the general effectiveness of their 1941 workshop. One consisted of interviews with a large and representative sampling of workshoppers. The other was a special questionnaire and rating form. The results from both procedures were very similar and are summarized herewith.

PERSONAL GROWTH AND DEVELOPMENT OF THE PARTICIPANT

Sources of Help

Outcomes	Workshop as a whole	6 general meetings with administrators	Organized group and subgroup meetings	Special interest meetings	Individual conferences with staff	Informal conferences with participants	Workshop committees	Library	Arts program	Field trips
New friendships formed	1		x		x	x			x	
Faith in cooperative action as a way of dealing with crucial school problems	2	x	x		x					
Better understanding of the needs and problems of children	3		x	x	x					
Better understanding of the problems of teachers and administrators throughout the system	4	x	x							
Inspiration and courage to attack problems	5		x		x					
Better understanding of the nature of democratic living	6	x	x							
New interests which are making and will continue to make my life more enjoyable	7		x			x			x	
Better understanding of the interrelationship of school and community	8	x	x							x
A better understanding of the directions in which I need to grow	9		x		x					
Greater skill in social relationships that may be carried over into my school situation	10		x		x					
Clarification and definition of problem	11		x		x			x		
A greater awareness of my own strengths and capabilities	12		x		x					
A better understanding of the nature and value of various sources of help	13		x		x			x		
Seeing the implications of my problem in its relation to the total program of the school	14		x		x					
Ideas, procedures, and techniques I can use in my class or school	15		x		x					
Greater confidence that persons in positions of leadership desire to use cooperative methods	16	x	x		x					
Insights into ways of bringing the arts in my classroom program	17			x					x	

One part of the questionnaire, given at the close of the workshop, included a list of "representative outcomes that workshop participants have suggested as coming from their experience in the Philadelphia workshop." After each item the participants were asked to rate the workshop as a whole and then, in appropriate spaces, to "rate each phase of the workshop as to its particular contribution to that outcome." In the table reproduced on page 341 the outcomes are listed in the order in which the workshop as a whole was judged to have contributed to them. The "x's" indicate some of the special sources of help that were mentioned most frequently.

As in the other workshops we have described, friendships and faith in cooperative action were among the dominant outcomes; group meetings and conferences with staff members were considered among the most helpful resources. Moreover, the fact that some outcomes and some resources were mentioned less frequently than others does not mean that they were unimportant. For example, 70 percent of the participants served on committees, 75 percent went on at least one field trip, 93 percent took part in the arts program, and practically all used the library; the large majority attributed definite values to these activities.

The impressions of what was accomplished at the workshop, gained by the person who interviewed representative participants, were very similar to the outcomes identified in the questionnaire. No attempt was made to list these interview impressions in the order of their importance:

1. We have been helped to work toward solutions of our professional problems.
2. We have learned how to define and attack professional problems, how to get help from other people and from books, how to work with other people and by ourselves in solving our problems.
3. Some of our groups have started projects at the workshop on which we intend to continue to work.
4. We have gained better understanding of democratic methods of working together and also, we think, greater skill in the use of these methods.
5. We have learned ways of teaching and working together which we intend to use in our own schools and classes.
6. We have experienced the breaking down of barriers which sometimes separate people who might and should work together.
7. We have been stimulated intellectually. Our viewpoint of education has been broadened. We have new enthusiasm for our work.

8. We have gained broader knowledge and greater appreciation of our own school system.

9. We have gained much useful information about our own community, and with it, a determination to know our community still better.

10. We have been stimulated to wider reading and personal study on our own initiative.

11. We enjoyed ourselves thoroughly in the arts periods. . . .

12. Each of us has greatly widened his circle of acquaintances, has made a number of close friends, and has learned how to get along better with all sorts of people.[8]

Both the interview and questionnaire techniques were more significant in giving a general appraisal of the workshop than in evaluating the attainment of individuals.

At the Stanford workshop in 1941

At Stanford University one major technique of evaluation was a special discussion by the whole group at the close of the workshop period. This evaluative discussion was concerned with the effectiveness of the workshop, the reasons for whatever success it was judged to have, and the implications of workshop procedures for the program of the School of Education.

At the outset the discussion revealed general enthusiasm about the values obtained from the workshop experience. This enthusiasm was expressed almost unanimously. The question was then raised as to what distinctive features of workshop procedure accounted most for its effectiveness. The following features were mentioned by the group and accepted by the large majority as being important:

1. The freedom from outside requirements, pressures, and rewards foreign to the problem at hand.

2. The basing of learning on that which is pertinent and functional in solving a real educational problem.

3. The cooperation and democratic atmosphere of the working group.

4. The opportunity to know other participants and staff members well.

[8] *The Story of the Philadelphia Workshop for Teachers and Administrators,* July 7 to August 15, 1941: A Report and an Interpretation, School District of Philadelphia, Board of Public Education, pp. 3-5.

5. The ability to work uninterruptedly on one's problem—without dashing from one class to another to study subjects none of which may be exactly pointed toward one's own concerns.

6. The opportunity to work with several staff members each bringing a different contribution to the problem.

7. The planning of art programs and recreational programs as an integral part of the whole learning experience rather than being "extras."

8. The goal of solving a problem rather than meeting requirements—with the consequence that one's reading is more purposeful.

9. The whole philosophy of education is reanalyzed under the workshop procedure. Therefore changes in point of view are more fundamental and far-reaching.

10. The degree to which self-appraisal goes on.

11. The opportunity for the learner to help plan learning activities to take advantage of what he needs to know and what he knows already.

The group then considered how such advantages could be obtained, at least in considerable measure, through modifications in the regular summer session or graduate program. The following suggestions from members of the group met with general approval:

1. Reducing the number of courses; for instance, instead of having five or six courses in different aspects of supervision each taught by a specialist, have one course with interest groups meeting on different phases with all the specialists participating.

2. Rethinking requirements and schedules in terms of large blocks of time.

3. Planning recreational activities, art programs, and get-togethers to develop a close spirit within the group.

4. Having student committees help plan the courses.

5. Basing instruction upon problems that are real to the students.

6. Substituting self-direction and self-appraisal for a large part of faculty direction and grading.

Evaluative discussions of this kind can produce a good deal of valuable information. Much depends, of course, upon the skill of the group leader and the quality of planning. In the discussion at the Stanford workshop a definite order of questions was followed. The first question was a very broad one and the answers were likewise general. The second question sought to bring out specific reasons for the generally favorable opinion of the workshop which the group held. And the third question turned the group's attention to the implications of what they had been saying for regular summer sessions and graduate programs. Moreover, as points were made in answer to these questions there was a definite attempt to determine their acceptability to the entire group. The result was not, therefore, merely a list of ideas held by the most vocal members of the group; it was a list of beliefs held by the large majority. When discussions are carried on in this way one can often get from them as much as or more than from a questionnaire which covers the same points. It is a technique of evaluation that might profitably be used more frequently; but it requires more skill and discernment than are often brought to group discussions.

THE QUESTION OF CREDIT

In almost all workshops for experienced teachers there are some, and often many, participants who wish graduate school credit for their work. They have come to the workshop instead of to the regular summer school. Many of them are working toward master's degrees. Generally the workshop is located on a university campus or if it is a school system workshop, arrangements with a local university are usually made for the use of services and registration for credit. These facts have a bearing upon evaluation in the workshop—particularly upon the evaluation of individual progress.

One fundamental question that has arisen is whether the kind of accomplishment aimed at by workshops is worthy of graduate credit. For the most part workshops have been set up to help teachers work on practical problems that have grown out of their experience. They do not offer "courses" in the usual meaning of that term. In this sense, the workshop is a service program rather than an academic one. Nearly all graduate schools, however, recognize the value of service programs for experienced professional workers; therefore the policy of granting credit for a professional degree in education for workshop experience is widespread. Many universities in fact make little distinction in this connection between the degrees of master of arts and master of education. Thus the basic question of whether workshop experience is deserving of credit toward an advanced degree has already been answered affirmatively by most degree-granting institutions.

The question then arises as to the quantity and quality of credit that should be given in individual cases. In graduate schools credit is ordinarily given for the study of some prescribed body of subject matter. The problems which participants bring to workshops, on the other hand, do not fall readily into definite subject-matter divisions. On the contrary, they generally require the bringing of material from a variety of fields to bear on some practical matter. Consequently, credit for specific courses is granted much less frequently than credit for general electives. Schools of education have generally followed the practice of granting up to six hours of credit toward an advanced degree for workshop study; this credit is usually listed under some such title as education workshop. In special cases, credit for specific courses is given subject to review and approval by the workshop adviser and a member of the graduate department concerned.

The question of what evidence one can use in determining the quantity and quality of credit has a special bearing on evaluation practices in the workshop. When cumulative records and reports such as we have described under the heading of "Individual Progress" have been kept, the evidence from which staff members can make an over-all appraisal of the participant's accomplishment is substantial; the basis for giving credit is available. There are the original and revised statements of his problem, his plans for working on it, the record of his activity during the workshop—interviews with his adviser and other staff members, readings, participation in his study group—sometimes a diary or log he has kept, and the final report he has prepared relative to his problem. It is necessary, of course, for the participant to keep such records and for the adviser to insist on it. If the participant feels that such record keeping, with its required writing, is merely a grade-getting device, a chore he must do to satisfy other people's purposes, he must frankly recognize two purposes in his attendance—to work toward the solution of his problem, and to receive credit. The latter purpose demands that he produce evidence of his achievement. It should be emphasized, however, that in the workshop these two purposes need not be in conflict. The participant has the opportunity to get credit for working on his own problem. And it is quite possible that he will find the process of furnishing evidence for credit in itself a helpful learning experience, a contribution to the clarification of his thinking with respect to his problem, and not inconsistent with sound self-appraisal.

VALUE OF WORKSHOPS

It goes without saying that the ultimate test of the values of workshops, or any other program of in-service education, lies in the extent to which they lead to improved classroom and administrative practice and to improved education for the boys and girls whom the schools serve. Some follow-up studies of workshops have been made and reported elsewhere.[9] In many workshops follow-up is difficult because the participants come from such widely scattered parts of the country. A unique opportunity for follow-up and self-appraisal, however, exists in the workshops conducted by school systems for their own teachers. There, as part of the regular supervisory service, continuous appraisal can be made. And, one may hope, many school systems will take advantage of that opportunity.

Meanwhile, from evaluations made during many workshops by participants and staff alike there has emerged, rather clearly, a picture of the main values which workshops seem to have. Among these values are the freedom of the environment, the chance to work on one's own problem, the opportunity to know staff members and other participants well, the social contacts and friendships, and the experience in cooperative and democratic procedure. In an environment characterized by these elements the practice of evaluation has, quite naturally,

[9] Kenneth L. Heaton, William G. Camp, and Paul B. Diederich, *Professional Education for Experienced Teachers* (Chicago: University of Chicago Press, 1940).

tended to reflect similar values. In the Commission's workshop, for example, the questionnaires were designed to stimulate the sort of analysis and reanalysis by teachers that would help them clarify their own problems. In all workshops, the emphasis upon close adviser-participant relationships and the accumulation of interview notes and progress reports is favorable to the development of self-evaluation. In short, evaluation should be, and in workshops generally is, not merely a summing up but a means for promoting progress and improvement.

SPECIAL IMPLICATIONS FOR EVALUATION IN SERVICE

In the descriptions of evaluation as related to study groups, secretarial records, consultant services, and workshops two elements which should be regarded as desirable characteristics of in-service evaluation can be identified. One of these is the attempt to seek evaluative evidence within, rather than apart from, the normal activity carried on in relation to the particular program. For example, within the secretarial records which a group might keep as a regular part of its work, it has been possible to find a great deal of data for the appraisal of the group's work. And in workshops, there has been the attempt to find evidence for the appraisal of individual progress from the sort of material which the individual, with his adviser, would naturally accumulate as part of a conscientious self-appraisal. The other element is the attempt to use evaluation as a means of contributing to growth and improvement as well as a method for estimating its amount. The procedures for evaluating individual progress in workshops were intended, for the most part, to contribute to that progress. The questions suggested with respect to consultant services were intended primarily as a guide in planning for the best use of those services and secondarily as a checklist to use after the consultant had left the campus. The secretarial records of the supervisors' group in Pasadena were used to consolidate gains and plan better meetings as well as to judge the amount of progress.

These elements are not new nor are they found solely in in-service evaluation. We indicated in Chapter VIII, however, that there has been a special need to emphasize them in connection with in-service evaluation. The reader may recall that many teachers, at first, tended to resist evaluation. They had associated it with special work which they had to do for someone else, and from which they had often gained little benefit. But as they came to see evaluation as something *they* did, and as an activity which contributed to the realization of *their* goals, their attitude changed. When these elements in evaluation were clear the teachers were warmly sympathetic with it.

When evaluation and learning are seen as closely related activities, and when both are motivated by the genuine acceptance of objectives to be worked for, the process of evaluation is an important instrument in the promotion of in-service growth and improvement.

X

Evaluation in the Educative Process

IN THE PREVIOUS chapters we described and commented on evaluative problems, techniques, and procedures in each of a sequence of topics which added together comprise nearly the whole of teacher education. Whether viewed from the standpoint of an individual's progress or as a progressive series of institutional activities, the sequence was a developmental one. It began with initial student selection, continued through orientation and guidance, general education, professional education, student teaching, follow-up, and concluded at the inservice level. A sequence implies continuity, implies that successive activities grow from and build on previous ones, and that earlier activities prepare for later ones. While events in sequence should have this character, it has not always been obvious in the activities we have described. For one thing, our descriptions have come from different institutions. For another, the activities have not always been recognized by the institutions as sequential. There is need, therefore, to focus attention on the coordination of evaluative activities. Moreover, whether evaluation is focused at the pre-service or the in-service level, whether it is directed specifically at general education or inservice workshops, there are common tasks, common problems of technique and procedure that will be faced. To draw these common problems together and to focus attention on the co-ordination of evaluation within a broad framework are the chief purposes of this final chapter. To begin, we shall review critically the highlights of the preceding chapters.

350

HIGHLIGHTS OF PRECEDING CHAPTERS

In discussing evaluation activities at the time of initial student selection we pointed out the need for developing a broad concept of the good teacher so that selection activities could be seen in proper relation to the larger problem of professional education and growth. In the selection programs we have described, an impressive mass of data was collected and used, but it was not clearly related to students' subsequent success or to any very well defined concept of the good teacher. In New York, New Jersey, and at Wayne University the chief criterion for determining the usefulness or validity of the selection tests was admission status. In other words, did the students who were admitted rate higher than the students not admitted? They did. But the criterion of admission status has limited significance. While there were plans for using more meaningful criteria they had not yet been carried out. One such criterion would be success in the professional education program. This would call for correlation studies. How well do the admission data predict subsequent college success? Success, of course, will need to be defined much more specifically than by convenient reference to the catchall of academic grades. Another, and more cogent, criterion would be success in the profession, in the actual job of teaching—judged perhaps by principals' and supervisors' ratings and follow-up studies of college graduates. This would call for a working together of pre-service and in-service personnel, for cooperative discussion and agreement on what constitutes success. In any program the question must always be asked, selection for what purpose? Selection practices will not make their maximum contribution to the improvement of teachers and teaching unless they are conceived, carried out, and evaluated in a framework that encompasses broadly the purposes of teacher education.

We noted a trend to combine selection programs with services in orientation and guidance. This is especially to be encouraged. From the students' point of view, yes-no selection procedures, whether based on elaborate batteries of tests or not, seem arbitrary. The institution which blocks many students from a career for reasons they do not comprehend is admitting its own failure to work personally and democratically with those who need and are seeking guidance. There is another reason for encouraging the combination of selection with orientation and guidance. One often hears the remark that students teach the way they were taught. Applying this axiom that example is more potent than precept, we might say that students will probably evaluate the way they have been evaluated. So it becomes important that the students' first college contact with evaluation practices be of the sort that the college itself wishes them to practice when they get into the profession.

We described orientation programs as fulfilling a continuous and personalized selective function that is preferable to automatic initial selection—preferable because such programs give fuller recognition to the personality and uniqueness of the individual. They give a central place to student motivation and planning. They help the student decide in full knowledge of the consequences. Teaching, learning, guiding, and evaluating are closely interrelated, and all are focused on the individual student. The student takes tests and studies job demands; moreover, he participates in the interpretation of results and plans in the light of them. Ideally, at least, this is what the Ohio State and Nebraska orientation programs sought to do. There may be some danger of developing in students a too intense self-curiosity and introspectiveness. The concept of readiness was therefore introduced. By readiness we meant the disposition of the student to face data about himself and to make or alter plans in the light of them. To judge student readiness for this kind of evaluation, teachers must know their students. The concept of readiness, in short, is a warning that cases must be treated individually. It is possible that many students do not need an orientation course. It is also true that students' test interpretations and plans often appear naive. But we felt that learning to do for themselves the sort of thing they will one day be called on to do with their pupils was important and worth while. The validity of student self-appraisal has never been adequately tested. What little research has been done on the validity of self-estimates has not been crucial. The judgments of uninformed students have been compared with the judgments of informed experts. But what is needed is a comparison of self versus expert appraisal when both parties have had access to the same data and a comparison of self-appraisal under guidance versus expert appraisal alone. Again in the chapter on orientation and guidance we stressed the necessity for widespread faculty participation and understanding. Orientation and counseling can leave the student frustrated unless other university resources are flexible enough to respond to needs discovered and plans made.

In the chapter on general education we discussed the problem of formulating objectives. Perhaps because the general education of teachers has less frequently been a subject for evaluation than other phases of teacher education and because vigorous debates have been in progress over the philosophy, organization, and content of general education, the typical approach in the Commission's cooperative study to evaluation in this area has begun with the formulation of objectives. Without in any way minimizing the importance of a statement of specific goals for a program of evaluation we questioned the wisdom of a direct philosophical approach to their formulation. Trying to define objectives in such detail that they can serve as a blueprint for evaluation has too often resulted in prolonged and inconclusive arguments. The evaluation gets postponed, sometimes indefinitely. Objectives that are developed at the outset of an evaluation program should set tentatively the general direction of faculty thinking; specific definition can result from carrying forward attempts to measure them. The experience and insight gained from trying to measure student attainment of general objectives can lead to more adequate formulation of specific objectives.

We also noted in the chapter on general education that the evaluation programs we described sought to collect evidence in relation to all or nearly all the goals professed. This search resulted in the accumulation of data from a great variety of sources and by a great variety of techniques: data from students, faculty, alumni and gathered through tests, questionnaires, opinion ratings, interviews, analyses of programs, and other means.

We considered some of these varieties of evidence further in the chapter on professional education. The School of Education at Stanford, for example, started to evaluate its program by systematically collecting opinions from students, staff, alumni. and employers. The State Teachers College at Milwaukee developed a battery of objective tests for its evaluation. The relative merits of subjective and objective data were then discussed. The collection of opinions can be useful in several ways. It can stimulate needed thinking about the purposes and outcomes of a program. It can give clues to the effectiveness of teaching procedures: teaching is a two-way process involving both a teacher and a learner; and the values students think they are getting are fully as important as the values professors think they are imparting. It can give an overview of a total program from which problems for more careful study can be selected. But it cannot give what in our judgment would be an adequate appraisal of the effectiveness of any college program. Opinion analysis may be a most profitable first step and may be uniquely suited to reveal certain factors operative in any program, but it does not tell us what the students have learned or how they act as a result of their learning. Actions speak louder than words. Conclusive evaluation must get evidence of student attainment from reliable tests and of student behavior from careful observation.

The importance of observation was stressed in the chapter on student teaching. In the final analysis one's ability to use his knowledge and training must be judged from actual behavior. Student teaching presents a unique opportunity for a college to appraise its pre-service program and the progress of its students, because it is a situation that more nearly than any other resembles the ultimate job. Of course, if student teaching is not in plain fact a significant part of the college's program, if it does not afford rich opportunity for students to reveal their competence, then there is little reason or urgency to launch a comprehensive evaluation of it. The character of the student-teaching situation determines in part the value of the appraisal. Because the situation can call forth a display of those actions that constitute teaching, it is not surprising that the most promising technique of evaluation is the direct observation of student performance. Some of the problems of accurate and valid observation were pointed out in connection with the program at Ohio State University. The combined judgment of student teacher and supervisor, arrived at through discussions following periods of observation, was believed to yield the soundest evaluation. The importance of frequent and open contacts between student and supervisor was also stressed. Evidence from sources other than observation is likewise needed—for example, evidence from the student himself, perhaps from his pupils, perhaps from his peers, and from his professors.

Follow-up studies provide a fertile meeting ground for pre-service and in-service interests. The ultimate test of any program is the character of its product. In follow-up studies this character is appraised under conditions over which the college has no direct control. This fact makes the appraisal especially significant and takes it a step beyond student teaching. Unfortunately, the potential contributions of follow-up studies have been capitalized to only a very limited degree. Most studies of this sort, beyond collecting some simple census data, have been limited to assembling opinions. While opinions are certainly suggestive and can be stimulating to college faculties, the evidence from opinions is by no means final. Adequate samples of behavior are needed. The Minnesota study illustrated some of the possibilities of behavior checklists, but beyond this we need observations of behavior and actual tests of achievement. Observations and tests cannot readily be arranged except in collaboration with public school systems. This is an opportunity, not a handicap. Many school systems have a probationary period for new teachers at the end of which a judgment must be made regarding their status and tenure. The school system and the college could explore ways of using this period to serve two purposes—one just mentioned for the school system and a follow-up appraisal for the college.

Evaluation of teachers in service and of in-service programs marked the climax of the sequence of topics we started out to discuss—a sequence that began with preparation for teaching and ended with professional activity. The transition from pre-service to in-service status is not always smooth, however. We suggested that the transition might be considerably aided if evaluation activities in the colleges were organized in such a way as to make feasible the building up of an educational history or cumulative record by each student. The record could ultimately be made available to principals and superintendents faced with the task of hiring new teachers.

As we viewed evaluation activities in service we noted that many of the problems confronted at the pre-service level were now accentuated, appeared in sharper relief. For example, when we described the use of the Ohio Teaching Record as a guide to the observation and evaluation of student teachers we concluded that the soundest evaluations resulted from discussions between supervisor and student teacher following the observation. This conclusion was even clearer when the Ohio Teaching Record was used among mature teachers. Supervisors and teachers, both adult, participated in the evaluation most satisfactorily when they were sharing decisions. Indeed, teachers were reluctant to take part in any evaluation if they felt that the results might be used against them. And contrariwise, teachers were eager to participate in evaluations which they could see as furthering their own professional competence. Teachers in Denver and Spokane were enthusiastic about an intensive study of pupil-teacher relationships—complex relationships, that is, between a single teacher and the pupils in his class—primarily because they personally benefited from it, because they learned a great many very useful things about themselves. It was felt necessary, however, to collect the data for this study in strict confidence through a special consultant from outside.

Our discussions of evaluation in workshops, conferences, and study groups all emphasized the need to view evaluation as *instrumental* to achieving the purposes of the participants or group. There was encountered, almost invariably, resistance to any appraisal which seemed tacked on to the main job or which seemed incidental to it. The close relationship between evaluating and learning thus became especially evident.

From this review of highlights and major emphases in the preceding chapters we can draw out for analysis several related and recurring matters. Evaluation consists of certain general tasks. In performing these tasks one employs certain technical instruments, he proceeds in certain ways, and he has certain ends in view—certain purposes to achieve. It is particularly the relationship among techniques and procedures and purposes that needs to be examined. By techniques we mean matters that are the special concern of the evaluator as a technical expert. For example, tests, questionnaires, rating scales, as instruments of appraisal, and questions of reliability, validity, and so on are illustrative. By procedures we refer to the organization of evaluation activities, to the question of who does what in a program of evaluation, to the role of the student, the teacher, and the specialist, to the whole range of interpersonal relationships found in the carrying forward of evaluative activities. Evaluation is an activity that is participated in by human beings; therefore it has consequences that must be viewed in the light of basic concepts about individual and group behavior, about personality and democracy. This fact confronts us with the question of the purposes and goals of evaluation, the human consequences.

Techniques are related to procedures, and procedures are related to purposes. In fact, all three are closely interrelated. One of the reasons we have paid so much attention in the cooperative study to the procedures of evaluation has been our conviction that such considerations have too often been ignored. Technical problems have been too often considered solely from a technical point of view. The technician has sometimes been reluctant to venture beyond his specialty. In actual fact a completely technical approach to evaluation is quite inadequate. Evaluation is like teaching in that the outcomes attained are definitely influenced by the techniques used. The quality of a technique very frequently depends on the way it is used. And often the questions of procedure influence the purposes or goals one is hoping to attain.

RELATION OF TECHNIQUES TO PROCEDURES

There are many examples in the cooperative study and elsewhere of the relationship between technique and procedure. The validity of responses to tests and questionnaires, especially attitude and interest tests, often depends on conditions surrounding their administration and use. It is easy to give misleading answers to most attitude and interest tests. If students have any suspicion that their answers will ever be used against them they will almost surely tend to respond the way they think their superiors want them to respond. Personality tests are a case in point. If one wants, he can often make himself out to be more extroverted than he is, or more dominant, or more well balanced, or what not. The bright student can usually perceive the intent of the test. At the in-service level, where mature adults may feel that their security and status depend to some extent on their answers, the tendency toward invalid response may be aggravated. Nor is the problem limited to tests of attitude and interest. It is not uncommon to discover rumors within a student body that the smart thing to do is to make a relatively low score on the academic aptitude test for then the professors will not expect such high achievement in their courses. The same type of beating-the-game attitude is sometimes expressed with reference to pretests of information when students think they will be graded according to the amount of progress they make. What is the solution? How can these potential sources of biased response be removed or their effect minimized?

There are two lines of approach to the problem. One focuses on techniques. It is not difficult, technically, to conceal the intent of an attitude, interest, or personality test. It can be done by giving a misleading or innocuous title to the test, by jumbling a variety of items under a general heading, or by the indirection of the test items themselves. There are many examples of such treatment. Stagner's test of fascist attitudes is labeled Attitudes toward the Depression. By avoiding a stereotyped word one avoids getting stereotyped answers. The Progressive Education Association's test labeled Scales of Beliefs is really a test to measure attitudes toward six different and specific topics—democracy, economic relations, labor and unemployment, race, nationalism, and militarism. The PEA Interests and Activities questionnaire is really a personality test designed to measure personal and social adjustment. Strong's Vocational Interest blank consists of items whose diagnostic value is not readily apparent. Washburn's Social Adjustment Inventory has a concealed group of items designed to reveal the probable truthfulness of student answers to other sections of the test. All these techniques are effective.

The other approach focuses on procedures. It asks, under what conditions will students be motivated to give honest and genuine answers to tests? The teachers and evaluators try to create those conditions. The orientation programs at Ohio State University and the University of Nebraska illustrated this approach. They reflected a sequence of beliefs somewhat as follows: students will give honest responses when they see in the test an opportunity to discover something about themselves which they honestly want to know. They want to know it because they believe the knowledge will help them gain insight for reaching decisions which they realize must be faced and which they are eager to face. They have no incentive to fool the teacher because they know the results are not going to be used against them and because they know that in so doing they will also be fooling themselves. From experience in the cooperative study we are convinced that this concentration on procedure, on the creation of an environment in which honesty of response flows naturally because the student knows it is to his self-interest, is also effective.

The two approaches are not mutually exclusive. They can and should be complementary. There are circumstances so charged with emotion and stereotyped reactions that the only way to measure attitudes with validity at the present time is through indirection. The necessity for the existence of such circumstances in schools and colleges is surely questionable. Meanwhile, one can adapt to circumstances as they in fact are and at the same time work vigorously for their modification. On the other hand, under the best of conditions there will doubtless be individual deviates for whom the only approach is a thoroughly clinical one. Neither approach is a panacea. The most promising point of view, it seems to us, is one that combines the desire to use the best that technical knowledge has developed with the determination to use it in an environment where democratic values and the individual's desire to learn are consciously and deliberately promoted.

Experience in the development and use of the observational form at Ohio State University affords another example of the interdependence of technical and procedural problems. The most complete and accurate account of what happened in a classroom will be one that is made on the spot. Yet teachers often do not like to have observers record notes in class. Willing permission to do so, however, can usually be gained from the teacher when the purpose of the recording is known and acceptable. The purpose will likely be acceptable when the teacher regards the observer as a help, not a judge. Moreover, the teacher is less likely to regard the observer as a judge if the interpretation of what occurred is withheld until teacher and observer have had an opportunity to discuss the events together and arrive jointly at their judgments. Thus, both the accuracy of classroom observations, and the validity of judgments based on them depend in part on the broader environment of interpersonal relationships and procedures within which the observations and judgments are made.

A third example is found in the construction and use of rating scales. No rating scale for judging the quality of teachers or teaching is self-explanatory or capable of automatic and objective application. A rating scale can be no more valid than the understanding of those who use it. One way to create this understanding is through conference and discussion. The meaning and definition of points on the scale can be clarified. General terms can gain specific and common connotation. Different categories in the scale can be seen in relationship. When those who will use the scale have participated in its formation, have gone through the arguments over meanings, and have had a meeting of minds, the validity of their judgments in using the scale is enhanced.

RELATION OF PROCEDURES TO PURPOSE

Just as technical problems can be dealt with adequately only in the larger context of evaluation procedure, so must these problems of method in turn be seen as related broadly to the goals and purposes of teacher education. Problems of method in evaluation occur throughout. They are not confined to any one area nor do they differ markedly from one area to another. Because this is true there is need for some over-all consistency and continuity in evaluation techniques and procedure throughout teacher education. There is, in short, a relationship between means and ends, and it needs to be made apparent.

IN DEVELOPING OBJECTIVES

Let us take, for example, the problem of developing a statement of objectives. Developing general objectives and defining them specifically, it will be recalled, were two of the five tasks which we said characterized any evaluation. The problem is a technical one, it can be approached in a variety of manners, and it has implications beyond the particular phase of teacher education one happens to be evaluating. The form in which objectives are stated is a technical matter. Objectives are double-barreled statements. They define what the institution is trying to accomplish. And they set goals for the students to attain or work toward. This dual purpose is achieved by phrasing objectives in terms of student behavior—that is, institutional goals are phrased so as to indicate the changes in student behavior that the institution hopes to produce. This phrasing is technically important for evaluation because it helps to define with some clarity the nature of evidence to be looked for. It gives direction to the task of developing or selecting tests, or other techniques, for evaluating student attainment of the objectives.

The procedures for developing objectives are important for on them partly depend the acceptability and validity of the resulting statement. Unless there is some meeting of minds among those who actually face students daily, statements of objectives may prove to be well meaning but ineffectual verbalisms. A college president does not ordinarily teach courses in psychology, nor does a school superintendent teach beginning reading. It is on the teachers and the others who work closely with students that the responsibility for helping students attain goals ultimately falls; it is therefore the teacher who should play a major role in developing any statement of objectives. In other words, the development of objectives needs to be a genuinely cooperative undertaking. It need not, however, follow the procedure of prolonged faculty discussion and debate. Comprehensive, specific, and functional statements of goals do not readily emerge full blown from such discussion. Rather there is a tendency for a staff to get weighed down by verbalisms and definitions. Specifics in a statement of goals can, and we believe should, grow out of trial-and-error attempts to measure student attainment. The task of defining objectives should be carried forward parallel to, and in interaction with, the task of trying to appraise student progress to the best of one's ability. This focus on the student and his progress minimizes the dangers of verbalism inherent in a philosophical approach to goals. Thought and discussion get firmly anchored to data about student behavior—his knowledge, interest, attitudes, and so on. In all these ways the procedures for developing objectives influence their value, meaning, and usefulness.

Those concerned with the task of developing objectives need to be aware not only of technical matters and of questions of procedure but also of the relation between their task and the tasks of others in teacher education. For example, a statement of objectives for a program of student selection should not have in it ideas that are in conflict with objectives for other programs. Goals for one aspect of teacher education should bear some recognizable relation to goals for other aspects. There should, in other words, be some apparent pattern and continuity in a program of teacher education. Unfortunately, while continuity is always presumed it is not always evident. It is not always evident in statements of objectives for different areas, or in the programs of instruction in different areas, or in the practices of evaluation.

IN USING EVIDENCE

The problems of identifying appropriate sources of evidence, of devising methods for getting it, and of interpreting the results gathered are likewise more than technical problems. These, it will be recalled, were the remaining three of the five tasks which comprise evaluation.

The way in which tests or questionnaires or other instruments are developed influences the way they will be interpreted and used. For instance, the Ohio Teaching Record was developed cooperatively to serve as a guide to observation and discussion between teachers and supervisors. The instrument has been used in some institutions without prior group discussion of its purposes with the result that it has served to create misunderstanding between teachers and supervisors. The mere fact that a test or other instrument is prepared has an implication for goals. If no technique is used to appraise student performance relative to some goal which has been deemed important, that goal will not seem important to students. From the students' point of view the most extensively appraised goals are the most important ones. Thus, the extent to which all the goals of a program are honored by attempts at evaluation is a question of more than technical import.

There are many examples of lack of relationship and of inconsistency in evaluation practices that tend to be confusing to students and staff alike. Precept and practice do not reinforce one another. Sometimes evaluation data are collected and used to promote learning. At other times data are filed away in an office and never get out to the students. Students may develop some competence in self-evaluation during an orientation program and find that in subsequent phases of the college program self-evaluation is ignored. The administration in a school system may wish teachers to plan evaluation activities with pupils, but in its own practices evaluation is something applied to teachers rather than developed with them. How can conflicting practices be reconciled? How can a greater degree of consistency and a clearer sense of sequence be developed? What might be found that could be an adhesive force, that could give perspective in viewing evaluation techniques and methods and their relation to goals of teacher education?

INTEGRATION THROUGH SELF-EVALUATION

One integrating focus for evaluation is the student himself. This focus is desirable in two ways: it can integrate different evaluative activities and it can promote the integration of educative experiences within the individual. How can the student be the center of evaluative activity?

Evaluation in teacher education focused on the individual becomes a sequence of self-evaluations under guidance. The student thinks he wants to become a teacher. So he is led to consider what the job of teaching includes. What do teachers do? He observes, reads, talks with others, and records what he finds out. What are some of the capabilities and traits that teachers apparently need in order to do these tasks? How does one get to be a teacher? And then he asks, what do I have, what assets and liabilities, what resources, what abilities, interests, and dispositions to justify my becoming a teacher? What, in short, are my potentialities for success? He tries to fit together the answers to these questions, to reach a decision that is satisfying to him. In doing all this, of course, he is learning not only about education and about himself but he is learning to evaluate—to collect data relevant to his purposes, to appraise data from different sources, to interpret data, and to make plans in the light of them.

He outlines, with his adviser, an educational program that he believes will help him acquire the competence he needs to become a good teacher. The program is not confined to college classes. It includes plans for summer work in a boys' camp. It includes teaching a Sunday school class. It includes reading newspapers, magazines and books, and listening to the radio, and going to the movies to keep informed about current events. It includes all these things because even though he plans to be a science teacher in a high school he has become convinced that dispensing facts about chemistry is only one small part of the job he will face. Perhaps he keeps a record of participation in campus and out-of-school activities, of books read, of scores on tests taken with comments as to their significance, of interviews with professors and counselors. Perhaps he begins to build a file of materials which he may be able to use eventually on the job.

Once on the job he continues to practice the habit of self-appraisal. His guides are the supervisors and principals instead of college professors. He in turn becomes the guide and adviser for the pupils in his classes. And he works so as to develop in them the habit of self-evaluation.

The focus of evaluation upon the individual and his progress makes of each person the natural repository of information and data relevant to educational and personal guidance. The student has selected education as his profession because he has studied about the profession and about himself. Therefore, he knows his scores or percentiles on college aptitude tests, reading tests, achievement tests, attitude, interest, and personality tests or whatever other sources of self-insight the college made available to him. He knows some of the judgments various counselors or professors have made about him. He has a record of their recommendations. He knows the outcome of his health examination. He is, in other words, the channel of communication between different educational agents and agencies. He has a cumulative record of his progress that equals in accuracy and exceeds in detail the college's own record. At least this could be true of the great majority of students. There would, of course, be students who are not yet ready to face all that their counselors know about them. In such cases, the counselor's appraisal is an essential supplement. In most cases, however, the individual's self-record would be complete and trustworthy because it would have been accumulated cooperatively by student and adviser, been discussed openly, and been the basis of plans which the student had made and was acting on.

In this focus upon self-evaluation under guidance, evaluative activity and learning for the student, and evaluation and instruction for the teacher, are closely related phases of the same over-all educative process. Evaluation is not an activity added on to instruction. Indeed, it is a method for improving and promoting instruction. And similarly, it is a method for promoting and improving learning.

INTEGRATION THROUGH COOPERATION

Inconsistency and lack of sequence are confusing to the faculty as well as the students. The faculty by devoting their energies deliberately to bringing pattern and sequence to the educational program can make of the program an effective integrating focus for evaluation. Probably any professor or college president could put down on paper a well conceived, logical, and sequential educational program. But an examination of this paper program would give no hint of the extent to which the actual program of that college was integrated. One would need to study the practices of the entire staff. A teacher does not readily direct his efforts toward achieving goals that are not clear to him or that represent someone else's thinking. If the parts of the program are to fit together easily those responsible for each part must see their task in relation to every other part and to the whole program. A faculty, working together on the task of clarifying their objectives and analyzing their activities in the light of them, can gain an invaluable perspective on the total educational program. They can attempt to see their goals, the experiences they provide students to promote the attainment of those goals, and their evaluation methods as related parts of a whole picture. They can work toward making their practices conform to their preachments.

It is quite apparent that any so-called integrating focus for evaluation will fail of achieving its purpose without a staff organization that permits and keeps open channels of communication. Consistency and sequence would be the products of sheer happenstance if the left hand did not know what the right hand was doing. Plans made in the orientation program will not readily be carried out unless those who teach subsequent programs know about and respect those plans, and have made their programs flexible to meet them. Staff talk about the desirability of self-evaluation will be compromised by staff practice in evaluation that is arbitrary. Stated objectives will be ignored by students unless evaluation practice honors those objectives with sincere attempts at measurement. The staff must be aware of all this. Faculty committees need to be familiar with each other's work. Too often, committees are not sensitive to the implications for others of what they recommend. They are unaware that other committees are approaching the same problem from a different angle. Evaluation, by focusing faculty and student thinking on the total program, and on their activities and practices and results, can help to bring order and sequence to the educative process. If it is to do this, evaluation must be a cooperative undertaking.

THE PURPOSE OF EVALUATION

Unconcern for the tensions in students and staff that arise from inconsistency, lack of continuity, and lack of knowledge has resulted, time and again, in the failure of an evaluation program to achieve its most important purpose, its very reason for existence—namely, to produce change, to make education more effective. If we were interested only in evaluation for evaluation's sake then much of what we have described and emphasized in the book would be irrelevant. It is precisely because evaluation has a purpose that the way it is carried out becomes important. Why do we evaluate? Because we are not now, never have been, and never will be, satisfied with our efforts, and because by analyzing them we hope to find ways of improving. Why do we evaluate teacher education? Because we want to make that education more effective. Because we believe that the more we can learn about the outcomes of our present practices the better qualified we will be to change those practices in the right directions.

Evaluation is of little worth unless the weaknesses it reveals are corrected. All evaluation reveals weaknesses as well as strengths. Who is to correct these weaknesses? Quite obviously, the students must correct deficiencies that apply to them, and the staff must correct deficiencies that apply to the educational program. But will they? They may not. They may produce an elaborate set of arguments to prove that the evaluation was untrustworthy, that the evidence it gathered was suspect and invalid. They are not likely to react in such manner to an appraisal which they have themselves carried out. That is why evaluation, to achieve its purpose, must be so conducted that confidence in the results is built up and readiness to change is fostered. Participation, making evaluation a genuine group enterprise, is one effective means of assuring that results will be put to good use.

THE AMERICAN COUNCIL ON EDUCATION

GEORGE F. ZOOK, *President*

The American Council on Education is a *council* of national educational associations; organizations having related interests; approved universities and colleges, technological schools, and selected private secondary schools; state departments of education; and city school systems. It is a center of cooperation and coordination whose influence has been apparent in the shaping of American educational policies as well as in the formulation of American educational practices during the past twenty-six years. Many leaders in American education and public life serve on the commissions and committees through which the Council operates.

Established by the Council in 1938, the Commission on Teacher Education consists of the persons whose names appear on a front page of this publication. It operates through a staff under the supervision and control of a director responsible to the Commission.